Agenda
for Action

A joint project of

*The Institute for African Studies
of the Academy of Sciences of the USSR*

*The African Studies Center
and the Center for International and Strategic Affairs
of the University of California at Los Angeles*

*and the School of International Relations
of the University of Southern California*

Agenda
for
Action
African–Soviet–U.S.
Cooperation

edited by
Anatoly A. Gromyko
C. S. Whitaker

Lynne Rienner Publishers   Boulder & London

Published in the United States of America in 1990 by
Lynne Rienner Publishers, Inc.
1800 30th Street, Boulder, Colorado 80301

and in the United Kingdom by
Lynne Rienner Publishers, Inc.
3 Henrietta Street, Covent Garden, London WC2E 8LU

Library of Congress Cataloging-in-Publication Data
Agenda for action : African–Soviet–U.S. cooperation / edited by
  Anatoly A. Gromyko and C.S. Whitaker.
    p. cm.
  Includes bibliographical references.
  ISBN 1-55587-196-8 (alk. paper)
  1. Africa—Foreign relations—Soviet Union. 2. Soviet Union—
Foreign relations—Africa. 3. Africa—Foreign relations—United
States. 4. United States—Foreign relations—Africa. I. Gromyko,
Anatolii Andreevich. II. Whitaker, C. S. (C. Sylvester), 1935-
JX1582.A517 1990
327'.096—dc20   89-29573
                                                              CIP

British Cataloguing in Publication Data
A Cataloguing in Publication record for this book
is available from the British Library.

Printed and bound in the United States of America

The paper used in this publication meets the requirements
of the American National Standard for Permanence of
Paper for Printed Library Materials Z39.48-1984.

Contents

Preface

This book is an important stage in an ongoing activity: Soviet–U.S. Cooperation for Africa, a joint project of the Institute for African Studies of the Soviet Academy of Sciences, the African Studies Center and the Center for International and Strategic Affairs of the University of California at Los Angeles, and the School of International Relations of the University of Southern California.

The idea for the project arose at a moment of unprecedented opportunity and significant need. In the period since the project's inception, relations have dramatically improved between the two global powers, while ongoing crises within the African continent have presented compelling reasons to transform the past of confrontation into a future of cooperation. To the extent that such currents persist, Africa may benefit and the entire world may profit from the precedent of African–Soviet–U.S. cooperation.

The spirit of multinational collaboration that has inspired these efforts emerged in the 1980s out of dissatisfaction on the part of Soviet and U.S. scholars with the global foreign policies of the past. Specifically, Professors Sklar and Bender, convinced that U.S. opposition to Soviet influence in Africa was outmoded as an imperative of U.S. foreign policy, decided to contact colleagues in the Soviet Union.

As it happened, Soviet scholars had begun about the same time to reassess the Soviet role in Africa in the light of African realities. Also arising in the USSR was the new orientation of glasnost, which was conducive to rethinking about Africa as a potential setting for Soviet–U.S. cooperation.

Professors Gromyko and Intriligator, known to each other through the series of Pugwash Conferences, discussed tentative proposals along these lines at a Pugwash gathering. Subsequently, Gromyko, in his capacity as director of the Institute for African Studies, USSR Academy of Sciences, asked Intriligator to invite a few U.S. colleagues in African studies to join with a group of Soviet colleagues in a Soviet–U.S. workshop in Moscow on the potential for Soviet–U.S. cooperation for Africa. These initiatives were then formally organized as a joint project of the Soviet Institute, UCLA's Center for International and Strategic Affairs and its African Studies Center, and USC's School of International Relations.

The project sponsored an initial workshop in December 1987 in Moscow, and a conference the following November at Airlie House, Virginia, near Washington, D.C. At the latter meeting, papers were presented by African, Soviet, and U.S. scholars and experts in nine different areas, each reflecting an issue of great concern to the future of Africa. Also present was a select group of Washington-based observers. This book is based on these papers and presentations and the discussions that followed.

The tone of these deliberations has been markedly positive; the outlook forward-looking and constructive. In this, the talks have reflected the atmosphere of changing attitudes in both the Soviet Union and the United States toward one another and the world. There evidently exists a new disposition to emphasize mutual interests, there is a fresh spirit of openness within the Soviet Union, and there is a continuing will on the part of often-beleaguered African countries to develop, notwithstanding their difficulties.

From the outset the participants have been guided by a broad consensus on at least seven fundamental points:

One: To succeed, the project requires African leadership, and to observe this essential condition must be a foundation of all other efforts.

Two: Great potential exists for substantive projects of cooperation among African countries, the Soviet Union, and the United States in many fields.

Three: Through cooperation, significantly greater results will be attained by all the national parties acting in concert than any of them acting alone or bilaterally.

Four: Of all the regions of the world, Africa is at present probably the optimum working arena in terms of the prospects and need for cooperative action.

Five: The Soviet Union and the United States are in a unique position, by virtue of resources, technology, traditions of anticolonial ideals, and national disposition, to assist development processes in African countries.

Six: Given the current hopeful state of Soviet–U.S. relations and the growing urgency of the situation in Africa, precisely now is the time for projects of cooperation in Africa.

Seven: The essence of the task as a whole is to support the constructive efforts of those African states that share the vision of comparative advantage through international cooperation.

This book, like the project itself, is intended to proclaim the vision and to stimulate the process.

The book is being published simultaneously in Russian and other languages, with the aim of reaching and informing the thinking of interested parties throughout the world.

It is to be emphasized that the publication of this volume is far from being the end-point of the project. Plans for the future include the establishment of study commissions of experts in each of the issue areas discussed in the book, with the goal of designing and implementing specific plans for joint African–Soviet–U.S. action.

In the longer term, it is hoped to establish institutional mechanisms of mutual African–Soviet–U.S. cooperative support. In the near term, the goal is to create channels of communication among the two industrial powers and African countries that will avoid the dismal past record of destructive conflict.

The participants are pleased to acknowledge, with deep gratitude, the help of organizations that have provided financial support for the project to date: The American Council of Learned Societies–Soviet Academy of Sciences Commission on the Humanities and Social Sciences (administered in the United States by the International Research and Exchanges Board [IREX]), The Carnegie Corporation of New York, and The Hunger Project. None of them is necessarily in agreement with all of the observations or suggestions made in this book, but without their generous backing, none of the project's achievements thus far would have been possible.

The editors also wish to acknowledge the tireless and expert assistance of Geoffrey Bergen, who wrote and assembled a first draft for consideration by the Editorial Board of the project, which met 1–7 July 1988, in Moscow; and of Owen Richelieu III, who helped prepare the manuscript for submission to the publishers.

Finally, warm thanks are due to all the participants in the 1987 Moscow Workshop and the 1988 Airlie House Conference. Their thoughtful comments and suggestions during the deliberations and in the course of the project generally have greatly enhanced the quality of the vision.

A. A. G.
C. S. W.

The initial group of U.S. participants in the project included GERALD J. BENDER, director, School of International Relations, USC; C.R.D. HALISI, assistant professor of political science, University of Indiana; MICHAEL D. INTRILIGATOR, director, Center for International and Strategic Affairs, UCLA (and project director); MICHAEL F. LOFCHIE, director, African Studies Center, UCLA; WILLIAM C. POTTER, executive director, Center for International and Strategic Affairs, UCLA; RICHARD L. SKLAR, professor of political science, UCLA; and C. S. WHITAKER, professor of international relations and dean, Division of Social Sciences and Communication, USC. The original Soviet participants included LEONID AKSIUK, leading scientific fellow, Institute for African Studies, Moscow; LEONGARD GONCHAROV, deputy director, Institute for African Studies, Moscow; VICTOR I. GONCHAROV, deputy director, Institute for African Studies, Moscow; STANISLAV RODIONOV, Space Research Institute of the USSR Academy of Sciences, Moscow; GLEB SMIRNOV, chief of department, Institute for African Studies, Moscow; YEVGENY TARABRIN, chief of department,

Institute for African Studies, Moscow; and ALEXEI M. VASSILIEV, deputy
director, Institute for African Studies, Moscow.

The expanded list of participants at Airlie House included ADEBAYO
ADEDEJI, executive secretary, Economic Commission for Africa, Addis
Ababa, Ethiopia; BOLAJI AKINYEMI, professor, Cambridge University;
LEONID N. AKSIUK, head of section, Institute for African Studies, Moscow;
RAYMOND AKWULE, editor, African Telecommunications Report,
Washington, D.C.; TAMARA ALIKHANOVA, senior research fellow, Institute
for African Studies, Moscow; PAULINE BAKER, senior associate, Carnegie
Endowment for International Peace, Washington, D.C.; ROBERT BATT, The
Hunger Project, New York; GERALD J. BENDER; GEOFFREY BERGEN,
doctoral candidate, UCLA; PETER BOURNE, Peter Bourne Associates,
Arlington, Virginia; NIKOLAI A. CHETVERTAKOV, Ministry of Foreign Trade
of the USSR, Moscow; MICHAEL GLANTZ, head of the Environmental and
Societal Impacts Group, National Center for Atmospheric Research, Boulder,
Colorado; LEONGARD GONCHAROV; VICTOR I. GONCHAROV; ANATOLY A.
GROMYKO; C.R.D. HALISI; JOAN HOLMES, global executive director, The
Hunger Project, New York; MICHAEL D. INTRILIGATOR; CRAIG JOHNSON,
doctoral candidate, UCLA; O. O. KALE, director, Community Health Pro-
gram, University of Ibadan, Nigeria; SMART R. KATAWALA, Ministry of
Foreign Affairs, Mozambique; VLADIMIR B. KOKOREV, head of section,
Institute for African Studies, Moscow; CAROL LANCASTER, director of
African Studies, Georgetown University, Washington, D.C.; A. M. LISEVICH,
Institute for African Studies, Moscow; MICHAEL F. LOFCHIE; CALLISTO
MADAVO, director, East Africa Department, The World Bank, Washington,
D.C.; SAMUEL MAKINDA, professor, The Flinders University of South
Australia; DONALD McHENRY, professor, Georgetown University, Washing-
ton, D.C.; SAM NOLUTSHUNGU, professor, University of Manchester; OYE
OGUNBADEJO, professor, Obafemi Awolowo University, Ile-Ife, Nigeria;
G. O. OLUSANYA, director-general, Nigerian Institute of International Affairs,
Lagos; JURI M. OSSIPOV, head of section, Institute for African Studies,
Moscow; DAVID OTTAWAY, the *Washington Post,* Washington, D.C.;
VALERIE PALMER, president, Third World Medical Research Foundation,
New York; WILLIAM POTTER; A. I. REZNICOVSKI, head of section, Institute
for African Studies, Moscow; STANISLAV RODIONOV, Academy of Sciences
of the USSR, Moscow; RICHARD L. SKLAR; GLEB V. SMIRNOV; PETER S.
SPENCER, director, Center for Research on Occupational and Environmental
Toxicology, Portland, Oregon; JOHN STREMLAU, former head of interna-
tional programs, The Rockefeller Foundation; CHEIKH TIDIANE SY, director,
Ecole National d'Economie Appliquée, Dakar, Senegal; FITIGU TADESSE,
director, Department of African Affairs, The Hunger Project, New York;
YEVGENY TARABRIN; ROBERT M. TINDWA, manager, Research and Develop-
ment, Zimbabwe Mining and Development Corporation, Harare, Zimbabwe;
ALEXEI M. VASSILIEV; and C. S. WHITAKER.

An Agenda for
Cooperative Action in Africa

C. S. WHITAKER

Africa: Let Us Cooperate. With this exhortation we convey the purpose of this book and the overall project of which it is a part. The project has the goal of promoting constructive cooperation among African countries, the Soviet Union, and the United States. The book discusses in detail nine different specific areas in which such cooperation promises to be beneficial.

The entire enterprise arises from a strong threefold conviction: that because of fresh and exciting new ways of thinking and movement away from traditional antagonisms, the time is ripe for the two global powers to act concurrently; that now, more than ever, the African continent can benefit from such an initiative; and that African–Soviet–U.S. collaboration can be an important first step toward wider constructive international cooperation.

For Africa, the cooperation envisaged involves potential benefits associated with the nine issue areas discussed: substantial gains in food production and distribution; protecting and maintaining the productivity of the environment; coping with the burden of external debt; enhancing the developmental potential of mineral resources; improving the state of communications; finding feasible solutions to epidemics and other health-related problems; preventing nuclear proliferation; stemming the flow of arms transfers that contribute to regional conflict; and promoting freedom and security in southern Africa.

For the Soviet Union and the United States the project could further bilateral political relations overall, setting the stage for constructive cooperation in other regions and in other areas of mutual interest, including arms control, cooperation in space, and scientific investigation. As an arena of action toward a more constructive relationship, the project looks beyond sectarian confrontation, distrust, and deterrence to a future of increasing cooperation with a view to benefiting the entire world.

A HISTORICAL BASIS FOR COOPERATION

Unfortunately, there is truth in the assertion that in the past the Soviet Union and the United States have frequently designed their actions on the African continent more with reference to each other than to the needs and interests of Africans.[1] At first glance, the record of Soviet–U.S. confrontation in Africa might suggest little hope for cooperation, or for benefits to Africa.

Yet, it is also true that the two powers have not always been on opposite sides of local conflicts; nor have they inevitably stood in the way of each other's efforts to provide developmental assistance or humanitarian aid. In fact, there have been important instances of overt cooperation.

The key question is whether Soviet and U.S. policies are *structurally* determined—hence inescapable—or whether there are at work other factors that might be altered through human agency.

As a practical matter, Soviet and U.S. policies have often mutated in response to particular institutional/political forces, personal biases of policymakers, and concrete experience with the roots and ramifications of events. Soviet and U.S. policies are not impervious to forces of change.

If any consistency can be discerned in both Soviet and U.S. policy toward Africa it is that both have attached minor importance to Africa in their foreign policies. Thus, in both countries, those who make vital policy decisions that may lastingly impact on Africa have often known or cared little about the continent.

Typically, the attention of policymakers has been drawn to Africa only when some crisis, or perceived crisis, forces it to their attention. Further, in periods of crisis, leaders have had little time to absorb new information, and thus there has been a tendency to make decisions based on popular fictions about Africa, or on experience in other places and times. Ignorance of local conditions has more than once led the two powers into support of opposing camps on the assumption—often fostered by the supposed beneficiaries of their aid—that in doing so they were supporting ideologically sympathetic actors in opposition to adversaries manipulated by the other. Yet, few if any of Africa's postindependence conflicts have been externally provoked.

Characteristically, both the Soviet Union and the United States have assumed that involvement in African conflicts represents relatively small stakes or at least low risks compared to potential rewards, only later to emerge badly bruised, or at best no better off, after large sacrifices of resources and reputation. Skepticism about the potential for constructive Soviet–U.S. cooperation grounded in this history is understandable. The skeptical still must be persuaded that fresh prospects have appeared, and that these can be translated into concrete action and institutional expression.

Those who discern grounds for optimism, however, will take heart from the evidence of precedent. Conventionally, relations between the Soviet Union and the United States in areas of the Third World are conceived as irreconcilable and ineluctably competitive, a "zero-sum" game of maneuver for power and influence. But historically, the two global powers have shared positions on a number of issues of importance to Africa. For example, both countries favored elimination of the colonial system in Africa, and each played a part in the decolonization process following World War II. In virtually every case, both took a stand in favor of diplomatic recognition of the new African states and their full participation in the United Nations and other international agencies.

Albeit in different ways, each also acted to promote schemes for African political and economic development, and to foster the creation of regional and continentwide institutions devoted to these values. Both have sponsored measures in opposition to the apartheid regime in South Africa and in favor of full political and other rights for the peoples of southern Africa.

In terms of local conflicts, certainly the postindependence history of Africa does include several notable instances of direct or indirect Soviet and U.S. support of bitterly opposing factions. But there were also important instances of joint support for one side. This was the case, for instance, in the Nigerian civil war, in which both the Soviet Union and the United States supported national unity under the established federal government.

Natural disasters have stimulated aid efforts by one side that have been accepted by the other. When drought and famine struck Ethiopia in 1985–1986, both countries rushed to provide assistance to afflicted areas. While such examples may not be indicative of the period, they do provide evidence to show that, at a minimum, the simultaneous presence of the Soviet Union and United States in the same area did not automatically lead to conflict.

There have even been cases of deliberate collaboration. A recent instance is the negotiated disengagement of South African and Cuban forces in Angola, coupled with South African withdrawal from Namibia. In this connection there were numerous high-level consultations between Soviet and U.S. officials in support of peace talks. Without taking anything away from the African heads of state and their ambassadors who initiated the process, it is doubtful that a positive result could have occurred without at least tacit Soviet and U.S. support.

To be sure, past Soviet and U.S. relations in Africa have been characterized by conflict, perhaps even enmity. But the record suggests that historical arguments that hold that this has been inevitable are flawed. In fact, the examples cited above suggest that even in the past the course of Soviet–U.S. relations has been subject to influences other than ideological or structural antagonism. That reality should serve to buttress new hope that the cold war in Africa and other places is in decline, perhaps even in a process of transformation.

THEORETICAL PERSPECTIVES

Theoretical arguments against Soviet–U.S. cooperation are typically rooted in one or another variant of the doctrine of "realism," the principal tenet being that the global interests of the two powers preclude their collaborating.

This school of political thought posits as inevitable that they will vie for influence, favored access to natural resources, military advantage, and strategic hegemony. A corollary axiom is that third parties end up bearing the brunt and paying the heaviest price for this rivalry. Accordingly, as salient factors, little room is left for any consideration of domestic politics, changing conditions and perspectives, or growing economic interdependence.

From an essentially structuralist point of view, the Third World is destined to be relegated to the vicissitudes of either global neglect or power conflict. Far from being completely reassuring to countries on the periphery of Soviet–U.S. relations, the paradox of nuclear standoff, making global war less plausible as an outcome of international relations, might well only magnify the temptation on the part of the global powers to dabble in lower-risk forms of conflict in places like Africa.

There is, however, an alternative point of view. The crux of this perspective is that motivations, attitudes, and perceptions, particularly of decisionmakers, play a role in determining a nation's behavior, as do popular orientations, and in the international arena not necessarily less than in others.

What appears to one era of policymakers to be "realistic" assessment may be idiosyncracy to another. Policymakers see the world through perceptual filters that sift phenomena, constructing a world that may or may not exist in those terms, or which perhaps was all along tinged with elements of delusion. The bitter experience of international politics and war in the first two-thirds of this century naturally instilled distrust. Yet the world has changed, and goes on changing. Over time, the realization of this fundamental fact does alter the perceptions of political leaders.

Both the United States and the Soviet Union have drawn hard lessons from their interventions in conflicts in Africa and elsewhere in the Third World. Their ability to learn from these lessons is demonstrated by an increasing willingness of both the global powers, jointly and unilaterally, to quench the flames of local conflicts they may previously have fanned. The learning process takes place.

Yet another factor contributing to the change in Soviet and U.S. perceptions of one another and the world is the "new thinking" inspired by Soviet President Mikhail S. Gorbachev.[2] For our purposes, the three most important aspects of this new thinking are (1) the spread of interdependence on a world scale, (2) the necessity to address problems through cooperation, and (3) the existence of significant limits to military methods of pursuing security.

The implicit significance of all this for Africa has been evident recently in conciliatory moves relating to long-term conflicts in Angola, Namibia, and, incipiently, Ethiopia.

The immediate challenge for the United States has been to respond constructively and responsibly to initiatives emanating from the Soviet Union, but there is more implied. As Hough states, "A new realism about the third world, about the Soviet role there, and about the very nature of international relations is vital. By failing to develop realistic expectations and rules of the game, the United States is setting the stage for a dangerous and unnecessary crisis sometime in the future."[3]

Not to respond positively is to court self-fulfilling and mournful prophecies. People *do* make their own history, and often they do so with the help of altered historical guidelines. However much yesterday's realism was "objectively real," the retention of a world view no longer current implies behavior that is apt to make matters worse than need be.

AFRICAN–SOVIET–U.S. COOPERATION

An underlying premise of this book is that ultimately Africans themselves should provide the solutions to Africa's problems. For example, while Soviet and U.S. participation was important to the recent negotiations over south-western Africa, the turn of events that were essential to success had nothing to do with either Soviet or U.S. involvement.[4] Furthermore, the lion's share of credit for the signed agreement itself belongs to African diplomats.

A crucial factor positively affecting the outlook for cooperation is major change in thinking and perceptions within Africa. The wind now sweeping Africa involves political change in the form of increasing attention by government officials to the concrete needs and aspirations of the citizens they have promised to serve.

Inherent in these changes is a growing insistence in Africa that its leaders must assume responsibility for the well-being of their countries, as opposed to attributing wholesale blame for Africa's problems on outside forces. In the words of one of the continent's most distinguished elder statesmen, General Olusegun Obasanjo, former Nigerian head of state, "In the last resort, only we ourselves know what is really amiss with us and what is more, only we as Africans can tell it as it is to ourselves. . . . Our destiny ultimately lies in our own hands."[5]

This increasing willingness to be accountable bodes well for the prospect of constructive, cooperative ventures. An encouraging aspect of this prospect is the recognition of Africa's leadership that, too often in the past, self-seeking elites have sustained their rule through recourse to the "great power game" of playing the Soviet Union and the United States against each other, threatening to switch alliances if the allied power is not forthcoming with material resources. Just this sort of ploy has permitted South Africa to sustain Western sympathy in its claims to be menaced by the specter of a Soviet-masterminded "total onslaught" that would turn the entire region into a dominion of an Eastern empire.

By signaling their joint determination to eschew pernicious games, the global powers will lend support to the democratizing trend already under way in Africa. It may be ventured that persisting in this direction will enhance the real political and economic capacities of African states. Few if any African states can go it alone as important players in hegemonic games; real African supranational influence will lie in collective action among and toward African countries.

Until now, the insecurity of African leaders has formed the principal barrier to joint action of the African states. Unsure of their domestic hold on power, they have not been about to relinquish control or welcome initiatives from regional or continental entities. Yet, in a climate of increased solidarity, Africa can only grow stronger. At the same time, instances of effective collaboration are likely to encourage both the Soviet and U.S. policymaking establishments to accord a higher degree of priority to African issues.

THE POTENTIAL BENEFITS OF
SOVIET–U.S. COOPERATION

While Soviet–U.S. cooperation for Africa may be attractive as a moral imperative, some will nonetheless cast a cold eye, asking what, if any, tangible benefits from the endeavor can truly be expected to accrue to the global powers and to Africa itself.

For Africa, the clearest benefits are the promise of a diminished level of destructive African conflict inherent in Soviet–U.S. enmity, plus the combined material and technical resources that might be realized through cooperation. For the Soviet Union and the United States, the payoff consists of the opportunity to avoid the costly policy misadventures that have persistently plagued them (in Africa and elsewhere).

Globally, cooperation in Africa may be a harbinger of increased international cooperation generally. To the extent that conflict is abated, bold programs of constructive purpose become more attractive as objectives of investment. The increased attention paid to the legitimate needs of Africa alone would help. Beyond that lies the potential yield of the sort of projects proposed in this book, and more.

The first step must be to establish regular channels of communication. Ignorance lies behind much of the unfortunate past, exacerbated by the utter lack of dialogue. Analysts employing so-called game theory have emphasized that in strategic games, and by analogy in the international system, cooperation is most likely to come about through the agency of repeated contact of the players. They have also stressed that there has to be a sufficiently "long shadow of the future" for players to be motivated to enter into mutually beneficial arrangements. Conversely, failure to develop institutional channels of contact tends to perpetuate past misconceptions and preclude productive coalition.

This project, we believe, is an important step toward the establishment of mutually rewarding communication.

AN AGENDA FOR ACTION

As noted earlier, a three-way discussion about priorities has been deemed essential to this project. The structure of this book therefore reflects that premise. Each chapter represents the individual and collective work of African, Soviet, and U.S. authors dealing with specific issue areas. The areas themselves were chosen on the basis of two criteria: first, that they represent a pressing issue in terms of Africa's current developmental crisis; and second, that they constitute areas in which the Soviet Union and the United States have the capability of achieving concrete results through joint action in the near term.

It was agreed, third, that our initial aims should be modest in scope. Confidence building is most likely to emanate in the context of feasible objectives pursued as nonintrusively as possible. It was further agreed, fourth, that the speedy translation of resolutions into action is critical. The contributions to this book, then, should be read as elements of a blueprint for action in the near term; the overall organization of the volume is designed to suggest this strategy as well.

Each section is introduced by a joint statement that was collaboratively developed by the African, Soviet, and U.S. authors of the chapters that follow. It is to be emphasized that these statements are not simply declarations of opinion or a wish-list, but guidelines for implementation by the project's participants, concerned individuals, and Soviet and U.S. officials. It should also be noted that the project's organizers are, of this writing, actively engaged in the process of establishing study commissions, with the intent of accelerating the implementation of its recommendations.

The Issue Areas

In the preliminary papers and ensuing discussions and debates, some of which were quite animated, the degree to which disagreements were practical and technical rather than doctrinal is quite remarkable. This reality is an indication of the mutual change of perception already at work. Absent were ideologically tinged, time-consuming, and futile disputes over interpretive issues such as the degree to which some African states are "capitalist" or "socialist." On the contrary, the overwhelming mood of the conference, which is embodied in the joint recommendations and individual papers, was pragmatic, enthusiastic, and action-oriented. The attitude of the participants was "roll up our sleeves" and "get down to [the practical] work" of constructive cooperation for Africa, without further delay.

In seeking to be guided by Africa's priority concerns, all agreed that foremost among the projects to be tackled was agricultural production and distribution. The problems associated with the lack of food self-sufficiency throughout most of sub-Saharan Africa, coupled with inefficiencies in food distribution, are well known. Drought and famine are acute and widely publicized ramifications, but chronic economic underdevelopment, underproduction, and maldistribution are also basic outgrowths. The Soviet Union and the United States have the skilled manpower, the specialized capital, and the technology available to help improve food production and distribution in Africa for the benefit of the peoples of Africa.

A second area of potential cooperation is the environment, including the prevention of further desertification in the Sahel and other areas. This is a matter of major concern in that desertification has many direct and indirect effects on food production, land use, transportation, housing, and weather patterns. The actual prevention of desertification is a task to which both the Soviet Union and the United States can bring considerable resources, including rich experience in Soviet Central Asia and in the U.S. Southwest. By pooling resources and knowledge it would be possible for the United States and the USSR to make a major contribution.

In particular, recent advances in computer-modeling and remote-sensing technologies furnish highly useful techniques applicable to African ecological problems. Another environmental concern is disposal of radioactive and other toxic wastes by industrialized countries in Africa. The Soviet Union and the United States can join in putting a halt to this odious practice.

A third area of potential cooperation is in the area of debt and development. While small in relation to the absolute amount of debt in other underdeveloped areas of the world, debt in a number of sub-Saharan African countries has imposed a crushing economic burden in relation to their ability to repay, thus impacting negatively on their ability to develop, and aggravating domestic and international political tensions as well. The Soviet Union and United States have the financial resources and informational capabilities to help resolve the crisis in ways potentially satisfactory to debtor and creditor nations alike.

A fourth area of potential cooperation is in mineral-production and extractive industries, which, for several African countries, are the major source of foreign earnings. A variety of external and internal factors have militated against the ability of sub-Saharan Africa's mineral-producing states to benefit for development purposes from their mineral wealth, for example, through the means of integrated industrial production. Again, the Soviet Union and the United States have the resources to help, in the form of training, technology transfer, technical assistance, and joint ventures.

A fifth area of potential cooperation is communications, including the use of satellites. Because of their large expanse, both the United States and the USSR have the experience of erecting communications networks over vast areas, which is also required for Africa. The development of communications in Africa, assisted by Soviet–U.S. cooperative efforts, could play an important role in the continent's economic, political, and social development.

A sixth area of potential cooperation is health and epidemics. A primary dimension here is again lack of resources, particularly shortages of severely needed medicines and equipment. Another dimension, however, is the brain drain of skilled medical personnel due to lack of adequate incentives and employment opportunities. Solutions lie in the search for locally available inexpensive treatments, and in the training and education of doctors, nurses, and other medical personnel, along with the provision of incentives to remain in Africa. Soviet–U.S. cooperation can help augment and allocate the needed human resources.

A seventh area of potential cooperation is that of nuclear non-proliferation. The introduction of nuclear weapons in Africa looms as a potentially dangerous development, with significant risks involved for Africa and the world. Whatever the state of their bilateral relations, be it cold war or détente, the United States and the USSR have traditionally cooperated in the area of nonproliferation, including support of the International Atomic Energy Agency (IAEA), cosponsorship (with the United Kingdom) of the Treaty on the Non-proliferation of Nuclear Weapons (NPT) and membership in the London Suppliers Group.

An eighth area of potential cooperation is with respect to arms transfers to and within African countries. A number of African states are experiencing severe problems in carrying out economic development as a result of the large proportion of national income being diverted to military expenditures, of which arms form the lion's share. Reassessing military outlays and alleviating the conditions leading to arms buildups are vital measures.

A ninth area of potential cooperation concerns the relationship between African development and African security, notably in southern Africa, where African states are in close proximity to the Republic of South Africa, creating special problems and needs. In all these countries there exists good prospects for Soviet–U.S. cooperation in the related areas of economic development and security. Above all, African–Soviet–U.S. cooperation in southern Africa would make clear that global ideological conflicts are giving way to more African-centered outcomes.

A Call to Action

Finally, we address in this book the need for foundations of mutual confidence building, in Africa to be sure, but also in the Soviet Union and the United States. This entails, among other sensitivities, not succumbing to voices of excessive caution. It also means stressing a results-oriented approach to problems. Confidence building implies not only appropriate rhetoric, but action.

We hope that through increased public awareness of the possibilities, which is one of this book's significant goals, constructive African–Soviet–U.S. cooperation may be promoted.

NOTES

1. See Gerald J. Bender, James S. Coleman, and Richard L. Sklar, eds., *African Crisis Areas and U.S. Foreign Policy* (Berkeley: University of California Press, 1985).

2. Mikhail S. Gorbachev, *Perestroika and New Thinking for Us and the World* (London: Collins, 1987).

3. Jerry F. Hough, *The Struggle for the Third World: Soviet Debates and American Opinions* (Washington, D.C.: Brookings Institution, 1986), 5.

4. See the analysis by Gerald J. Bender, "Peacemaking in Southern Africa," *Third World Quarterly* 11, no. 2 (April 1989): 15–30.

5. Quoted by Flora Lewis, "Straight Talk in Africa," *New York Times*, Editorial Section, 30 October 1988.

PART 1

The Agrarian Sector

A critical problem for Africa is that of food availability and distribution, highlighted by declines in food production, widespread hunger, and famine. There are several interrelated sources of this problem, both domestic and external. Among them are ecological deficits, engendered by climatic and natural conditions, and depletion of land fertility in many regions of sub-Saharan Africa. Related conditions include the extreme scarcity of financial resources, accentuated by the debt burden and falling terms of trade; a deficit of investment goods and research and development facilities needed for agricultural development; and weaknesses in rural infrastructure, both economic and social. Unbalanced interaction between rural and urban economies, as well as archaic socioeconomic structures, also affect food distribution and production adversely.

The complex problems of food production and distribution in Africa present at once a major challenge to Africa and an opportunity for Soviet–U.S. cooperation in this field. There is, in fact, wide scope for such cooperation, both in research and development and in direct collaborative action. Specific recommendations for Soviet–U.S. cooperation include:

• Joint research, of an applied nature, with results transmitted directly to appropriate organizations and individuals in African countries. This joint research might focus on topics such as economic policies that affect agricultural production and low-cost methods of controlling desertification.

• Joint technical assistance. A preliminary inventory of feasible projects for the near term includes the following:

• The creation of cadastral (land use) and water availability surveys using satellite imagery; and demonstration programs of soil regeneration that will economically enhance soil fertility

• Demonstration programs of resource-sharing agricultural technology, including zero-tillage and comparable low resource methods of animal husbandry for small and medium farms (this latter being especially critical inasmuch as overgrazing is a major cause of desertification)

• Demonstration of testing projects for intermediate technology, including the building of medium-size irrigation systems, the sinking (and testing of the environmental effects) of pencil wells, and the creation of rural low technology agrotechnical and veterinary services

• Projects for inexpensive agricultural storage and the building (or rebuilding) of infrastructure

- Projects to develop economically feasible means of processing and packaging agricultural products for home market consumption
- Establishment, maintenance, and supplying of farmer's cooperatives (for marketing, credit provision, and technical services)
- Establishment of training centers for medium-level specialists in African agriculture

• Joint Soviet–U.S. action at various international fora, including the United Nations, in support of collective positions of African developing countries with respect to the interests of exporters of tropical agricultural products and importers of industrial products.

• Establishment of institutional linkages, including conferences and joint technical missions among Soviet, U.S., African, and multilateral agencies concerned with research and action for agricultural production. Priority concerns to be addressed by these conferences include the following:
- Consideration of specific projects in drylands agriculture, which would develop a detailed agenda of specific projects for desert reclamation and food production under conditions of environmental stress
- Consideration of land tenure systems in light of Africa's ever-shrinking land and resource base

• The organization in Africa of a permanent Soviet–U.S. agency with the technical and logistic capacity to develop an early-warning system against locust invasion and the capacity to render timely and adequate assistance to African countries.

• The creation of a joint Soviet–U.S. consulting firm that could render engineering and consultative services in a variety of fields, including food storage systems based on regional systems of food supply and utilization, the efficient utilization of land and water resources, and waste storage and disposal. Such a joint Soviet–U.S. mission has already been formed to investigate deforestation in Madagascar.

• The creation of a joint facility for waging medical warfare against Africa's tropical parasitic diseases. While this may not appear at first glance to be a priority concern as an agricultural topic, it remains the case that in this sector, as elsewhere, Africa's most precious resource is its people. Africa's human resources are needed for agricultural recovery, but they are deeply imperiled by the rampant parasitic and viral diseases that plague the continent.

2

Food Deficits in Africa: Causes and Remedies

MICHAEL F. LOFCHIE

The dramatic recurrence of famine in Sudan underscores once again the perilous fragility of Africa's agricultural sector and the bitter paradox of an agricultural continent recurrently unable to feed its own population. The imagery is cruelly familiar: unutterably painful news photography of starving children; the weary mobilization of private voluntary organizations, many of whose workers and staff have seen failure before; the instant and fleeting involvement of famous entertainment figures, some of whom unscrupulously exploit the situation to abet personal notoriety; and a belated response by variegated official agencies, both national and international. All this is too easily criticized as "too little, too late"—as if any level of governmental and private reaction could be sufficiently timely or adequate.

According to a recent study by the Food and Agriculture Organization (FAO) of the United Nations, Sudan is only one of a number of African nations where the problem of food supply has once again reached desperate proportions.[1] A severe food crisis continues, for example, in Mozambique, primarily because of war-related disruption and turmoil. Its long-standing civil war pitting the Front for the Liberation of Mozambique (FRELIMO) government's forces against a bewildering resistance movement calling itself the Mozambican National Resistance (RENAMO, or MNR) has for several years not only prevented normal cultivation in the countryside, but also severely restricted the rural distribution of food aid and vitally needed agricultural inputs. Political instability and the destruction of the country's rural infrastructure are so advanced that Mozambique is unlikely to receive more than a small fraction of the grain it requires to feed its rural population. The problem of food deficits is critical in Ethiopia, where widespread death due to famine appears again to be inevitable. In Angola, the food requirements of the urban and displaced population for 1988/89 will have to be met almost entirely by imports.

The African countries threatened by dire food emergencies are primarily those afflicted by ongoing civil wars: Ethiopia, Sudan, Angola, Mozambique, and Chad. At first glance, this seems to indicate that internal strife, more than any other factor, is responsible for the chronic problem of food deficits and that the solution lies essentially in finding ways to bring political peace to these troubled lands. There is much reason to accept this proposition. But the list of countries that today face extreme food emergencies is by no means confined to these, and in recent years it has included nations once considered virtually immune to famine, such as Botswana and Malawi.

The fact that acute food shortages recurrently affect a wide range of African countries suggests that this problem cannot be confined to idiosyncratic events such as civil wars and drought, though these are most certainly precipitating factors. For example, a severe locust infestation in northern and western Africa has recently begun to pose a severe danger to the food supplies of a number of Sahelian countries.

Although it is still unclear precisely how great the actual damage due to locust invasion is, experts estimate that the crop loss may be as high as one million tons, an amount equal to about 10 percent of total grain consumption in Sudano-Sahelian Africa during the period 1979–1981.

Despite the obvious importance of such local factors as civil war and crop pests, Africa's problems have deeper, more systemic, or structural roots. During the three-year period 1966–1968, per capita grain production for all the countries of sub-Saharan Africa (not including South Africa) averaged 119 kilograms per person/year. During the three-year period 1982–1984, average per capita grain production had fallen to only about 98 kilograms per person/year. These figures confirm an early study by the United States Department of Agriculture that showed that per capita food production in sub-Saharan Africa was falling by about 1 percent per year.[2]

The future implications of this decline are ominous. According to a study by David Norse of the FAO, Africa's self-sufficiency ratio for cereals (the ratio of grain produced to grain consumed) is likely to drop from about 90 percent in 1961 to as low as 50 percent by the year 2010.[3] Total grain production in that year, however, is forecast to be only about 100 million tons. With annual grain deficits of this magnitude, African countries will require massive imports to enable grain consumption to keep pace with basic human needs. To compound the need for imports still further, grain preferences in Africa have been shifting gradually away from cereals such as maize, sorghum, and millet, which can be grown relatively easily in almost all countries, to wheat and rice, which only a tiny handful of countries can grow in any significant volume.

Because of the debt crisis and the continent's acute balance of payments difficulties, African countries are unlikely to be able to finance their grain needs through commercial imports. Thus, the declining self-sufficiency ratio is, for all practical purposes, an increasing ratio of dependency upon food aid. There seems little doubt that the international donor community will respond by providing generous amounts of food assistance. Whether this response will be adequate to the continent's needs is another matter. Some observers have already begun to comment on "donor fatigue," the tendency for aid organizations to become impatient when food deficits continue to re-cur year after year. At the very least, Africa's perennial need for food assis-tance will render African governments ever more vulnerable to the policy conditionalities of both national and multinational donor organizations.

Africa is the only one of the world's major developing regions where food deficits have been growing in severity in recent years. In both Asia and Latin America, for example, per capita food production has risen steadily since the mid-1960s, and both of these regions are now significant food exporters. Asian and Latin American countries that were once heavily de-pendent upon food imports have become wholly self-sufficient during the past twenty years. Both India and China, for example, no longer depend upon food imports, and even Bangladesh, once considered the global nadir of food deficit countries, is now expected to attain food self-sufficiency before the turn of the century.

Africa's decline in per capita food has exacted a high price in both human and economic terms. The human price is all too visible when attention is directed to heart-rending images of starvation due to inadequate supplies. Less visible over long periods of time is the fact that significant proportions of the populations of affected countries continue to suffer caloric and nutritional deficits. As early as 1970, the FAO estimated that as much as one-fourth of the population of sub-Saharan Africa was suffering from inadequate caloric intake. And this estimate may have been low because it did not take into account the impact of income inequality on the distribution of a country's food supplies. Declining per capita food production, coupled with chronically inadequate caloric intake, has meant that there is little margin for human error, natural disaster, or political turbulence.

The already intractable nature of Africa's food problems has begun to show signs of increasing, especially given international donors' impatience over the need to provide regular supplies of concessional or humanitarian aid. There is a growing conviction on the part of many donor nations that Africa's food deficits are the product of a combination of poor policy and poor management and that the appropriate remedy, therefore, is not food assistance, but political or policy reform. Donor country development experts have also become sensitive to the extent to which food aid is itself a part of the problem because it serves as a disincentive to come to terms with low agricultural prices. As well, donor organizations have been offended by the tendency of some African political leaders to use food aid for political purposes or as a means for elite corruption.

The crisis of African agriculture is by no means confined to the food-producing sector. It includes the production of exportable agricultural goods as well. Indeed, Africa's food crisis is deepened further by the inability of many countries to provide for high levels of food imports out of their own financial resources. Export-oriented agriculture should provide the foreign exchange earnings necessary to finance food imports, but stagnating produc-tion mitigates that solution.

Africa's share of the world market for an extensive array of agricultural exports has fallen steadily since the 1960s. The list of such commodities includes coffee, tea, cotton, bananas, and oilseeds. Since world demand for these commodities is projected to grow only slowly at best, Africa's prospects of recreating an adequate stream of foreign exchange earnings from agricultural exports depends upon the introduction of policies that will enable the continent to recapture its former share of the world market for these products. But increased exports into a world of relatively fixed demand could simply result in the suppression of already low prices.

The faltering production of export agriculture has had profound reverberations for other economic sectors. Most fundamentally, it has posed a serious constraint on the performance of Africa's urban industries. Since much of Africa's industrial sector is based on import substitution, hard currency agricultural exports are necessary to finance needed inputs. As the earnings from export agriculture have in fact stagnated, diminishing reserves of foreign exchange have been available to finance the purchase of other vitally necessary imports such as food and energy. Consequently, Africa's urban industries have begun to suffer from the lack of replacement capital goods, spare parts, and raw materials. The most conspicuous symptom of these shortages has been a falling rate of capacity utilization, already as low as 25 percent or 30 percent in some countries. But other symptoms of the problem are high rates of inflation (due to a shortage of imported consumer goods), increasing rates of urban unemployment (caused by industrial closures), and a falling real wage rate caused principally by the concomitant fall in labor productivity.

One of the more portentous outcomes of Africa's broad agricultural malaise is a debt crisis of steadily worsening proportions. During the past decade, African countries have accumulated an enormous debt burden, which diminishes the prospects of economic recovery because debt servicing has now become an additional drain on dwindling foreign exchange reserves. As late as 1974, the total outstanding debt of Africa's low-income countries was only about $7.5 billion and the debt service ratio for these countries (debt payments as a percentage of foreign exchange earnings) was only about 7 percent. By the mid-1980s, the debt burden of this group of countries had increased nearly fourfold, to over $30 billion, and the debt service ratio had increased almost four and a half times, to well over 30 percent. Today some of the countries most seriously affected by debt have completely unmanageable debt service ratios. Tanzania's, for example, is well over 60 percent, as is Egypt's. More than 95 percent of Egypt's foreign exchange earnings are utilized for debt service and food imports!

THE CAUSALITY DEBATE

Africa's agricultural crisis has given rise to a wide-ranging debate about the root causes and real remedies for the problem. Within this debate, four dominant positions can be identified: (1) the critical importance of episodic factors, (2) the environmentalist view, (3) emphasis on external factors in the international economic environment, and (4) emphasis on the agricultural policies of African governments.

Episodic Events

Transitory factors such as domestic insurgency have an impact, as the close correlation between civil war and famine in Africa demonstrates. Wars diminish agricultural production by disrupting planting, harvesting, the maintenance of infrastructure, and the delivery of inputs; they also generate an atmosphere of economic unpredictability and extreme personal insecurity. Civil wars create refugee populations, thus reducing the number of persons productively engaged in agriculture. At the same time, war increases the number of those who depend upon already fragile food delivery systems. In areas where agricultural production has declined, a civil war can make the difference between a crisis and a disaster. Civil war is not the cause of poor agricultural performance, but it *is* the cause of death due to famine.

Drought, as Ethiopia and Mozambique illustrate, is also among the episodic events that contribute to poor agricultural performance in African countries. Africa has experienced two particularly severe droughts during the past twenty years. The first was the Sahelian drought of 1968 to 1973, which severely affected the West African countries lying along the southern border of the Sahara desert. The human impact was so severe that it stimulated an outpouring of international assistance to the Sahelian countries and the formation of a multinational donor organization devoted to redevelopment of the region, the Club du Sahel. A second drought, centered closer to the Horn of Africa in Sudan and Ethiopia, occurred between 1983 and 1985; it may still be affecting parts of southern Africa, including Botswana and the Republic of South Africa.

The critical question is whether Africa's recent droughts are part of a long-term shift toward a more arid climate. The Sahelian drought was initially viewed as a unique event. The more abundant rainfall in 1974 was therefore seen as a return to "normal" conditions. Climatologists analyzing the 1983–1985 drought, however, concluded that the low levels of mean annual rainfall during the sixteen-year period (1970–1985) were unprecedented in this century, a finding that suggested the possibility that a new, more arid, era was under way. The evidence for this point of view is unpersuasive, however. Historical rainfall data for Africa is fragmentary at best, and much of the case rests on flimsy archaeological evidence about the incidence of drought in previous centuries. The weight of expert opinion views climate change as an extremely gradual process, extending over several millennia. It is a development that would, therefore, allow much time for human adaptation.[4]

This suggests that the critical factor is not rainfall alone, but, rather, the interaction between rainfall patterns and changing patterns of human settlement. Africa has experienced massive population growth since the beginning of the colonial era during the last quarter of the nineteenth century. This explanation is itself the product of numerous factors, most notably the end of the slave trade, which is generally dated at around the 1880s for West Africa and slightly later for East Africa. Also important was the introduction of bioscientific medicine, which drastically reduced infant mortality and has helped to extend life expectancy. The result of population growth has been enormous pressure on the continent's potentially productive agricultural areas, some of which have begun to experience population densities as high as any in China, India, or Western Europe.

As population has grown, some people have sought economic opportunity in agriculturally marginal areas, principally semiarid regions where rainfall has always been less in volume and more unpredictable in pattern. Population growth may also have exacerbated the effects of climatic irregularity by inducing a change from cultivation methods suitable to low rainfall conditions to agrarian systems that are dependent upon more abundant and predictable patterns of precipitation.

As Africa's population has increased, the escape mechanisms that permitted localized adjustment to drought conditions are eliminated. Shifting cultivation is now extremely rare; in most regions, there is simply not enough land to allow significant acreage for fallow. More importantly, population growth has increasingly precluded the possibility of cultivating more than a single piece of farmland. If such land is located within a drought-affected climatic zone, there is no backup in the form of family agricultural plots in less affected locations. It has also become less and less possible for the vast majority of African farmers to move their farms to regions where drought conditions are less severe, because such regions are in all likelihood already densely populated.

Explanations of agricultural decline that focus on drought alone, without taking these additional factors into account, miss the complexity of the problem. Part of that complexity lies in the fact that rainfall patterns are simply one feature of the physical environment within which agriculture in Africa must be carried out. If it is difficult on the evidence available to make the case that Africa's rainfall levels are undergoing a long-term decline, there is compelling reason to believe that other elements of the continent's natural environment have, in recent generations, been intensely subjected to processes of physical depletion. There is little doubt that broad patterns of environmental degradation have had a profound effect on the productivity of the continent's agricultural systems.

The Environmentalist Viewpoint

Policy debates about the causes of Africa's agricultural crisis often omit one of the most important long-term factors: the degradation of Africa's physical environment. The omission is singularly regrettable. Damage to the continent's fragile ecosystems has become so severe in some areas that the prospects of agroeconomic recovery would be extremely poor, even should other causes be corrected. As this issue is the subject of C. S. Whitaker's chapter in this book, it may suffice here merely to state certain of the central aspects of the environmental analysis.

The process of environmental degradation is most conspicuous in the Sahel, where vast regions of once arable land have been converted to desert wasteland within the last century. But damage to the continent's physical base can also be discerned in a wide range of countries throughout the eastern, central, and southern regions of the continent.

Agricultural systems introduced during the period of European colonialism have been partly responsible for this problem. To understand the genesis of the process, it is useful to recall that much of Africa's land area is not well suited to intensive agricultural development. Throughout much of the continent, the soil cover is typically thin, deficient in vital nutrients, and low in organic content. In addition, Africa's rainfall patterns are typically characterized by extremes of high and low precipitation and by a frustrating degree of unpredictability from one season to the next. As a result, African soils are easily susceptible to rapid depletion of capacity to sustain intensive cultivation. Methods of agricultural production that were developed in temperate latitudes, where the soil base is more dense and rainfall patterns more regular and predictable, have proven to be highly destructive under these conditions.

In Africa's tropical regions, preservation of the soil base typically depended upon the presence of a perennial ground cover consisting of forests of year-round grasses and scrubs. Africa's physical environment may have consisted of a relatively dense green cover during the precolonial era. But this was only possible because of the highly delicate balance between organic decomposition of surface vegetation and the growth of new plant materials. Colonial agriculture, however, frequently required the clearing of this ground cover in order to introduce crops that have an annual harvest cycle. Crops such as cotton, groundnuts, and tobacco have proven to be especially harmful, for they require that vast amounts of land be cleared of original cover, which interrupts the natural cycle of organic replenishment. Once such annual crops are harvested, the earth is laid bare and exposed to the baking action of the sun. Desiccated soils have virtually no capacity to store moisture, and when rainfall does occur, even in modest amounts, its effects are typically to cause erosion and gullying. Deprived of the stabilizing benefit of tree and shrub root systems, the soils are easily washed away, leaving behind a barren terrain wholly unsuitable for agricultural production.

It would be incorrect to place the entire responsibility for this sort of environmental destruction on colonially introduced agricultural systems, because certain of the rural practices of African peoples have also proven harmful. As Africa's population has expanded, African communities have been forced to abandon traditional agricultural practices such as shifting cultivation, which allowed for long fallow periods during which the soil could regenerate. In addition, rapid population growth has generally been accompanied by a rapid growth in the size of the continent's herds of domesticated animals. This has resulted in widespread overgrazing, further stripping the soil of its protective cover of grasses and shrubs. Deforestation also continues to result from the fact that wood continues to be Africa's most common cooking fuel and construction material. Yet, for some countries, such as Ivory Coast, timber exports are a critically important source of foreign exchange.

The end product of the processes is desertification, the conversion of once arable land to desertlike conditions. This process is most dramatically under way in the Sahel countries, where the southern movement of the Sahara desert has sometimes been estimated in the magnitude of kilometers per year. According to *National Geographic* magazine, desertification in this region has consumed nearly 250,000 square miles, an area the size of France and Austria, during the past fifty years.[5] Desertification is by no means confined to the Sahel, however. It can be observed in every major region of the continent, including eastern and southern Africa. Indeed, desertification is so widespread that its effects are virtually impossible to measure precisely. But the cumulative impact of various processes of environmental deterioration is certainly enormous. To this extent, Africa's prospects for agricultural recovery are all the more bleak because the process of environmental decay is seemingly irreversible.

According to one theory, desertification may even have contributed to changing Africa's rainfall pattern, since an area that is vegetated is more likely to receive rain, if the possibility exits, than one that is not. If correct, this theory suggests that Africa's droughts emanate from the destructive manner in which human populations have interacted with their physical environment.

The portentous implication of the environmental factor is that it appears to rule out so many frequently suggested solutions to the continent's agricultural crisis. A readaptation of certain historical forms of agricultural production would be wholly impractical, for example. Not only would traditional agricultural practices be completely incapable of supporting today's population levels, but those practices depend upon ecological systems of soil preservation and replenishment that, in many areas, have all but ceased to be a part of the physical environment. Africa's unique environmental problems also cast doubt on the viability of further developing intensive agroscientific production systems, because these have the potential to wreak disastrous effects on the continent's fragile topsoils and to further accelerate the tendency toward desertification. It seems imperative that future solutions to Africa's agricultural crisis be based on sound environmental as well as economic principles. But there is as yet very little sense on the part of African governments or among donor organizations of exactly how this can be done.

The Externalist Viewpoint

Proponents of the externalist viewpoint tend to assign primary responsibility for the agricultural crisis to salient features of the international economic system, including the declining terms of trade for primary agricultural exporters. There is a general consensus among observers of Africa's present economic predicament that the continent has suffered badly because of adverse changes in the international terms of trade and that its current perilous state can be traced in large measure to the rising costs of the goods that African countries need to import in relation to the prices of the goods they export. Recent World Bank research on Africa's terms of trade shows an especially sharp downward trend beginning in 1979. The Bank's report assesses economic effects of this decline in stark terms.

> Between 1980 and 1982, prices of non-oil primary commodities declined by 27 percent in current dollar terms. The loss of income due to deterioration in the terms of trade was 1.2 percent of GDP for sub-Saharan Africa; middle-income oil importers suffered the biggest loss (3 percent of GDP) . . . and low income countries a loss of 2.4 percent of GDP.[6]

This trend toward declining terms of trade helps account for the critical scarcity of foreign exchange that the overwhelming majority of African countries now experience.

For countries suffering critical food deficits, the potential benefits of increased production of export crops are completely eroded by the declining prices of these products. Sudan, for example, was able to increase cotton production by about 50 percent in the early 1980s, but a sharp drop in the world market price for this product meant that its foreign exchange position deteriorated badly. World Bank economists now anticipate a continued fall in the terms of trade for sub-Saharan Africa throughout the 1980s, with real price levels for Africa's key exports falling at least 15–25 percent, to prices even lower than those that prevailed in the 1960s. Price declines of this magnitude make it extremely difficult for governments to implement policy reforms, such as price increases, to improve production. An increase in domestic producer prices could easily result in enormous budget deficits if the world market prices of any particular commodity were to drop after a government had raised its official price to the producer.

Externalists believe strongly that critics of African governments generally fail to distinguish between poor pricing policies and the depressed price levels of primary agricultural commodities on world markets. They argue as well that the drop in foreign exchange earnings resulting from falling prices has constrained the implementation of infrastructure improvements intended to facilitate increased exports. The building of improved transportation systems and storage and processing facilities and the acquisition of upgraded port facilities are heavily dependent upon the availability of foreign exchange. If foreign exchange earnings fall due to lower world prices, vital infrastructural improvements must be postponed.

The scarcity of foreign exchange is compounded by another salient feature of the international economic system: the markedly low demand elasticities for Africa's key agricultural commodities. World demand for such critically important agricultural exports as coffee, cocoa, and tea has been virtually static for the past decade or more and is generally expected to remain so for the rest of this century. The World Bank's study of anticipated demand for Africa's principal agricultural exports over the next decade presents a gloomy picture, suggesting that world consumption of these products will increase by only about 3 percent per year, or less, for the foreseeable future.

African countries are therefore compelled to operate in a highly perverse environment. Their efforts to increase the production and export of these commodities could well turn out to be self-defeating. If increased supplies enter an already overcrowded market, the result might well be a drop in prices far greater than the percentage increase in exports. The net result would be a fall in foreign exchange earning such as that experienced by Sudan when it increased cotton exports in 1981 and 1982.

Internal Factors

Analysts who emphasize the internal sources of agricultural decay are inclined to attach great importance to the economic policies pursued since independence by African states. Chief among these is the continentwide tendency to control and suppress agricultural prices. Robert Bates has made this particular observation central to his analysis of Africa's agrarian crisis. In his classic study, *Markets and States in Tropical Africa,* for example, Bates notes that "the producers of cash crops for export . . . have been subject to a pricing policy that reduces the prices they receive to a level well below market prices."[7]

The policy of price suppression has had an especially marked and destructive impact on the continent's food production. It is probably rooted in a variety of objectives, including the desire to provide a low-cost food supply for cities. For export crops, it stems from the belief that agricultural exports should generate an economic surplus adequate to finance the development of an industrial sector and to provide for the import needs of the public sector. It now seems clear that this policy has had effects that are precisely the opposite from those intended: it has become a major factor in accounting for the stagnation of agricultural exports. The disincentive posed by low food prices has severely constrained the available supplies of marketed food staples. Indeed, suppression of agricultural producer prices may well be the single most important factor in accounting for the sharp decline in Africa's share of world trade in agricultural commodities, relative to other developing areas, and for the skyrocketing increase of food imports.

A second major policy with adverse effects on agricultural production has been a ubiquitous tendency toward currency overvaluation. The effects of this policy have been most severe in Africa's anglophone countries, whose currencies are not directly tied to those of a major European power; but it also occurs even in the francophone nations whose currencies are officially pegged to the French franc. Currency overvaluation operates as a hidden tax on the financial return to the producers of export goods and thus has precisely the same effect on agricultural exports as the suppression of producer prices. It also depresses the availability of marketed food staples for local consumption. By artificially cheapening the value of imported goods, including foodstuffs, currency overvaluation sets up an unfair competition with domestic food producers. The broad impact is to subsidize the cost of living of urban consumers at the expense of rural producers.

The widespread use of parastatal corporations has also had a substantial and deleterious effect on Africa's agricultural sector. Africa's parastatals are characterized almost everywhere by destructive levels of corruption, inefficiency, and mismanagement. In some cases, the expenses of the parastatal corporations are actually higher than the returns from crop sales, leaving no margins whatsoever with which to pay the producers. The result has been a consistent and growing tendency toward nonpayment, late payment, or partial payment of farmers, a major disincentive in itself to the production of marketed agricultural surpluses. In a number of African countries, agricultural parastatals are also given responsibility for the implementation of key agricultural services such as the provision of fertilizers and pesticides. Here, too, the record of parastatal performance is, with rare exceptions, a uniformly poor one.

A poor choice of development strategies has also contributed to the present crisis. Some observers believe that the decision to pursue a policy of industrialization through import substitution, for example, may be held at least partially responsible for the continent's deteriorating agricultural performance. This form of industrialization has sapped away capital and other resources that might otherwise have gone into financing needed agricultural improvements. Michael Roemer, for example, has criticized import-substitution strategies in Africa because "they focus development efforts on industrialization although it is agriculture that remains the base of the economy and that employs the majority of workers."[8] One of the factors that has undermined Africa's position in world agriculture trade has been the continent's inability to respond to changing market conditions by introducing new, high-demand crops or more productive varieties of old ones. This rigidity seems rooted largely in the scarcity of capital for agricultural reinvestment, and this scarcity is fundamentally the product of an industrial policy that is not oriented toward the generation of its own sources of foreign exchange.

Industrialization by import substitution has also required high levels of tariff protection for the infant industries. This, in turn, has meant that Africa's farmers have been confronted with extremely high prices for consumer goods and for the agricultural inputs that are manufactured in the new industries.[9] Moreover, in many cases, Africa's import-substitution industries have been marked by inefficient management and this has sometimes resulted in severe scarcities of essential agricultural inputs. Urban industries that are highly protected also diminish agricultural performance by competing in the same labor markets; by bidding up wage levels, they can create severe labor bottlenecks in the countryside.

CONCLUSION: AREAS OF COOPERATION

The possibilities for fruitful cooperation to help in remedying Africa's food shortages are considerable. They begin with the need to identify projects for environmental reconstruction in areas where agricultural recovery is hampered by the process of agroecological decay. They include the necessity for broad international cooperation to help alleviate the disastrous fall in the terms of trade that has so badly undercut efforts to improve the production of export goods. And they include, most importantly, the need for concerted international pressure on African governments to remedy those domestic policies that have suppressed production below reasonable levels. The Soviet Union particularly is in an excellent position to assume a leading role in this latter process. The gradual introduction of agricultural reforms intended to allow greater scope for market forces is potentially an instance of leadership by example.

NOTES

1. Food and Agriculture Organization of the United Nations, *Food Supply Situation and Crop Prospects in Sub-Saharan Africa: Special Report* (n.p., June 1988), iii.

2. United States Department of Agriculture, Economic Research Service, *Food Problems and Prospects in Sub-Saharan Africa: The Decade of the 1980s* (Washington, D.C.: World Bank, 1981), 46.

3. David Norse, "Population, Resources and Food in Africa," *Population Bulletin of the United Nations*, nos. 21/22, 1987.

4. The author is deeply indebted to Michael Glantz of the National Center for Atmospheric Research for these observations.

5. William S. Ellis, "Africa's Sahel: The Stricken Land," *National Geographic* (August 1987): 144.

6. The World Bank, *Toward Sustained Development in Sub-Saharan Africa: A Joint Program of Action* (Washington, D.C.: World Bank, 1984), 11–12.

7. Robert Bates, *Markets and States in Tropical Africa* (Los Angeles: University of California Press, 1981), 28.

8. Michael Roemer, "Economic Development in Africa: Performance Since Independence," *Daedalus* (Spring 1982): 132.

9. Bates, *Markets and States,* 62–67.

3

Development of Food Production and Distribution in the Agrarian Sector

GLEB V. SMIRNOV

The backwardness of the agrarian sector and the declining production of food sufficient to feed fast-growing populations are among the most acute economic and social problems in the vast majority of African countries, particularly those south of the Sahara. Most of the Third World has suffered from food shortages and hunger in the past fifteen to twenty years, but the situation in Africa is especially critical.

In the Third World as a whole, the average rates of agrarian production increased slightly between 1961 and 1985, with national food production growing by an average of 0.5 percent a year. In Africa, however, agricultural production, food included, substantially dropped in the 1971–1985 period. Even taking into account high population growth rates, favorable weather conditions, and a record high harvest registered in 1984–1985, per capita food production in Africa decreased between 1970 and 1986 by over 17 percent, and by 20 percent in countries south of the Sahara.

REASONS FOR THE CRITICAL SITUATION IN AFRICA'S AGRICULTURE

It would be wrong to attempt to arrange in order of importance the causes underlying the decline and stagnation of Africa's agrarian sector. Explanatory factors vary in terms of time and place. Generally, however, three groups of reasons for this critical impasse can be identified: (1) environmental, (2) external, and (3) internal. Each of these should be considered in identifying ways and means to overcome the difficulties encountered by the agrarian sector of African countries.

Natural and Man-Made Environmental Problems

A considerable part of Africa lies in arid and semiarid zones with dry subtropical and tropical climates. With rainfall varying from year to year, these zones suffer from droughts, which have led to drastic declines in agricultural production, food shortages, and famine. Observations conducted in the past ten to fifteen years reveal that the area affected by catastrophic droughts has increased. In the 1982–1984 period, droughts hit the Sahelian countries and also Ethiopia, Somalia, Kenya, Uganda, Zimbabwe, Rwanda, and some other nations. In total, about 150 million people, or 30 percent of the continent's population, were implicated, with the rate of decline in food production being more than 26 percent in Gambia, 25 percent in Senegal, 21 percent in Zimbabwe (1982/83), nearly 25 percent in Uganda, and 15 percent in Kenya (1983/84).

Droughts are due to both weather changes and the global effect the world's economic activity has on the atmosphere (recently, widespread attention has been drawn to the greenhouse effect, said to result from concentrations of carbon dioxide and other compounds in the atmosphere). But this is not the only ecological factor negatively affecting the rehabilitation and development of agriculture in Africa.

Ecology, particularly soil systems in arid zones, is sensitive to external factors, and equilibrium is easily upset. Desertification is a result. Desertification connotes the depletion and partial or complete degradation of ground ecological systems: destruction of vegetation cover, water and wind erosion of soils, growing compactness of ground layers, salinization, and an ultimate loss of fertility. Increasing desertification is a direct result of economic activity: the felling of trees for fuel, overgrazing, absence of crop rotations, archaic farming techniques (such as slash-and-burn), and ill-planned or mismanaged irrigation systems.

Such human factors affect soil fertility, especially in African countries with humid tropical climates. Forests are cut in those countries for fuel and timber exports. In addition, the traditional method of protecting the fragile fertile layer of tropical soil is deprived of its natural protective defenses of mulching leaves and grass. Crops such as cotton, groundnuts, and tobacco require removal of natural vegetation cover, thus depriving the soil of its normal supply of organic fertilizers. After harvesting, bare soil is dried up by the sun, its fertile layer is washed away by rain, and gullies are formed.

In conditions of fast population growth, African communities depart from traditional farming methods of shifting fields, thus damaging soil regeneration. Regeneration is also inhibited by domestic cattle raising, which depletes the grasses and shrubs that protect the soil from erosion.

Some efforts to increase agricultural production and solve the food problem further damage ecological systems. Methods of intensive agrarian production, such as those that produced the "Green Revolution," can hardly boost agricultural output unless the ecological situation is improved, desertification is arrested, and soil fertility is restored.

Most African countries have insufficient labor, material, and financial resources to put an end to this vicious circle. The problem can be solved only by the joint efforts of African and industrially developed countries.

The developed countries can contribute to scaling down and removing negative ecological factors by, first, finding more rational ways and methods of controlling desertification; second, by restoring soil fertility; and third, by properly using land and water, all with due account being given to meeting the specific needs of various regions and countries and to rendering economic and technical assistance in the most efficient manner.

External Factors

Even a general analysis prompts the conclusion that, more and more, external factors and conditions have been seriously inhibiting progress in African agrarian production.

The terms of trade, which were favorable on the whole for African countries in the 1970s, have considerably deteriorated in the current decade. As a result of this factor alone, between 1980 and 1987, sub-Saharan countries lost about $8 billion, recording no less than a $20 billion loss in export revenues (estimated on the basis of UN Conference on Trade and Development [UNCTAD] data). A reduction in the international market prices of exports, along with price increases for many imported industrial products, brought about a substantial decline in the purchasing power of those countries. There are reasons to believe that the structural changes occurring in Western economies and the related decline in their demand for raw materials and energy resources will continue to have a negative effect on the terms of trade for African countries, which will nonetheless continue to stress the export of raw materials for many years to come. Deterioration of the terms of trade restricts the import of goods and services and has a negative effect on the development of the economy as a whole and the agrarian sector in particular. This external constraint can be removed only by international action.

Foreign debt is a major factor contributing to persistence of the crisis of food production and distribution. In 1987 foreign debt equaled more than two-thirds of Africa's aggregate gross domestic product (GDP); servicing that debt consumed over a fourth of export revenues.

Of no less importance is the fact that beginning with 1983 (1984 for countries south of the Sahara) African countries in effect stopped receiving finances for development. This came about because financial inflows were more than matched by outflows in the form of debt servicing and payment of returns on direct foreign investments. An international political will is therefore needed to help solve this problem as well.

There are yet other external factors to include in the picture. In a number of cases foreign donors, especially the United States, prefer providing African countries direct food aid rather than aid designed to boost local food production. Food overproduction in the West will continue to minimalize Western investment in agriculture and agroindustry in Africa. Recent evidence suggests that the widespread consumption of nonindigenous grains, partly as a result of their availability through importation, has led to underproduction of traditional crops, which might otherwise be cultivated and to which appropriate conditions and techniques apply.

Regional conflicts are a still weightier factor contributing to the deterioration of the agrarian sector in a number of African countries. Such conflicts have involved over a dozen developing countries, accounting for more than 25 percent of Africa's population (outside South Africa). In all these countries, per capita food production declined, most critically in Mozambique, Angola, Ethiopia, Sudan, and Somalia. It would be wrong to suppose that all conflicts in Africa are due to external factors. They often are related to internal ethnic, political, and other causes. It must be recognized, however, that all these conflicts have involved foreign forces, even if indirectly. In this respect, too, the world community can make a major contribution by seeking solutions to these conflicts and their negative consequences.

Internal Factors

It is hard to identify the most important internal factors, but it is a fact that it will be extremely difficult, if at all possible, to solve the food problem without addressing internal factors in terms of their effect on the agrarian sector.

African countries have often suffered from erroneous views concerning the role of the agrarian sector in the economy, particularly with respect to development. Such mistaken views frequently underlie the strategies, plans, and programs of economic development during the first decades of independence. Stress was placed on industrial development as the principle and the primary method of overcoming backwardness and ensuring independence. Investments were geared to the same objectives.

It was only in the late 1970s that new concepts and ideas forced their way to the attention of policymakers. These concepts stressed the relationship between agrarian and industrial development, arguing generally for a redistribution of resources toward agriculture. In other words, this reorientation was directed toward setting up agroindustrial complexes to process locally produced agricultural inputs, produce tools and consumer goods for the rural population, and enhance national infrastructure. Concrete economic policy measures (prices, taxes, credit, etc.) have taken shape in accordance with these concepts.

In a majority of African countries, commodity-monetary relations between rural and urban economies are underdeveloped. In this sphere, too, a kind of vicious circle has been formed. The underdevelopment of commodity-monetary relations inhibits the application of economic measures (indirect economic regulation) to boost agrarian production. On the other hand, rural producers have neither the stimulus nor the opportunity to increase production of commodities in the absence of sound government policies involving prices, taxes, and credit.

In most cases this vicious circle creates conditions that make the development of export agricultural production a difficult task. It goes without saying that African countries themselves should map out and use means of developing commodity-monetary relations between rural and urban economies and of boosting the production of agricultural commodities. Nevertheless, recommendations by more developed countries may prove useful.

Other conditions that adversely affect African agriculture include the common practice of currency overvaluation. This diminishes the competitiveness of African exports, reduces revenues from agricultural products exported, and creates greater incentives to import rather than to produce food. In addition, the agrarian sector is often adversely impacted by the involvement of parastatal corporations with their corruption, low efficiency, and bad management.

It stands to reason that many of the agricultural conditions cited are the result of Africa's general social and economic underdevelopment, lack of experience in state administration, political instability, ethnic contradictions, and so forth. Overcoming all these negative factors will require time, experience, and training of national personnel. Foreign aid to improve the internal climate for the purpose of agrarian development is both possible and advisable. This aid should be offered in measured and cautious fashion, and should not take the form of interference with the internal affairs of African countries.

4

Food Production and Distribution: The Case of Senegal

CHEIKH TIDIANE SY

The crisis of the Senegalese economy is that of its agriculture. Because its economy has not yet escaped its colonial legacy, Senegal is listed among the countries that have registered the lowest rate of GDP growth since 1960 (2.3 percent). Groundnuts and millet have remained the basic crops, the latter being used for domestic consumption and the former for export. Groundnuts are the largest earner of foreign exchange. Since 1970, however, Senegal has been exposed to a series of climatic variations leading to a quasi-permanent drought. This has resulted in the accumulation of structural and financial constraints in the rural economy, which have reduced the volume of agriculture production by 40 percent. These structural constraints can be identified as: (1) the lack of a consistent agricultural policy, and (2) the deteriorating resource base of the rural economy.

The lack of a consistent agricultural policy is the main cause of the negative growth rate of the rural economy and appears to be the major problem facing Senegal, as the authors of the Medium and Long Term Economic and Financial Adjustment Program have recognized:

> Not only . . . must the agricultural sector undergo a whole series of adjustments, but given its importance, its restoration lies at the heart of any revival policy. Indeed, agricultural development can furnish important elements in the overall adjustment of the economy, as well as the basis for accelerated growth in other sectors and the best means of ensuring productive jobs for the majority of the population and contributing to slowing down the drift to the cities.[1]

In Senegal, most of the population is located in the Peanut Basin, which has registered very low rainfall in the last decade; in the same area, the soil has been deteriorating considerably. Not only has groundnut production decreased, but the price paid to agricultural producers in general has not increased for many years, especially for food crops. The resulting lack of incentive to producers has disfavored the expansion of food production. As a result—and this is a distinguishing feature of monoeconomies—food production has decreased, forcing the Senegalese government to import food to cover deficits. The heavy dependence of the country upon a single crop for export, and the costs of the 1977 drought, has forced Senegal's leaders to undertake a crop diversification program. This step did not, however, involve the substitution of new crops in expanded production areas outside the Peanut Basin (see Table 4.1). Thus, in the north irrigated rice, vegetables, wheat, and sugar were promoted; in the eastern region the program was based on the increase of cotton and corn; and in the southern region the approach was to expand the production of tropical fruits, cotton, peanuts, and corn.

Table 4.1
Evolution of Groundnut Production Between 1978/79 and 1982/83

	1978/79	1979/80	1980/81	1981/82	1982/83
Output[a]	1,061	676	523	872	1,164
Area cultivated[b]	1,175	1,069	1,075	1,016	1,167
Value of yield[c]	0.9	0.6	0.5	0.9	1.0

Source: Ministry of Planning and Cooperation, Dakar, November 1984.
Notes: [a] Thousands of tons
　　　　 [b] Thousands of hectares
　　　　 [c] Billions of CFA

As can be seen from these data, the crop diversification program did not alter the "strategic" role of peanuts in the economy.

In the fifth four-year Development Plan (1977–1981) agricultural development was given the highest priority; yet, ironically, the total investment in crop production dropped from 48 percent to 41 percent of the total for the agricultural sector. More than half of the investment in crop production (56 percent) was directed toward irrigation projects in the northern and southern regions in support of the two major parastatal agencies' programs in rice production.

According to Ministry of Planning sources, total food production in 1980 covered less than 50 percent of national cereal needs, and in 1981 millet production decreased by about 40 percent. The reduction of cultivated land and a decrease in the volume of fertilizer going to producers were the principal causes of the decline. As for rice—farmed principally in the Fleuve and Casamance regions—production declined dramatically: between 1979 and 1983 it fell from 147,000 tons to 92,000 tons, the decrease resulting largely from reduction of land area devoted to rice cultivation.[2] Table 4.2 provides the evolution of output for major cereals between 1978/79 and 1982/83.

Table 4.2
Production of Major Cereal Crops, 1978/79–1982/83
(Thousands of Tons)

	1978/79	1979/80	1980/81	1981/82	1982/83
Millet & sorghum	802	503	553	986	585
Rice (paddy)	147	97	68	127	95
Corn	50	46	50	79	82
Niebe (cowpea)	23	19	17	46	11

Source: Ministry of Planning and Cooperation, Dakar, November 1984.

The cereal deficit of the country continued to be a major concern for the Senegalese government, as reflected in the sixth four-year Development Plan (1981–1985), in which rice production was expected to increase from 112,000 tons in 1980 to 220,000 tons in 1985, with average national consumption being estimated at 531,000 tons. But because of the high costs of domestic rice production, compared to the cost of imported rice, the objective was not reached.

Senegal's stated development objectives, which have always given priority to agriculture, have never been matched in the allocation of national resources in the various development plans. The state's financial contribution to its own development policy has decreased from one plan to the other, not only for the agriculture sector, but overall.[3] It is therefore easy to conclude that the government's ambition, in the sixth Development Plan, to increase food production from 732,000 tons in 1980 to 1,037,000 tons in 1985—an annual increase of 7.2 percent—was highly unrealistic, if not pure slogan.

Another factor having a destabilizing effect on agricultural growth in Senegal is the outflow of labor from the rural sector and the resulting expansion of the urban population. This problem is illustrated by the massive migration out of the two most peripheral regions (Fleuve and Casamance), where economic opportunities generally are lacking. While in some Fleuve villages about 80 percent of the men aged seventeen to fifty have migrated, in Casamance the heaviest drain occurred among young educated men and women aged thirteen to twenty-five. The rural economy is obviously affected by this outflow of labor, which benefits mainly the urban sector.[4]

In many cases migration has become a necessity; it is also a strategy for the rural migrants to earn cash income and to escape from the heavy labor required in agriculture, especially in rice production. In October 1983 a Diola peasant was quoted as saying:

This year I must go to Dakar, but this is not what I wanted. The rice yields are not good and we will have to buy rice. The price of peanuts will decrease to 10

CFA the kg. Ordinarily it is the cash received from the sale of peanuts that serves to pay the local tax and to buy clothes. This year the cash is to be provided from the sale of the rice. I must go to Dakar to help the women.[5]

This outflow of labor from the rural economy is not a transitory phenomenon. Given the young age of the migrants, it must be regarded as a long-term disengagement of the nation's youth from agriculture, which as a vocation they consider to be not only backward and disreputable, but insufficiently remunerative as well.

The country's long-term productive capacity, particularly in the Peanut Basin, has been seriously affected by a rapidly growing population, increased pressure on rangelands, and above all by continuous deforestation. These factors have been unfavorable to agricultural development in Senegal; indeed, they tend to undermine any and all efforts to increase agricultural production. Senegalese leaders are inclined to explain the deterioration of the environment and the depletion of the soil as "a fact of nature," ignoring the fact that the areas concerned have been subject for centuries to a form of "extractive agriculture," that is to say, intensive peanut cultivation, resulting in the degradation of the land. Moreover, not only has the government granted special authorizations to Muslim brotherhoods, particularly the Murids, to cultivate on lands traditionally reserved for sylvo-pastoral activities, but it has facilitated their migration to the southern part of the country, where the land is still wet and fertile.

In addition to these factors underlying the deterioration of Senegal's productive capacity in agriculture, the practices of bush burning for fields and tree cutting for fuel have resulted in serious desertification. In this area, too, the government's response has been uninspired: antidesertification measures remain burdened by top-heavy bureaucratic mechanisms and involve no community input or participation in planning or implementation.

PRICE AND DISTRIBUTION POLICIES

Price policy plays a fundamental role in any agricultural strategy, and in most African countries the tendency is to tax the agricultural sector or to lower prices for food crops. While it would be unrealistic to rely entirely on the price-setting mechanism of the free market to reform state policy, it is true that the state is unlikely to withdraw from what it accepts as a fundamental responsibility.

Since 1983 it has been a policy to encourage the production of cowpeas, through allowing the price to be determined by "market forces." Initially, this resulted in a price increase of 83.3 percent to producers, who responded with a production increase of 45.3 percent. Yet, although producers benefited from temporarily higher prices, consumer demand shrank accordingly, leading to a next swing of the pendulum in the magnitude of a 10 percent drop in the price paid producers between 1985/86 and 1986/87. The effect was a decline in production of over 30 percent in 1986/87.

This case illustrates the difficulties encountered in leaving developmental priorities to market mechanisms alone. In fact, the problems of food distribution and marketing are extremely complex. There are two major issues involved. First, in many African countries the official marketing channel measures only the tip of the iceberg of real flows of goods and money. The real distribution system involves a vast network of "traditional" channels in addition to the official one. This "parallel market" easily accounts for the bulk of food produced and marketed in Senegal. According to the Inter-State Committee for Combatting Drought in the Sahel (CILSS) data, the official marketing channel has never captured more than 10 percent of the millet produced—an important statistic given millet's role as the staple food in rural areas. Second, government policy treats different segments of society, and different subsectors of rural production, differently. In particular, food crops have never benefited from the official attention accorded cash crops.

THE FOOD PLAN AND ITS LIMITATIONS

As with most African countries, Senegal has suffered from a very severe food shortage since the early 1970s. Between 1961 and 1984, food production grew at an average annual rate of only 0.9 percent, while the population growth rate was 2.8 percent. This has led to increased food imports, as shown in Table 4.3.

Table 4.3
Quantities of Food Imported 1970–1984
(Thousands of Tons)

	1970/72	1973/76	1977/80	1981/84
Quantity	295	328	455	488
% growth of imports	—	11.1	38.7	7.2

Source: Plan céréalier - Ministère du Développement Rural, May 1986.

Only 52 percent of the food Senegal needs in the early 1990s is produced locally; the remaining 48 percent consists of imports (40 percent) and food aid (8 percent). If the current population growth rate is maintained, it is expected that by the end of this century Senegal's food requirements will amount to 1,700,000 tons, an increase of 54.2 percent over current levels. During the sixth four-year plan (1981–1985), total food production amounted to 675,000 tons; this means that for food needs to be satisfied at the end of this century, production will have to more than double.

The pattern of Senegal's food consumption is characterized by widespread demand for rice, of which little is produced locally. Indeed, rice production accounted for only 10 percent of food needs during the fifth four-year plan. On the other hand, the quantity of rice consumed increased from 35.7 percent of total food consumption in 1977–1979 to 39.7 percent in 1982–1984. The negative impact of this consumption pattern on Senegal's foreign exchange situation is obvious enough.

The last two four-year plans put a strong emphasis on the need to arrive at self-sufficiency in food production. In fact, the slow growth of food production, which actually resulted in the doubling of food imports in the 1970s, indicates that vast structural changes are needed in the rural sector. The new Food Plan constitutes a major element in the New Agricultural Policy undertaken by the Senegalese government.[6] Its objective is to reach 80 percent of total self-sufficiency in food by the end of this century.

Meanwhile, the following actions have been designed to achieve this challenging objective:

• *An improvement in the productive quality of land.* This would be achieved through widespread use of fertilizers, along with the introduction of high-yielding seed varieties and a more appropriate technology.

• *A reformulation of pricing strategy.* Prices for food crops have been maintained for a long time at a very low level compared to cash crops. The new pricing policy, which aims to give more incentives to producers, should provide for:

  • The setting of prices at a minimum level. Following good harvests, the Food Security Service will buy surpluses to avoid a sharp decrease of prices. On the other hand, when the market price is higher than the minimum price, the Food Security Service will not intervene.

  • Action directed toward gradually changing consumer habits in favor of the locally produced food crops. To that end, there should be created more facilities for the processing of high-quality products, yielding at least as much value for the consumer as the crops replaced. Target prices should be set up for the processed output. To increase the consumption of locally processed products, actions being taken should result in a high-quality, reasonably priced, and readily available product. At the same time, the price of imported food should gradually be raised.

• *The creation of food banks at the village level.* Surpluses should be purchased locally and stored at the village store. This stock would then be resold to the villages during periods of shortages.

• *The establishment of a new credit system.* Its main goal is to allow producers to have easy access to inputs (seeds, fertilizers, pesticides, etc.) and equipment.

• *A greater emphasis on irrigated agriculture.* The objective is to increase the portion of agricultural land under irrigation from 11 percent in 1985 to 38 percent in 2000. Rainfed agriculture has become less and less reliable as rainfall has decreased; thus the long-term solution lies in the use of surface and underground water.

• *Land resource management and environmental protection.* Senegalese authorities have been convinced of the need to encourage community-based action for the protection of the environment and for the management of local land resources on a more equitable basis. These community actions should support local initiatives that contribute to the objective of self-sufficiency.

The achievement of these objectives depends on many factors over which policymakers have little or no control. The Food Plan, for instance, relies a great deal on an increase in the production of rainfed food crops. The rainfall trend is such, however, that expectations should not be high. Moreover, to increase the irrigated lands by 5,000 hectares a year is a really challenging objective, considering the relatively high financial costs of such programs.

NOTES

1. Ministry of Planning and Cooperation, *Medium and Long Term Economic and Financial Adjustment* (Dakar: Ministry of Planning and Cooperation, October 1984).

2. It is important to note that rice production has been the most inefficient in the Fleuve, where there operates one of the major parastatal agencies, SAED.

3. Because of low productivity increases, domestic savings is unchanging, requiring that 85 percent of the budget for development be provided by external sources over the last decade.

4. The case of Senegal confirms Michael Lipton's analysis of the "rural skill drain," a process wherein the young leaders for agricultural development move to cities. See his *Why Poor People Stay Poor* (Cambridge, Mass.: Harvard University Press, 1977), 259.

5. CIEPAC, *Aménagement de la Valée de Bignona* (Dakar: CIEPAC, June 1984), 51.

6. For an assessment of the New Agricultural Policy see *Crise du Développement Rural et Désengagement de L'Etat au Sénégal,* ed. Cheikh Tidiane Sy (Dakar: Nouvelles Editions Africaines, 1988).

PART 2

The Environment

Africa's environmental problems are numerous and the result of complex and interacting causes. While desertification looms as the most widespread and pressing environmental problem, others merit joint African–Soviet–U.S. action. One problem calling for immediate attention involves attempts by industrialized areas to dispose of their toxic and nuclear wastes in African countries. That issue draws urgent attention to the international scope of Africa's environmental problems. In the list of recommendations that follows, those dealing with the issue of industrial wastes are listed separately, since they involve special steps.

The complicated ecological and socioeconomic situation in the arid and semiarid zones of Africa calls for new, large-scale, comprehensive inter-disciplinary studies and long-term programs of cooperative action that cannot be achieved within the current institutional framework. The Soviet Union and the United States, however, are well positioned to help Africa combat desertification, given their resources and their experience in the prevention of further desertification and in the utilization of deserts in areas such as Soviet Central Asia and the U.S. Southwest.

A campaign against desertification entails a number of prerequisites in attitude and organization: elevation of desertification to the status of a global priority; adequate conceptualization of the complex human and material interaction involved in causing desertification; coordination of action in local, national, and international arenas; systemization of analysis, including exploration of computer-modeling techniques; creation of well-established and well-funded institutions with the capacity to institute long-term plans; formulation of flexible strategies capable of responding to specific local conditions; application of recent developments in technology such as remote sensing; and sensitivity and respect for the needs of local people in areas of action, including provision for their participation and education in the campaign against desertification. Specific recommendations for Soviet–U.S. cooperation in this area include:

• Creation of provisional task groups that would include scientists and specialists from those African countries that will be involved in pre-investment research or development projects of this kind.
• Organization, in the Soviet Union and the United States, of educational centers for the training of African participants in specific Soviet–U.S. projects in desertification control. Specialists in the fields of

soil sciences, meteorology, hydrology, and other technical fields will be the most urgently needed trainees.

• Establishment of procedures for information exchange in the areas of ecology and agriculture among African, Soviet, and U.S. scientists who will take part in desertification control projects in Africa.

• Institution of a complementary investigation by African, Soviet, and U.S. scientists of the problem of population-carrying capacity in arid and semiarid areas of Africa.

• Systematic examination of stronger and weaker aspects of programs for Africa administered by the United Nations Environment Programme (UNEP), with the aim of working out proposals to increase the effectiveness of complex long-term programs of combating desertification.

• Creation of a joint African–Soviet–U.S. commission to assist African countries in their fight against desertification. This commission should include specialists and representatives of state agencies from the Soviet Union, the United States, specific African governments, and representatives from African regional and subregional organizations. This commission would provide functional and consultative support and coordination for the measures detailed above.

• Communication of the problems touched upon, on behalf of this project, to UNEP and UNESCO.

The disposal in Africa of radioactive and toxic wastes from industrialized countries has become one of the most pressing ecological problems for a number of African countries, calling for close attention and active efforts by the developing countries themselves, and by the entire international community. As industrialized countries, the Soviet Union and the United States have accumulated ample experience in this area, and could render substantial aid to African states. Among other things, such cooperation could include (1) joint Soviet–U.S. efforts in various international forums dedicated to the responsible disposal of industrial wastes in Africa and elsewhere; and (2) assistance in drafting national legislation on environmental protection and in establishing or consolidating administrative mechanisms to control its enforcement.

5

Activities to Foster Environmental Protection

ADEBAYO ADEDEJI

Of the fifty member states of the UN Economic Commission for Africa (ECA), thirty-six are desertification-prone countries; and of these, nineteen are classifiable, even by Third World standards, as least developed countries. About 200 million people live in these drought-stricken areas, of whom 10 million have become displaced persons or environmental refugees. Thousands of them suffer from famine, malnutrition, and related diseases. Millions of cattle and livestock have died, striking a serious blow to the rural economies of these largely pastoral countries.

Environmental protection is a priority area for development management, for the simple reason that Africa is facing serious problems of environmental degradation, including risks arising from the dumping of hazardous industrial wastes that Africa has not produced. Furthermore, analysts must give more attention to desertification as they study the African economic crisis of today.

However, Africa has not been totally insensitive to the problems of environmental protection, particularly those related to desertification control. In fact, in 1971, just before the Stockholm Conference on the Human Environment of 1972, there was the first All-African Seminar on the Human Environment, which was convened under the auspices of the ECA. The recommendations of this seminar were adopted at the third session of the ECA Conference of Ministers by its Resolution 264 (XII) on desertification, urging the ECA to take steps in collaboration with the international community to seek solutions to the problem.

In 1979 the ECA organized, with the assistance of UNEP, a workshop entitled "Alternative Patterns of Development of Life-styles," which also highlighted the urgent need for Africa to tackle the problems of environmental degradation, particularly desertification. The recommendations of this workshop provided very important inputs into the Lagos Plan of Action for the social and economic development of Africa. This plan devoted Chapter 9 to problems of environmental management.

In the same spirit, and recognizing the need for a multinational approach to desertification control, countries south of the Sahara have been taking a number of actions to organize themselves for the purpose. Inter-governmental organizations they have established to combat desertification include CILSS, (in eastern and southern Africa) the Intergovernmental Authority on Drought and Development (IGADD), and the Southern African Development Coordination Conference (SADCC). At the regional level, there is the African Ministerial Conference on the Environment (AMCEN).

SOVIET–U.S. COOPERATION AND THE ENVIRONMENT

I am gratified to note that the underlying reason for Soviet–U.S. Cooperation for Africa is "to find ways, on the basis of fresh political thinking, of transforming the well-established pattern of competition between the two countries in that area of the World into one of collaboration for the mutual benefit of both parties and Africa."[1] This cooperation is in the spirit of perestroika and is part of the search for a new approach to relations between the two countries. This new Soviet–U.S. relationship should "not be at the expense of Africa, but rather [be directed toward] improving understanding and better relations."[2]

We in Africa must, therefore, also rethink and adopt a new approach to international relations to make sure that the new wind of perestroika will not be at our expense. This is particularly important in the area of environmental management, where the lack of adequate capabilities to monitor environmental degradation is being taken advantage of by some industrial establishments in the advanced economies.

COMPREHENSIVE AND INTEGRATED
LARGE-SCALE STUDIES

In Africa today, efforts are being made to study environmental management, including desertification control. These studies are based in government ministries such as Agriculture or Planning, in national institutes of research, or in institutions of higher learning. Among these are the Desert Research Institute in Cairo, Egypt, the Institute of Environmental Studies of Makerere University in Uganda, and the Environmental Protection Council in Ghana, to name just a few. However, these studies are not well coordinated either nationally, subregionally, or regionally. The exchange of methodologies and technology across cultural and national boundaries has not received the level of attention that it should have. This is a field of activity where an injection of Soviet–U.S. support would be of considerable benefit to Africa.

Land-Use Systems

In Africa the agricultural sector contributes most to the desertification process. Shifting cultivation and slash-and-burn systems are still commonly used and result in the destruction of extensive areas of vegetation cover. Intensive agriculture, with characteristic heavy mechanization, has always been encouraged by external donors in areas where the topography allows. But through this mechanization, soils are plowed deep and made fragile. If intensive agriculture is not followed by the appropriate soil management and conservation technology, large portions of the land lose fertility and are subject to soil erosion, eventually being abandoned by the farmers. Since natural regeneration of plant life is not rapid, particularly in the semiarid and arid zones, the ground is left bare and desertification immediately sets in.

The other type of agricultural activity that encourages desertification is agropastoralism. Here, the supply and demand argument is also relevant. In the drought- and desertification-prone subregions of Africa, livestock raising has a strong sociocultural connotation, whereby social position is enhanced by large herds. These, added to human population increase and nomadism, aggravate the situation. The systems of raising very large numbers of livestock and permitting extensive grazing has very serious implications with regard to desertification, through overgrazing.

It is common knowledge that the law of diminishing returns also begins to operate on poorly managed land as the carrying capacity is reduced and the soils are degraded in fertility. Soil degradation and desertification usually go together. In Africa, soil degradation, in the majority of cases, results from the pressure on land as a consequence of the supply and demand factors earlier mentioned. Extensive areas of forested land that are cleared for agriculture or other purposes are usually not rehabilitated, and soil erosion, a major factor in the desertification process, sets in. Trees felled are only slowly replaced, through natural regeneration, by shrubs and grass, but these replacements are easily destroyed by wild animals or domestic livestock.

To further assist active soil conservation and soil rehabilitation programs of member states and multinational organizations in the region, support needs to be given to carrying out studies for more effective soil conservation and rehabilitation measures.

At the national level, antidesertification activities often take the form of afforestation, reforestation, or sand dune stabilization. In most cases, there is little formalized research on desert plant species and their reactions under varying climatic and seasonal conditions. Nor is there research into the various methods and results of dune stabilization. In other words, programs for combating desertification in Africa are based on trial-and-error rather than on research results.

In the majority of countries in Africa, landholding systems discourage long-term investment. This is especially true of the desertification-prone zones of sub-Saharan Africa—the Sudano-Sahelian zone particularly— where the populations are still highly nomadic. In these areas, land management is not a priority. Nomads move on in search of new pasture when the land on which they have "squatted" becomes overgrazed and can no longer support the flocks they herd. They leave behind land in the process of desertification.

Soviet–U.S. experience is needed in carrying out comprehensive and integrated large-scale studies to better understand the implications of these factors. The goal is to increase food production, while also practicing environmental conservation within the context of local capabilities. Rural land use is especially important considering that desertification is largely a rural phenomenon.

Energy Requirements and Desertification

Apart from agricultural practices and landholding systems that encourage further desertification, the demand for energy, particularly fuelwood, merits serious consideration. In most of Africa fuelwood is the main source of energy, if not the only source of energy for most people. Fuelwood has become so accepted as a traditional source of fuel that suggested alternatives such as biogas are never fully accepted as an alternative. Many factors are responsible for this resistance to change, including the attitude that fuelwood is traditionally gathered freely (although labor and time are entailed) and the common belief that food prepared with fuelwood tastes better.

The search for socially acceptable and sustainable alternatives should be guided by what Nash and Bowers refer to as revealed preferences, alternative costs, and the stated preference of the populations concerned in relation to their capabilities to afford those alternatives.[3] Alternative sources of energy that should be fully examined for use include:

- Solar energy for cooking, heating, lighting, water pumping, radio, and television
- Biogas for cooking, lighting, running small diesel engines, and heating
- Geothermal sources for electricity and heating
- Wind power for water pumping and electricity

Added to studies into alternative sources of energy, there is a need to intensify the search for cheap building materials in connection with low-cost housing. This should lead to greater success in afforestation and refor-estation activities that would relieve pressure on the forests by supplying an alternative to wood as a building material.

The Need for Further Studies in Meteorology

Related to agriculture and energy resources is meteorology. The morphology and behavior of the atmosphere during any given period determines the amount of precipitation, which, in turn, accounts for the availability of water resources. In other words, meteorology and its applications are key areas for a better understanding of the desertification processes.

More often than not, meteorology is taken for granted in discussions on the sustainability of ecosystems. Its importance seems to become manifest only when there are serious shortfalls in agricultural production as a result of drought.

The seasonality and duration of weather and climatic conditions depend on global atmospheric patterns that are not easily predictable. Even when they are, it is only for very short periods. Constant monitoring of the behavior of the atmosphere is actually required. In the economically more advanced countries of the north, research and development have improved the capability of monitoring atmospheric behavior through highly sophisticated technology and techniques that are backed by elaborate networks. Unfortunately, in Africa, all of these have not, as yet, been fully realized. The recent spells of very severe drought have highlighted the dire need to step up studies in meteorology and its applications in order to reduce the impacts of drought. This will in turn enhance desertification control programs.

With this in mind, African countries, through the ECA Conference of Ministers, adopted in 1984 Resolution 518 (XIX), which led to the establishment of the African Center of Meteorological Applications for Development (ACMAD). The feasibility of establishing such a center was first examined by the ECA in close collaboration with the World Meteorological Organization (WMO), and the modalities for the establishment of the center were then recommended. The center was subsequently established, and by its Resolution 621 (XXII) of April 1987, the ECA Conference of Ministers decided to locate it in Niamey, capital of the Republic of Niger.

The ACMAD will collect meteorological data, process and analyze the data received, make the information systematic, and periodically disseminate it to users for application to agricultural production, water, weather, and climate. The center will also enhance program activities being undertaken by the following intergovernmental organizations: CILSS, AGRHYMET, HYDRO-Niger, IGADD, SADCC, and AMCEN. It will also complement the activities of the following ECA-sponsored institutions: the African Regional Remote Sensing Center, Ouagadougou; the Regional Center for Services in Surveying, Mapping and Remote Sensing (RCSSMRS), Nairobi; the African Regional Center for Technology (ARCT), Dakar; and the

Regional Center for Training in Aerospace Surveys (RECTAS), Ile-Ife. The work of the WMO regional network in Africa, of FAO's Global Information and Early Warning Systems on Food and Agriculture, and of the International Livestock Center for Africa (ILCA) in assessing the performance of cultivable, arable, and pasture lands in member states are all of direct relevance to the planned activities of ACMAD.

The area of meteorological applications for desertification control in Africa needs urgent support. Soviet and U.S. experience, within the context of Soviet–U.S. cooperation for Africa, is definitely needed.

Studies in Environmental Economics and Desertification

Human ecosystems and their internal economic systems ultimately depend on the maintenance of the biospherical life support system.[4] In this vein, the law of supply and demand has very strong environmental management implications. These postulations are demonstrated in Africa where economies presently depend on the exploitation of the natural ecosystems, which, in most cases, has led to severe natural resource degradation.

The Human Factor in Desertification Control

The greatest resource for the implementation of desertification control programs is *people*. They must be convinced, through education, of the objectives of the programs in which they are requested to participate. Targets must be set and the people must be committed to the implementation of strategies chosen to achieve these targets. The effectiveness of alternative approaches must be demonstrable in order to satisfy social and economic needs.

FORMULATION OF MASTER PLANS

What makes the current inability to cope with the tasks of desertification control in Africa so poignant is that the countries most affected are the least organized to combat it. To change this, master plans must be drawn up within the context of existing plans of action. Master plans should delimit zones for desertification control or sand fixation, or both, according to the immediate needs of the populations concerned. These needs should generally center on:

- Agricultural practices
- Pasture land conservation or rehabilitation
- Alternatives to fuelwood for energy

Built into these master plans must be instruments for monitoring and evaluation. Desertification is a slow process and, like any slow process, it is difficult to reverse when it is advanced. The cooperation of member states in early transboundary monitoring and evaluation, using techniques such as remote sensing and mapping, is absolutely essential.

RESEARCH AND DEVELOPMENT

Allow me to underscore further the importance of desert research as an integral part of activities to prevent further desertification.

The behavior of ecosystems changes across time and location, depending on the stress to which they are subjected. This is particularly the case in semiarid and arid regions. The nature of this behavioral characteristic has not yet been fully studied in the semiarid and arid subregions of Africa. Worse still, institutional and manpower capabilities have not yet been adequately mobilized for desert research. The area of institutionalization and manpower development is therefore of great importance. In this connection, the feasibility of strengthening ACMAD, to include a division for desert research, should be examined. If instituted, the Division of Desert Research would comprise the following sections:

- Desertification and wind-sand research
- Dune fixation research
- Rehabilitation and land use research
- Monitoring and mapping
- Information

A division of desert research within ACMAD would have subregional or regional experimental/pilot stations at the subregional or regional levels, or both, side by side with the subregional intergovernmental organizations dealing with desertification control: CILSS, IGADD, SADCC, and AMCEN.

Based on these research activities, priority should be given to pilot demonstration projects that would emphasize land use practices in semiarid zones. These projects should also be centers for demonstrating the following: methods of land preparation for cultivation in desert areas to avoid soil erosion and salinization; techniques for developing water reservoirs and lake areas for agriculture and afforestation; ways to make greater use of solar and wind energy and biogas; afforestation practices; and methods to develop water resources, particularly for small-scale irrigation.

Within this framework, each of the affected countries could become an experimental ground for research results from the pilot projects. In so doing, objectives of the subregional intergovernmental organizations, as well as those of the desert and arid lands committee of AMCEN and the Conférence Ministérielle sur le Désertification (COMIDES), will gradually be achieved.

RESOURCE IMPLICATIONS

Another crucial area for consideration in desertification control activities is the availability of financial resources and scientific manpower. These are determining factors in the success and sustainability of the propositions advanced so far. On the other hand, in Africa today one of the most serious problems in implementing desertification control programs is the lack of financial and technological resources. Heavy initial investments are usually needed for programs such as sand dune fixation, water resources development and management in semiarid and arid lands, and alternative sources of energy—and for the necessary infrastructure to back up all these measures. This is an added area on which Soviet–U.S. cooperation for Africa should be focused.

In regard to scientific manpower, Soviet–U.S. cooperation for Africa is greatly needed in the area of desertification control manpower development. This should be not only in training scientists but also in providing reorientation and specialization opportunities for the existing manpower working on desertification control. Therefore, it will be necessary to support both existing institutions and those that might be developed as need determines. There is an urgent need, at the national, subregional, and regional levels, to develop three categories of manpower: scientific, technical, and general.

There already exists a core of African scientists in the field of ecology and related sciences, such as biology, botany, forestry, and geography, that can be mobilized almost immediately with minimum reorientation for desert research. Thereafter, a more specialized program should be developed and specializations expanded to include arid land agriculture and horticulture as well as animal husbandry. The focus must be on operational research into the different species of desert flora and fauna.

To enhance local scientific knowledge and to share experience on desertification control research activities in Africa, African scientists need to initiate and sustain a dialogue among themselves as well as with their Soviet and U.S. counterparts.

Regarding the implementation of desertification control programs, little middle-level manpower for extension services and implementation of desert-related programs exists. There is therefore a need to mobilize those workers, and develop more where the need exists, and to provide them with directly relevant skills.

CONCLUSION

I have touched only the tip of the iceberg concerning the possibilities and challenges that face Soviet–U.S. cooperation for Africa in the area of environmental conservation, particularly activities to prevent further desertification. The Stockholm Conference on the Human Environment in 1972 made the world realize that all aspects of international relations (trade, investment, transport, technology and cultural transfers, communications, and information) affect the environments of both developed and developing countries as well as the global commons. This realization has created a host of new opportunities that have, for the most part, not been seized.

For Soviet–U.S. cooperation for Africa "not to be at the expense of Africa," it must take advantage of these opportunities and work toward concrete support activities within the context of the collective development strategies of African countries. In so doing, Africa must not sacrifice the principle of mutual self-interest in international relations. In other words, while regarding Soviet–U.S. cooperation for Africa as an "important confidence-building measure in reducing tensions, correcting misperceptions, promoting mutual understanding, fostering improved bilateral Soviet–U.S. relations, and creating trust,"[5] great care must be taken that the course of common interests for the United States, the Soviet Union, and Africa is served.

Within this context of cooperation, I must alert African governments to organize themselves to face this new challenge in international relations.

NOTES

1. *Soviet–U.S. Cooperation for Africa: A Report on the Moscow Workshop, December 1987* (Los Angeles: Center for International and Strategic Affairs, 1988).

2. Ibid.

3. C. Nash and J. Bowers, "Alternative Approaches to the Evaluation of Environmental Resources," in *Sustainable Environmental Management*, ed. R. K. Turner (Boulder, Colo.: Westview Press, 1988), 102–117.

4. Turner, *Sustainable Environmental Management.*

5. See *Soviet–U.S. Cooperation for Africa*, 16.

6

Environmental Problems in Africa: Disposal of Industrial Wastes

TAMARA A. ALIKHANOVA

Man's negative impact on the environment is an increasingly severe problem for the African continent today. What's more, the number of difficulties associated with this pernicious state of affairs is growing all the time. Desertification, already one of Africa's gravest crises, has been compounded by the problems of environmental pollution resulting from man's industrial activities. Although few in number, the industrial enterprises (oil refineries, chemical works, etc.) in African countries generate a sizable amount of wastes that in most cases are not properly disposed of.

But the gravest danger for the region in the past few years has been the burial on African lands of toxic and radioactive wastes brought in from industrialized Western countries.

The question of industrial waste disposal is acute at the moment in France, the United States, Italy, and other Western countries. In particular, France "produces" each year some 50 million tons of so-called banal industrial wastes (analogous to domestic wastes) and 18 million tons of specific industrial wastes, most often toxic and extremely hazardous. French soil is already oversaturated with wastes, while the capacity of its waste-disposal facilities (incineration, decontamination, recycling) is too low. There are about fifty enterprises specializing in this field, with no more than ten plants having the facilities for recycling more than 50,000 tons of wastes a year, which is obviously insufficient.[1]

The United States generates a great share of the toxic wastes produced by the industrialized capitalist countries (83 percent, to be exact) and faces grave difficulties, too, with disposal on its own territory. One might also mention the spiraling cost of waste recycling. Whereas in 1976 it stood at $10 per ton, in 1988 it had exceeded $140 per ton for storage and reached almost $2,500 per ton for neutralization.[2]

In these conditions, the removal of industrial wastes to developing countries, including those of Africa, has begun to be a sizable temptation for France, the United States, and a number of other industrialized countries. The most attractive places in Africa in this respect are the coastal states, and especially those with extensive desert territories. In particular, Mauritania is a subject of great interest among traders in industrial wastes. The latter, however, do not confine their search to desert locations; they also focus on many other countries whose geographic position is convenient in terms of transportation costs.

African countries often consent to the burial of others' industrial wastes on their territory because of their difficult financial position. A parliamentary inquiry filed by West German Bundestag deputies A. Grossmann and D. Schanz describes the logic of such decisions in the following way:

> The countries in question have a huge foreign debt and, worse still, have almost no hopes for foreign-exchange earnings because of the drop in the prices of commodities. That is why many Third World countries cannot resist such tempting financial propositions. This is a new form of economic colonialism inadmissible from the ethical point of view.[3]

One example is Guinea-Bissau's agreement to the burial of 500,000 tons of highly toxic pharmacological wastes at Binta, nine kilometers from the Senegalese border. Under this agreement, Guinea-Bissau was to receive $40 for each ton of wastes. (The current price for disposal of such wastes within European Community [EC] states ranges from $160 to $1,000 per ton). Given that the annual per capita income in Guinea-Bissau ($180) is one of the lowest in the world, the promised sum for the waste disposal looked quite attractive. It was twice as high as the country's external debt and twenty-five times higher than its annual export earnings.[4] Details of the deal became known to a Europarliament deputy, François Roland Du Vivier (of the EC's environmental protection organization). It was revealed, among other things, that in the warm and humid tropical climate the metal drums containing toxins would rust away very quickly, releasing toxic substances into the ground water. The indignant people of Guinea-Bissau, including those at Binta, demanded that the contract be canceled, which was done in due course.

The burial of wastes is fraught with grave consequences for the recipient countries. *The Reference Book on the Elimination and Recycling of Industrial Wastes*, published by the French ministry for the environment, puts those hazards into three categories: (1) contamination of potable water resources through the seepage of pollutants into the soil; (2) direct threat to the lives of people, animals, and plants; and (3) unpredictable future consequences.

In the case of the burial of such wastes in Africa, the local population is faced with all three types of hazard. The problem of water supply, especially drinking water, is intense in the arid and semiarid regions, which are the most attractive of all for the burial of toxic and radioactive wastes. Contamination of drinking water resources, very limited in the first place, can result from disregard for waste burial rules, a frequent occurrence in

Africa, and from the rupture of waste containers.

There is a particularly grave threat to ground water in those areas where the population draws water exclusively from wells, which is typical of the Sahel countries. Traders in industrial wastes persuade Africans that the buried materials will stay above the aquifers, which lie 200 to 250 meters deep in these regions. This does not rule out certain risks, however. Sooner or later, the soil, which does not always remain impermeable to water, may release some of the wastes, either pushing them up to the surface or down to the ground water.

The latter danger is no less serious than the former. There is already a recorded case of damage to the health of people, animals, and plants. In that case, 15,000 tons of industrial wastes brought to and buried in Guinea desiccated all plant life on the Los Islands.[5] The storage of industrial wastes in Nigeria, where toxic and radioactive wastes had been illegally kept on the outskirts of the port of Coco for ten months, proved just as detrimental to the health of the local population. Experts from an international consultancy service have revealed that some of the chemicals stored there can provoke malignant tumors and serious nervous disorders. During the elimination of that storage depot, eighty-seven Nigerian workers were poisoned and a fire brigade officer was taken to the hospital with a nervous breakdown.[6]

It is hard to predict now what problems the African states that make their territory available for the burial of hazardous wastes will face in the future. The poisoning of the Los Islands in Guinea, for example, was not discovered until four years after the waste was dumped. In Nigeria, after the first nine months of the storage of toxic and radioactive wastes, the area around the storage site was declared unsuitable for farming, and ground water was found to be contaminated as a result of the leakage of wastes. It cannot be ruled out that future generations of Africans will have to face such phenomena as desiccation of plants, soil infertility, and congenital defects in humans and animals.

The burial of hazardous wastes in arid zones will complicate the struggle against desertification in the future. The minister-delegate for the environment of Senegal, Moctar Kebe, has commented on the problem in the following way:

> At the moment the Ferlo area [in the center of Senegal] is virtually a desert. All that grows there is skeleton-like shrubs whose leaves are eaten by camels. In a few years, however, due to the dams at Manantali and Diama, it will be possible to channel water from the Senegal River to that area and it will become good for farming. We certainly do not intend to pollute it. If anything, let them leave us at least our deserts. After all, they are not dumps.[7]

The removal abroad of industrial wastes often becomes a kind of illicit business. According to expert estimates, the volume of illegal removal of wastes is seven times the official figure for legal removal.[8] Wastes are often removed under fictitious pretexts. For example, an Italian national obtained a license in Nigeria on 16 May 1987 for the import of building materials, which were actually industrial wastes, to that country. No less than five consignments of wastes, with a total weight of 3,800 tons were unloaded at Coco and then transferred to a so-called "exemplary" African storage site. It was a vacant lot on the outskirts of the port of Coco surrounded by a simple fence. The owner of the lot was paid a hundred dollars a month for the lease.[9] In June 1988 the Nigerian paper *The Guardian* unveiled this story to the public. The reaction of the federal military government was all the more violent, since shortly before this revelation President Babangida had made a call for a "clean" Africa at a session of the Organization of African Unity (OAU). About forty Italians and Nigerians were arrested and found themselves threatened with a firing squad. To avert further scandal, the Italian government took the wastes away. The Nigerian chemist K. Akporohonor evaluates the damage caused to the environment, people's health, and the economy of the region at a billion naira (about $250 million).[10]

The conflicts that have resulted in a number of African countries from the burial of industrial wastes have prompted those countries to turn their attention to the absence or inadequacies of national laws regulating such issues. Nigeria, for one, prohibited in 1988 the import of any industrial wastes into the country. In the Liberian senate a bill was introduced in July 1988, envisaging capital punishment for any person found guilty of unloading toxic wastes on the country's territory. That bill also provided for punishment for the transport of such cargo.

African leaders are increasingly realizing the danger threatening their countries when toxic and radioactive industrial wastes are buried on their own and neighboring territories. In particular, many leaders in West African countries understand the regional dangers posed by the plans of Benin and Guinea-Bissau to have industrial wastes buried on their territories. This problem has been extensively discussed at various international forums—notably at the session of the assembly of the OAU heads of state and government in Addis Ababa in May 1988, and at the fifth session of the Steering Committee of the Convention on Environmental Protection and the Use of Sea Waters and Littoral Zones of West and Central Africa (Nairobi, May 1988). The parties to this convention—all littoral states, from Mauritania to Angola—have been joined by Burkina Faso, Mali, and Niger (all with observer status). However, of the twenty-one member states, only seven have ratified the convention.

At the eleventh Economic Commission of West African States (ECOWAS) summit in Lomé in 1988 a special Waste Disposal Control Service was set up. The participants in the meeting called for an immediate adoption by the countries of the region of laws declaring the burial of toxic industrial wastes on their territory a criminal offense.

The movement against the import to the African continent of lethal substances has been headed by Nigeria. At the initiative of Senegal, a conference on environmental pollution issues was called in Dakar in October 1988. It was attended by foreign specialists and representatives of U.S. and West European ecological movements who informed the Africans about the dangers associated with the burial of industrial wastes on their territory. The idea of the conference was strongly supported by the executive director of UNEP.

A new phenomenon in Africa is widespread public protest against the conversion of the continent into a dump for toxic materials. In 1988 Nigeria, for example, set up an organization called "Concerned Nigerians Against Nuclear and Toxic Wastes in Africa." They have set themselves two tasks: to promote greater public awareness of the danger of toxic wastes and to attract the attention of the people of all developing countries to the problem.

Qualms about the removal abroad of industrial wastes is reflected in legislation enacted in all industrialized capitalist countries. In particular, under U.S. laws any removal of toxic wastes requires a permit from the Washington-based Environmental Protection Agency (EPA), which has mandated control over toxic waste disposition. For its own part, the EPA, through the appropriate U.S. embassy, requests the consent of the government of the country to which wastes are to be removed. If no consent is given, the deal is canceled. This is exactly what occurred, for example, with the planned export of wastes by the U.S. company Lindaca to Guinea-Bissau.

In 1986 the EC issued an instruction permitting the removal of industrial wastes abroad only if two major conditions are met: prior consent from the recipient country, and the existence in that country of a technical capacity for the reception, treatment, and destruction of toxic wastes. So far, however, only Belgium, Denmark, and Greece have included these provisions in domestic legislation.

This question is under close scrutiny by a number of public organizations and, first of all, by the European Association for the Protection of the Environment. Its members have carried out a survey of operations by industrial waste traders in Africa. In May 1988 the association's chairman, Du Vivier, circulated copies of a memorandum detailing the terms of two contracts signed by the government of Guinea-Bissau with three European firms (London-based Bis Import-Export, Hobdey Limited from the Isle of Man in Britain, and Intercontract from Fribourg in Switzerland). He also circulated copies of contracts signed by the govern-ment of Benin and by the Gibraltar-based company SESCO on the burial of 1.5 million tons of toxic wastes, including radioactive substances, in Benin. This information aroused well-justified protests from around the world, especially from African countries, and resulted in the cancellation of a similar contract by Guinea-Bissau. On 19 May 1988 the European Parliament passed a resolution demanding a ban on large-scale removal of toxic wastes to developing countries and calling for stricter observance of the existing rules for their removal.

A sizable contribution to the struggle for an ecologically clean Africa is being made by the UN. The report "A System-Wide Medium-Term Environment Programme for 1990–1995" speaks about the inadmissibility of the "settlement of the ecological problem, caused by industry, by simple removal of industrial wastes or replacement of its consequences from one region to another."[11] Utilization and disposal of wastes and their trans-national carriage are seen as questions demanding increased attention.[12]

The resolution of the UN General Assembly of 11 December 1987 and a report of the World Commission for the Environment and Development point to the

> need for strengthening by developed countries and appropriate U.N. bodies and organizations of technical cooperation with developing countries in order to enable them to set up and broaden their potential in the exposure of ecological problems, their monitoring, analysis, prevention and settlement in accordance with their national development plans, priorities and values.[13]

No less important for the cause of environmental protection is its legal regulation. The medium-term plan of UNEP for 1990–1995 names one of the program's priority tasks to be support for developing countries in the introduction of appropriate environmental legislation and in the establishment of an administrative mechanism or in the consolidation of the existing one.[14]

Speaking at the forty-third session of the UN General Assembly, Soviet Foreign Minister Eduard Shevardnadze suggested discussing the question of conversion of the environmental protection program into an ecological council capable of passing effective decisions to safeguard ecological security. The Soviet Union regards it as advisable to hold a series of international meetings on the coordination of efforts in the field of ecological security.[15]

Today the burial of industrial wastes (especially toxic and radioactive) has become the most pressing ecological problem for a number of African countries, calling for close attention and active efforts by the developing states themselves and by the whole international community. As industrialized countries, the Soviet Union and the United States have ample experience in this field and could render appreciable aid to developing African states.

NOTES

1. *Jeune Afrique* (Economie), June 1988.

2. *Le Point,* 29 August 1988.

3. *Izvestia,* 8 October 1988.

4. Ibid.

5. *Jeune Afrique* (Economie), June 1988.

6. *The Guardian* (Lagos), 6 August 1988.

7. *Jeune Afrique* (Economie), June 1988.

8. *Le Point,* 29 August 1988.

9. Ibid.

10. *The Guardian,* 6 August 1988.

11. Global Medium-Term Environment Programme for 1990–1995 (UNEP/GCSS 1/2, 1 December 1987), 100.

12. Ibid., 111.

13. Resolution 42/187 of the UN General Assembly of 11 December 1987 on the report of the World Commission for the Environment and Development (UNEP/GCSS, 1/6/dd.2), 4.

14. Proposed Medium-Term Plan of the UN Environment Programme for 1990–1995 (UNEP/GCSS, 1/3).

15. *Pravda,* 28 September 1988.

7

Addressing the Crisis of Desertification in Africa

C. S. WHITAKER

The Moscow papers on this subject identified the insidious and complex character of the phenomenon of desertification. The crux of the problem is the emergence of a malign biosphere or negative ecosystem, in which the destructive use of a dwindling supply of arable land is reducing the capacity to sustain human life.

Effective counteraction involves a variety of measures, each requiring that strong sources of resistance to action or tendencies toward inaction be overcome. The longer the problem remains unaddressed, the greater will be the effort required to achieve an increasingly small degree of success. The dimensions of the problem are particularly disturbing for Africa, which suffers from unusually severe climatic conditions, extreme demographic pressure, and a paucity of resources. The need for action is therefore urgent; yet efforts to date have been mostly misplaced or inadequate.

The process of environmental deterioration is painful to witness, not only because of the immense human suffering it causes, but also because it involves a natural and human disaster that is within our capacity to mitigate, if not control. The destruction of the earth's productive potential, which is what the process of desertification means, is so far a classic case of missed opportunity for creative and humanitarian public policy.

Ironically, the record of attempts to halt desertification is characterized by a significant degree of success with respect to a number of specific projects. Paul Harrison has recently detailed several such projects—in Kenya, Burkina Faso, and Niger.[1] The common elements of success in these instances were careful and informed planning at the national level, low cost, a minimization of risk on the part of governments and local people, and benefits that were clearly visible in the near term.

The same record also suggests, however, that given the scope of the problem of desertification, the broad lessons of specific efforts have not been identified and applied elsewhere. An earlier paper outlined the problems that seemed to frustrate effective intervention against desertification.[2] Here this focus is adjusted to highlight the challenge of overcoming barriers, with special emphasis on measures that the Soviet Union and the United States might take in concert to help mobilize existing and potential resources.

It is crucial that these opportunities be seized while there is still time to intervene in advance of a further series of events and acts of neglect that could well render the situation hopeless for ever larger areas. This chapter stresses the broad principles and themes of coordination and action that experience suggests should be employed, and it also attempts to focus attention on the chief sources of resistance to effective efforts and the need to overcome them.

THE CAUSES AND SCOPE OF THE PROBLEM

The causes of desertification are well known but poorly understood. It is well established, for instance, that desertification is the result of a combination of natural patterns, such as cycles of drought, and poor human practices of land use.[3] Exactly how much of the problem is natural and how much man-made is another matter; nor is the issue trivial. In fact, the implications in terms of the effective deployment of resources in combating further desertification are crucial. While recent scientific advance in the use of space technology, for example, has led to vast increases in our understanding of weather patterns, much remains to be discovered about the extent to which atmospheric conditions may induce situations of desertification.

To reflect extensively on the nature-man equation is to understand the saliency of both factors. While seemingly impersonal elements are implicated, the phenomenon of desertification also requires an understanding of the complex motives, needs, and wants that drive people to use land in damaging ways. The human contribution is not always clear either. Common misconceptions abound, for instance, concerning the supposed "irrational" dimension of custom and ignorance of herd-maximizing techniques on the part of pastoral nomads. Frequently cited as a major contributor to desertification, this accusation is now giving way to the insight that, under the circumstances, quite rational and environmentally sensitive motives account for the prevailing patterns of pastoral land use in many cases. Yet, large sums of aid money have been spent on projects designed to persuade pastoral nomads to abandon traditional practices of animal husbandry, projects that have usually failed.[4] Frequently they fail not so much because of lack of response as because of ill-conceived attributions of cause and effect.

Part of the problem is the tendency of individuals and groups to blame others for the failure to combat desertification. But the reality is far too complex to justify such a simple analysis.

The Moscow workshop dealt with three discrete levels of responsibility and potential action in the fight against desertification: local, national, and international.[5] This scheme of analysis is also pertinent to the theme of this chapter and should be briefly restated here.

Local residents of desertified areas usually receive not only the attention of desertification experts, but also, often for reasons that are less well elaborated, much of the blame for the situation.[6] It is true, of course, that the inhabitants of these areas often perform poorly as stewards of their own local resources, sometimes to their impoverishment. To a degree, this reflects elements of sheer ignorance;[7] more often it stems from a calculated application of an instinct to survive in an insecure environment. Thus, practices that are at present environmentally harmful or even disastrous have in the recent past been beneficial. They have been *rendered* damaging by a rapidly changing political, economic, and demographic situation.[8] The advice of many experts that the attack on desertification should take place from the "ground up," by allowing local residents a voice in the implementation of development schemes, is the laudable result of this insight.[9] The implication is not that designed projects[10] are irrelevant, but that no matter how well conceived implemented local projects may be, they must be accompanied by a national commitment to coordinated planning, investment, and reform.

At the national level what is required above all is effective distribution of resources and long-term planning. These perspectives are rarely in force under existing conditions of the African states.

Despite the call in 1977 of the United Nations Conference on Desertification for submission of national plans, one purpose of which was to elicit funds from the entire international community, only two plans had been submitted worldwide as of 1984, and only one from Africa. The basic problems at this level are essentially threefold: financial, political, and institutional/legal. They suggest that African states are in need of *help* to respond adequately.

The African states are chronically strapped for resources. Faced with a host of allocative priorities, many of which are more pressing in the immediate perspective than the fight against desertification, what little may be left over for that purpose is often spread too thin to be of much use. Further, the hold on a number of African states by essentially self-regarding individuals and groups virtually guarantees that a large measure of what resources might be available (e.g., credit facilities for irrigated agriculture) is already appropriated for use in consumption rather than for the enlightened and farsighted investment required for effective control of desertification.

In addition, the weak national institutions and often inappropriate legal structure of many African states constitute barriers to effective action. The legal structure of some African states can serve as a disincentive to proper land use, where, for instance, insecurity of rights of land tenure often leads local people to cut down trees in order simply to gain access to wood before someone else does the same thing.

What seems clear is that if government policy in Africa is often the source of insecurity at the local level—which impacts adversely on the environment—then the basis for such policy is equally the result of the insecurity of leaders at the national level. Resources are siphoned away from investment against desertification. Rural areas most directly threatened by desertification are neglected in the allocation of national revenues, in part because African leaders are compelled to hedge their bets against political opposition by investing resources in arenas that yield immediate political support.

The international side of this coin involves the uncertain nature of external resources available to the African state. Most African states are dependent for revenues on receipts from exports of commodities whose value on world markets is volatile and beyond their control. Uncertainty on the part of national leaders about resource flows, which are typically crucial as a means of acquiring some measure of legitimation, reinforces the tendency to disburse scarce resources to the surest sources of political support. In the process of bolstering support in the short term—a reflection of uncertainty—long-term ruin is courted through the failure to invest in such seemingly less troublesome areas as antidesertification programs. A cycle of denial and destruction is thus played out.

If, as seems clear, the threat of desertification is worldwide in scale, the parsimonious nature of the response by the world community is perplexing. The United Nations has estimated that to bring desertification under control will require $4.5 billion a year for twenty years. Contributions by the international community to a special account set up in 1979 for the purpose of collecting funds to support the fight against desertification have amounted to only $50,000.

In addition, conventional pressures underlying most assistance to the Third World will defeat the purpose of aid insofar as it is applied to desertification. There remains a clear preference on the part of international donors for "showcase" projects. Halting desertification essentially involves maintaining the land as it is, as opposed to exploiting opportunities to project novel or spectacular results.

Another apparent reason for lack of funds is the problem of desertification's status as a latecomer to world attention. Desertification "must elbow its way into a global complex of development activities to which all the available funding has already been assigned. Unless development financing shows a net increase, desertification projects have to displace other action which will already have an institutional base."[11]

To address the problem of desertification, a conscious and concerted determination to push it forward on the world agenda must emerge. Powers external to Africa are best positioned to achieve a higher status for the issue.

Having identified responsibility for combating desertification as arising in three discrete realms—local, national, international—what remains to be emphasized is that in practice these realms are much more closely interlinked than this conceptualization might otherwise suggest.

First, there are common elements mainly—perception and will—that affect the ability to combat desertification at all three levels. Without a clear notion of the task at hand and the realization that it is imperative to act, little or nothing will be accomplished. The will to implement effective techniques and policies depends in part on attaining a level of security in the decisionmaking environment to make pertinent choices of strategy, and in part on being able to predict returns on investment made in the fight. People made insecure at the local level by the failures or equivocations of government are often, in turn, the source of the political and economic insecurity of leaders. This cycle of insecurity is at least partially due to the uncertainty and lack of commitment in the international environment from which resources are needed.

Second, actions taken in the fight against desertification must occur not sequentially but concomitantly at all three levels. Changes in agricultural practice by individuals at the local level will not be forthcoming without reform at the national. Nothing good will happen without pointed action or assistance from the international community. In this light, there is a great deal the Soviet Union and the United States can do, but not by themselves. Effective action will require that steps be taken by nations who together have the accurate sense of being threatened by the specter of desertification; passivity at the national level will mean that Soviet–U.S. cooperation can have little more than superficial effects.

OPPORTUNITIES AND CHALLENGES FOR SOVIET–U.S. COOPERATION IN HALTING DESERTIFICATION

The point of these observations is to make clear the financial, technical, and educational capacity to weigh against desertification. The open question concerns the model of action that must be mobilized. The major challenges to the effective mobilization of resources, and ways in which the Soviet Union and the United States might cooperate in meeting those challenges, can be stated.

The first challenge involves perceptions of actors at all three levels. At the local and national levels, understanding the long-term benefits of proper husbandry of the land will be required. The key barrier to a long-term view of things in Africa today is the insecurity of not only the physical, but also the political and economic environment—for rural inhabitants and governments alike. Here, Soviet–U.S. cooperation can be marshaled in areas not evidently directly related to, but nonetheless essential to, desertification control. Acting in concert to stabilize commodity prices internationally and providing joint aid with the goal of enhancing national economic self-sufficiency are two pertinent means of enhancing the security of governments, thereby providing them with an expanded opportunity to invest in longer-term national projects such as environmental upkeep.

The second challenge is that of increasing our knowledge of causes, effects, and counteractions. In this regard, there is an immense potential for beneficial Soviet–U.S. cooperation. A key challenge lies in sorting out the relative importance and incremental impact of the various factors known to result in desertification. In addition, as Leongard Goncharov has suggested, there is a critical need for studies of desertification region by region.[12] Both the United States and the Soviet Union possess expertise in such studies, based on their own experiences with arid lands (e.g., desertification in the Aral Sea region of the Soviet Union and in the U.S. Southwest).

Cooperation in the form of weather research, using the advanced technology available to scientists in the Soviet Union and in the United States, can also be of enormous benefit. An encouraging factor here is the already impressive record of cooperation in space. A transference of these experiences may bring about advances in the technical and organizational means of desertification control. A compelling reason for this sort of effort lies in a concern noted above: the efficient use of scarce resources. A more precise knowledge and understanding of the specific causes, incremental effects, and applied remedies for desertification will allow allocation of resources to proceed in the most feasible scenario.

A third challenge involves overcoming the very *un*cooperative character of conventional project aid, not just between the Soviet Union and the United States, but including most other donors of aid to African countries as well. The purely opportunistic single-state approach to aid may enhance the particularistic interests of donors, but it also typically creates as many problems for recipients as it solves.

With respect to desertification control, there is an opportunity for the Soviet Union and the United States to act jointly, with the active and equal participation of African countries involved, in planning and implementing projects against desertification on a large scale. The potential relevance of Soviet–U.S. cooperation in this sphere is inherent in the physical endowments of the two countries. Both possess enormous assets applicable to combat desertification; together, they have, in effect, a "comparative advantage" in action of the sort that involves long-term planning and forward investment. The strategic combination and concentration of these assets directed to desertification would yield economies of scale and appropriate coordination of the multiple levels of community and administration that are absolutely essential in this realm of global imperative.

THE CAMPAIGN AGAINST DESERTIFICATION

Having presented these policy dilemmas, challenges, and options discursively and critically, the implications may now be spelled out as a set of principles and recommendations that I am suggesting must underlie a campaign for African–Soviet–U.S. action.

General Principles and Priorities

- *Reprioritization*: The effort must deliberately aim to elevate the status of the problem as a priority of the global agenda, recognizing that it is more difficult to motivate people to assess a deteriorating situation than to pursue a positive goal.
- *Adequate conceptualization*: The heart of the problem is the articulation of the complex relationship of human and natural influences, as opposed to either element in isolation.
- *Coordination*: Action on several levels must be consciously coordinated, i.e., local, national, and international, and also with respect to different kinds of measures, e.g., financial, informational, technological, legal, and administrative.
- *Systemization*: Analysis must comprehend all factors at once; in this connection advanced computer-modeling techniques should be employed.
- *Institutionalization*: The long-term nature of the challenge requires the creation of ongoing structures of response in Africa and elsewhere.
- *Contextualization*: Flexible strategies of response must be formulated; different local situations will call for different emphasis and deployment of types and levels of support.
- *Research and evaluation*: Each measure must be grounded in the effort to generate new knowledge and evaluated in terms of salience and cost. Master-planning techniques should be applied.
- *Demonstrability*: To the extent possible, opportunities to demonstrate locally the salience of measures must be promoted; the use of computer graphics as a demonstration technology should be explored.
- *Broad participation*: The people affected in the formulation of strategies of action must be involved.
- *Education and training*: The campaign should strive for results not merely in terms of global statistical impact but should emphasize the increased capacity of local people to gain control.

All of this would also be of help in obtaining a comprehensive knowledge of the role of climatic and anthropogenic factors in the spread of desertification, among other phenomena.

Recommendations

- *Set up provisional task forces* of groups that include scientists and specialists from those African countries that will be involved at the preinvestment stage of research and development of projects in specific African countries.

- *Organize, in the United States and the USSR, educational centers to train African nationals* as specialists who will later participate in specific African–Soviet–U.S. desertification control projects. Specialists in the fields of soil science, climatology, meteorology, and hydrology are most needed.
- *Establish suitable procedures of information exchange* in the areas of ecology and agriculture among African, Soviet, and U.S. scientists who will take part in the implementation of desertification control projects in Africa.
- *Initiate a comprehensive joint investigation* by African, Soviet, and U.S. scientists of the problem of *population-carrying capacity* of various arid and semiarid areas.
- *Design and execute a pilot project* in a pertinent area of Africa that will demonstrate the efficacy of the approach suggested in the call for African–Soviet–U.S. cooperation.

At least since the 1977 UN Conference on Desertification, many of these principles and recommendations have enjoyed a general currency and acceptance. Yet virtually no progress has been made in mounting a systematic effort to undertake the tasks implied in the understanding of what needs to be done.

The most significant aspect of the project of African–Soviet–U.S. cooperation in the field of desertification is that it offers a fresh occasion and an appealing framework for long-overdue action on a profoundly important yet manageable problem.

The summons is to proceed.

NOTES

1. Paul Harrison, *The Greening of Africa: Breaking Through in the Battle for Land and Food* (New York: Viking Penguin, 1987).

2. C. S. Whitaker, "Missed Opportunities for Intervention in the African Desertification Crisis." Paper presented at the conference Soviet–U.S. Cooperation for Africa, 1–5 December 1987.

3. This process of "biogeophysical feedback" is described in fuller detail by Sharon Nicholson, "The Climatology of Sub-Saharan Africa," in *Environmental Change in the West African Sahel* (Washington, D.C.: National Academy Press, 1984).

4. See the discussion of Kenya's Group Ranching scheme in Phylo Evangelou, *Livestock Development in Kenya's Maasailand: Pastoralists' Transition to a Market Economy* (Boulder: Westview, 1984).

5. The notion of three levels of analysis for purposes of examining the process

of desertification is inspired by the earlier work of Michael Glantz, "Man, State and Environment: An Inquiry into Whether Solutions to Desertification in the West African Sahel Are Known but Not Applied," *Canadian Journal of Development Studies* 1, no. 1 (1980): 75–97.

6. This is particularly the case of pastoral peoples, whose traditional livelihood entails maximizing herd size, a practice that leads to the rapid overgrazing of land. See, for example, Evangelou.

7. Studies of the understanding by local peoples of practices that lead to or prevent desertification produce differing results in areas that are equally desertified. A survey of pastoralists in northern Kenya, for instance, revealed that 85 percent did not know that soil could be degraded (cited by Daniel Stiles in "Camel Pastoralism and Desertification in Northern Kenya" [unpublished manuscript]). Yet, others have shown an extraordinary awareness of the environment's demands, as evidenced, for example, in many of the traditional practices of sedentary and pastoral peoples alike. Cf. Harrison, *The Greening of Africa.*

8. A good example of this is the practice of transhumant grazing by pastoralists. While this was an environmentally sound practice in the days of broad and accessible rangeland, the squeezing of pastoralists onto ever smaller parcels of land makes this and other traditional herding practices outright damaging. See Evangelou.

9. See the argument by Reinhard Adelhelm and Johannes Kotschi, *Towards Control of Desertification in African Drylands* (Eschborn: Commission of the European Communities, Bundesministerium für wirtschaftliche Zusammenarbeit, and Deutsche Gesellschaft für Technische Zusammenarbeit, 1986).

10. See UNEP, "Rehabilitating Kenya's North—The Baringo Pilot Semi-Arid Area Project," in *Desertification Control Bulletin* 14 (November 1987): 55–58.

11. James Walls, "A Summons to Action," *Desertification Control Bulletin* 10 (May 1984).

12. Whitaker, "Missed Opportunities."

8

Measures for Desertification Control

LEONGARD GONCHAROV

The urgency of the environmental problem in Africa is well illustrated by recent estimates showing that over half of all the land in Africa is vulnerable to desertification. Although the problem has enormous proportions, the governments of African countries and international bodies have so far failed to find the means to tackle the problem effectively. The situation urgently calls for the immediate mobilization of all available resources and the use of up-to-date technology for an effective system of protection from desertification. Every year of delay intensifies the danger of completely losing control of the situation.

Of course, directions, forms, and techniques of desertification control must be based on objective information on the causes, nature, scale, and consequences of the phenomenon. In his chapter, C. S. Whitaker points out that of Africa's multiple crises, the environmental crisis must be singled out as bearing most heavily on the inhabitants of this continent. This crisis is caused by a combination of natural and human factors.

The human factors that cause and then accelerate desertification in Africa include destruction of soil cover through mechanized tillage of land; shortening of fallow periods in systems of slash-and-burn cultivation; overgrazing in traditional stock-farming areas and migration of nomads to new areas where some degree of overgrazing soon recurs; and deforestation due to the extensive use of wood as fuel, road construction, and so on.

Many factors that exert pressure on traditional crop and stock farming tend also to destabilize ecological balances. Among such factors are increased population densities per unit of cultivated land and the spread of cultivation to virgin marginal lands, and the decline of the ratio of unexploited land to land under cultivation.

It is certainly erroneous to believe that the heavy use of technical cultivation methods will contribute to checking and reversing the destruction of the natural environment while fully utilizing the potential of arid regions. In fact, the application of purely "technological" methods, if carried out under the fragile conditions of Africa's drylands, may actually result in negative ecological consequences.

To have reliable approaches to environmental protection and effective measures of desertification control it is necessary to consider all factors, including local ones. An objective analysis of the role of natural and human factors is indispensable for avoiding mistakes in choosing alternate courses of action to check and prevent further desertification. More attention must be paid to devising a new approach, one that recognizes the necessity of combating soil erosion and desertification on the scale of individual states, even of entire regions.

The UN-sponsored conference held in Nairobi in 1977 adopted the Plan of Action to Control Desertification for the period up to 2000. Unfortunately, this plan has met with serious difficulties and is heading for failure. Indeed, it is all too common that measures to control desertification are outstripped by the rapid occurrence of environmental disasters, while funds are often misallocated.

The 1977 plan is basically oriented to narrow technological means of tackling individual areas and ignores the problem of rational management of the entire system of natural resources. The human factor in desertification is underestimated; as a result, methods of control that are reactive are vested with more importance than those that emphasize prevention. Any preventive approach must take into consideration the specific local character of the natural environment, along with economic activities and social conditions. A narrowly technical approach can, in fact, lead to perverse results. According to Soviet scientists I. S. Zonn and S. B. Rostotsky, in periods of severe drought—that is, in periods of accelerated desertification—efforts to keep it in check are sharply intensified; however, with favorable weather changes such efforts are slackened to the point of futility. In the opinion of these scientists, in times of abundant rainfall the population of marginal areas tends to forget the lessons of previous years and ecological disasters reemerge.

More attention should be paid to the problems entailed in opening up virgin lands and managing water resources. At present, construction of water reservoirs, canals, and large irrigation systems is costly, and not always efficient, because of high levels of evaporation and water seepage. Having analyzed the experience of water construction, experts from the OAU and the ECA have come to the conclusion that many irrigation systems in Africa are unproductive. Typically, such systems tend to begin deteriorating as they are about to show profit. In the opinion of Soviet specialists of the research institutes Zagubezhgeologia and Glavzarubezhvodstroy, this is due partly to the deficiency of water resources and partly to lack of involvement on the part of rural inhabitants who are just not interested in running irrigation systems that are mostly oriented toward industrial crops.

Any large-scale use of fresh groundwater resources encounters a number of obstacles. Ranking first among such obstacles, according to these experts, is a lack of adequate hydrogeological information, which hampers planning of groundwater prospecting and makes such prospecting less than efficient. The second obstacle is associated with inadequate scientific investigation of the problem, as a result of which the use of groundwater resources often leads to their speedy exhaustion and to lower quality water. In addition, the use of groundwater on marginal lands is associated with increased population densities in the immediate vicinity of water-supply points and overgrazing, which results in soil degradation and further desertification. Under certain conditions, the apparent benefits of providing a groundwater supply are not lasting.

Effective water prospecting and an efficient use of groundwater resources are possible, as a rule, only within the framework of well-planned projects. Such projects may be elaborated both for individual countries and for groups of adjoining countries. Identification of the essential character and costs of water projects largely depends on the adequacy of hydrogeologic surveys in a country (or group of countries), on the scale of projected use of groundwater, and on the aims of the project.

In the sphere of water resources there are still some untapped possibilities, for example, intergovernmental cooperation in the use of rivers and lakes. Programs of intergovernmental cooperation take place in such contexts as the construction of dams supplying electric power to participating countries and the development of shipping and irrigation for the adjacent areas. However, the full potential for intergovernmental cooperation for environmental protection remains unrealized.

In some countries, schemes for environmental protection—desertification control in particular—incorporate mass planting of trees with the aim of checking the desert's advance; Algeria and Libya are good examples. However, on the whole the tempo of afforestation in Africa lags far behind the tempo of deforestation.

Some projects of desertification control have made use of cloud-seeding techniques, but these projects were local in character, did not provide for lasting effect, and were rather costly.

The study of different environmental protection projects for Africa quite clearly shows that neither individual countries nor regional or international organizations have agreed on a continental-scale approach to these general problems, much less on solutions to specific local problems of desertification and drought control. Environmental planning is usually restricted to separate countries or to groups of countries. Projects to be implemented under the Plan of Action to Combat Desertification and those initiated by African countries themselves are often uncoordinated, even chaotic, and the need to create a single, scientifically well-grounded system is ignored. To raise the effectiveness of the desertification control effort, environmental protection policy must be made an important component of an all-African strategy of agricultural development.

This strategy must incorporate the development of diverse technologies so that both modern and traditional farming techniques may be used. It should be emphasized that a development strategy of this kind must be matched by progressive social and economic transformation of the African agrarian sector. Experience has shown that whenever social and ecological problems emerge, they are proof positive of a lack of balance in the development of water and land resources, of effective management of these resources, and of effective social policy.

The present ecological situation in arid and semiarid African areas imperatively calls for assistance in environmental protection on the part of the international community, including the United States and the Soviet Union. These two countries are quite capable of rendering aid to Africa in this area, since they can rely on their own experience of desertification control and development of arid regions, such as in the U.S. Southwest and in Soviet Central Asia.

It should be mentioned in this connection that in the first days of October 1988, the city of Ashkhabad hosted a visiting session of the Scientific Council on African Problems of the USSR Academy of Sciences, held jointly with the Turkmenian Institute of Deserts and the Institute for African Studies. A program of biosphere reserves is being worked out jointly by U.S. and Soviet scientists (the latter from the Institute of Evolutionary Animal Morphology and Ecology of the USSR), and a program of arid ecosystems protection is being carried out by U.S. scientists from Utah, Washington, and Arizona jointly with the Institute of Deserts of the Turkmen SSR Academy of Sciences. In our opinion, both sides might intensify their research on desertification control and promote Soviet–U.S. cooperation in Africa in this area of concern.

A prominent place in this cooperation undoubtedly should be accorded to the development of cartographic techniques, adapted to the specific conditions of the African continent and making use of both airplane and satellite surveys. An important task is to map current African water and land resources for use in finding practicable ways of holding desertification in check. We should be able, for instance, to determine areas suitable or not for irrigation or land conservation projects, to discern where pastoral stock farming has some potential and where it has to be restricted, and where afforestation has the best chances for success.

Assistance to African countries in their fight against desertification provides a good opportunity to combine Soviet and U.S. aid. Useful efforts would begin with participation in international projects and with education and training of a larger number of African specialists. In addition, special attention should be paid to field work. All this would help to identify and estimate properly the role of climatic and human factors in the spread of desertification.

PART 3

Debt and Development

Africa's debt crisis has been grave since the early 1980s. It has impeded economic growth, aggravated domestic sociopolitical problems, and exacerbated tensions in debtor nations' relations with their neighbors and the rest of the world. The crisis stems from a combination of internal problems and external factors, over which debtor countries have little control. These problems have inhibited production, investment, and growth and impaired the health of the world economy. In reality, to resolve international indebtedness there is no alternative to collective action at the international level.

In contemplating joint action, the Soviet Union and the United States should keep in mind several facts, and they should observe guiding principles. First, the debt of many especially low-income countries of Africa stands in the way of their economic recovery and renewed growth. Existing relief measures are welcome, but they will have little impact on the basic magnitude of sub-Saharan African debt or the burden of debt servicing. Measures must be implemented that would reduce the stock of debt and relieve the servicing burden, especially for those low-income African countries committed to sound economic reform. These measures should be equitable for creditor and debtor alike, and they should take into account the debtor's capacity to service debt without depressing growth and investment; they should be flexible enough to adjust to changing economic circumstances in the country; and they should result in minimal drain of already scarce human resources. Specifically, the Soviet Union and the United States should:

• Systematically exchange information concerning the profile and terms of debt owed by each African country and identify relief measures already in place.

• Explore measures for both governments, with the cooperation of other industrial countries and institutional creditors, to shape further debt relief initiatives for low-income African countries in a manner consistent with economic growth.

• Develop accurate means of forecasting the debt situation in Africa and facilities for expert groups to address the issues in a timely and effective manner.

• Support continuing export credit with terms appropriate to the abilities of low-income countries to repay; devise effective multilateral schemes for the stabilization of the price of raw materials, including the UN Common Fund for Commodities; and promote adjustment policies that reflect due regard for the interests of African states.

• Support research and exchange views on the results of structural adjustment in African economies, with a view to working out methods that render this process effective and sustainable.

9

The African Debt Crisis, Structural Adjustment, and Economic Development

JURI M. OSSIPOV

Since the early 1980s, the problem of African countries' external debt has assumed the distinct features of a grave chronic crisis, aggravating the already instable economic growth of those nations, increasing sociopolitical tensions, and exerting a negative influence upon African regional relations with the wider world.[1]

GENERAL CHARACTERISTICS OF THE PROBLEM

According to the ECA, the African debt (without South Africa) exceeds $200 billion. A particularly critical situation has taken shape in the countries south of the Sahara: tentative International Monetary Fund (IMF) data show that their aggregate debt by the end of 1987 was about $138 billion, or over two-thirds of their total gross national product (GNP). In these terms, sub-Saharan Africa surpasses all other regions of the world, even Latin America, which has accumulated an enormous debt (61 percent of GNP).

Nearly 85 percent of the African debt is concentrated in fifteen states; over half of it is owed by Egypt, Nigeria, Algeria, Morocco, and Ivory Coast. Despite the disparity in levels of indebtedness, even those countries with a relatively modest outstanding debt encounter persistent difficulties with its servicing. A striking illustration of this fact is an accumulation of overdue debt payments, which in 1986 reached the figure of about $6 billion for sub-Saharan countries.

Between 1980 and 1987 alone over sixty agreements within the framework of the Paris Club were concluded on easing the terms of the official debt for twenty-four countries, mainly involving the least developed group. However, even if this relief is taken into account, the actual rate of debt servicing, which in sub-Saharan Africa hovers around the level of 26 to 30 percent of export receipts, exceeds the "tolerance" level of the overwhelming majority of the countries in that area. According to the IMF, this rate (which does not include write-offs and other preferences), was expected to jump to 50 percent or even higher by 1988/89.

Specialists estimate that the majority of the least developed and most debt-burdened countries south of the Sahara will be unable to achieve solvency in the near future without substantial assistance on the part of donor countries.

INTERNAL FACTORS INFLUENCING THE CRISIS

The debt crisis in Africa is rooted in errors of national strategy and economic policy, substantially reducing the effective utilization of both external and domestic resources in the course of economic restructuring.

African states made the mistake of orienting their economic policies toward import-substituting industrialization, which led to a host of structural distortions, particularly in stimulating investment in inappropriately capital-intensive industrial projects. Ignoring the needs of the agricultural sector, and of its potential role in planning for integrated national industrialization, African states embarked on policies that led to decreased food production, with the result that later they were forced to draw down reserves of foreign exchange to pay for food imports. At the same time, this one-sided policy paralyzed the development of new and more effective export-oriented industries. A considerable portion of external loans were frozen in the projects ("white elephants") that, according to the nearly unanimous opinion of specialists, "ignored the basic facts of African life." A great number of state-owned enterprises became totally dependent on subsidies, an intolerable drain on the finances of debtor countries.

While production capacity in these projects was often underutilized, there was practically unrestrained import consumption on the part of elites, along with illegal transfers of scarce foreign currency abroad. With respect to such leakages abroad of investable financial resources (nearly $29 billion by the end of 1985), Africa is conspicuously worse, for example, than the Asian region and second only to Latin America.[2]

Finally, military expenditures, often as a result of conflicts not wholly of the states' own making, have ballooned, putting further pressure on available reserves. Unable to cover all of these growing expenditures, state authorities have had little option but to print money. The resulting two-digit inflation, further aggravating economic distortions, undermines savings, stimulates a "shadow economy," and contributes to the deterioration of the sociopolitical climate—all factors that make it even more difficult for the state to generate resources for either productive investment or debt service.

EXTERNAL FACTORS INFLUENCING THE CRISIS

The relatively beneficial state of international markets for African exporters in the 1970s was followed by the harsh external shocks of the 1980s. The cyclical crisis in the world economy of 1980–1982 harmed African exports in the form of an unprecedented drop in the prices of fuels and raw materials. It was particularly disastrous for sub-Saharan countries, whose export receipts fell by nearly one-third. Due to deteriorating trade conditions alone, these countries (not counting Nigeria) lost no less than $2.9 billion annually between 1979 and 1987.[3]

The protracted decline in export receipts, combined with the social welfare obligations of African states, led necessarily to an increasing reliance on foreign sources of finance. After 1981 the net influx of capital (i.e., minus debt service payments) in all its forms to sub-Saharan Africa steadily shrank. In 1984 it dropped to a low point of $13.8 billion, while in 1986 its level was still approximately $3 billion lower than in 1981.[4] A particularly large drop occurred in private bank credit (Africa was denied any access to the Euromarket), export loans, and financial interrelations with the IMF. Beginning in the mid-1980s, sub-Saharan countries actually became net creditors on an annual basis: payments to the IMF alone in 1985–1987 exceeded $2.2 billion. At the same time, private investments dropped by about $200 million between 1979 and 1987 (Nigeria excluded).[5]

Parallel to the dramatic decline in influxes of fresh capital, the burden of interest payments on credit from private sources became much heavier. While in the late 1970s the African clients of the Eurocurrency market could borrow at practically negative real interest rates (caused by high rates of international inflation), the switch-over to floating interest rates by banks in the 1980s, followed by the stabilization of inflation, sharply raised the real cost of debt. In particular, the cost of servicing the U.S. dollar portion of the African debt (over two-thirds of the total) grew through the mid-1980s because of the dollar's overvaluation.

The real burden of annual payments on all types of debt incurred by sub-Saharan Africa (i.e., with due account taken of grace periods, write-offs, and other privileges) in 1984–1986 grew to $10 billion, of which about $4.5 billion was for payment of interest. This sum was expected to reach $15.5 billion by 1987–1989, with $5.6 billion going toward interest.[6]

The external financing mechanism not only failed to help Africa weather the debt crisis, but under conditions of severe market instability in export prices it actually resulted in an outflow of capital from the region. In this situation, the "extension" of debt service payments granted African countries a temporary respite. In partially putting off the burden of its service, however, this "relief" led to a general rise in the costs of resources.

THE PROBLEM OF RESTORING SOLVENCY

Thus, both in its origin and in its consequences the debt crisis of African countries goes far beyond domestic factors. It is also an integral aspect of expanding asymmetry in the interdependent development of the world economy. That is why the African debt crisis cannot be solved by the debtor countries alone but must be addressed by a comprehensive approach on the part of donor and recipient countries.

Resolution of the debt crisis in its initial stages was based primarily on a combination of IMF stabilizing credits and Paris Club decisions, entailing strict deflationary actions, rapid correction of balance of payments imbalances, and a cutting of domestic demand in borrower countries. The IMF's orthodox therapy ignored the structural nature of Africa's external debt, reducing it chiefly to a short-term problem of liquidity. The IMF's "bitter medicine" only reinforced the disease instead of curing it. More and more countries became dissatisfied with its monetarist philosophy, which suppressed the incentives for development and thus, ironically, further weakened the ability of African countries to repay debt.

Therefore, in the mid-1980s (the pressure of criticism on the part of developing countries being a major factor) there occurred a changed way of thinking, directed toward a comprehensive interpretation of the adjustment process. The problem of restoring stable economic growth in Africa became of paramount importance. In other words, the main goal was to stimulate the medium-term attainment of a relatively stable growth rate of GDP (its currency component in particular) to external debt, thus ameliorating the solvency problem.

The concept of so-called structural adjustment is mainly based on the universalist canons of contemporary neoliberalism, complemented with elements of the "supply theory." In practice, this approach, obviously spearheaded at encouraging market-oriented development in Africa, is embodied in working programs coordinated within the framework of the IMF and the World Bank. The approach includes permitting an unlimited liberalization of prices and tariffs; allowing exchange and interest rates to be set by the market; abolishing or drastically reducing food subsidies and other types of social assistance to the population; eliminating or substantially reducing support to farmers; and finally, relaxing control over private investment and trade in currency.

Measures to reorganize the state sector along "free enterprise" lines are part and parcel of the adjustment model. Here the stress is laid on privatizing enterprises, pumping resources into the private sector via development banks and finance corporations, and providing technical assistance and other services. Finally, the overall package of reforms includes the following components: the rationalization of administrative institutions, taxation, credit, and budgeting mechanisms; improvement in the efficiency of state investment programs; better management and control over state funds; and improvements in debt management.

These policies, which have been implemented in over thirty African countries under the supervision of the IMF and the World Bank, do not enjoy unanimous approval. A number of experts have found fault with the approach detailed above—and with good reason.

African economies contain structural impediments to development that these policies actually reinforce. In "dual economies" of the African type, that is, those recognizable by the parallel existence of subsistence economies and advanced industrial enclaves, it is relatively easy for privileged strata to seize both wealth and power. Lacking state intervention on their behalf, traditional producers are unable to gain the economic momentum necessary to develop and modernize local production.

Under these conditions, policies of unlimited liberalization can hardly overcome the structural dualism that stands in the way of development. Deregulation carries the danger of further weakening the foundations of small-commodity production. Indeed, is it really possible to deny government assistance to a huge number of stagnating peasant households? Even highly developed countries annually allocate billions of dollars to agricultural subsidies and price supports. The market alone is too imperfect to remove structural limitations and extraeconomic obstacles hampering Africa's agrarian development. The "free market" may instead serve as an invitation to those with the power to do so to exploit broad sections of the population, through, for example, monopoly pricing. Not surprisingly, sober-minded scholars persistently recommend that "adjustment with a human face" be imparted to programs of reforms in Africa.

In short, the logic of a comprehensive approach must avert the excesses of neoliberal extremism. As Vassily Leontiev, Nobel Prize winner, put it figuratively, the sail of the economic ship needs a wind. Personal interest and market initiative make up this wind. But the ship's movement must be controlled, and it falls to the state to steer through skillful implementation of macroeconomic policy. Skill at the helm can considerably accelerate the movement of the economic ship on its prescribed course, judging from the experience of South Korea, India, and other Asian countries. The state's proper role is to correct market mechanisms rather than suppress them. In short, the impetus for development should come both from above and from below: market mechanisms must reflect social dynamics.

A PROGRAM FOR STRUCTURAL ADJUSTMENT WITH GROWTH

Structural adjustment in Africa is expected to continue for a relatively long period (at least five years). However, some results are already visible. A World Bank study shows that only a few countries have made substantial progress. A number of countries (including Egypt, Mauritius, Botswana, Niger, Uganda, and Rwanda) have accelerated their economic growth rates. But on the whole, structural adjustment policies have failed to stem the economic decline of the first half of the 1980s. Moreover, in 1987 the economic situation deteriorated. According to the ECA, the average growth rate of the region's GDP was only 1.5 percent, or half the population growth rate. For the bulk of sub-Saharan Africa, real economic growth rates are still close to zero and in some instances are even falling.

Why, then, is adjustment policy in the region not very effective? One important reason lies in a too general approach to the conditions of development in the countries of the region. The slow pace of reform in the state sector is an even greater factor, however. Large bureaucracies, big business, and other influential factions seeking to retain their privileges all tend to hinder solutions.

There is no doubt, however, that the main destabilizing factor in the adjustment process is the growing asymmetry in the economic relations of industrial centers with a large number of raw materials–producing agrarian countries of the region. Further aggravation of the financial crisis threatens to bring many countries south of the Sahara even closer to catastrophe, with a number of unpredictable consequences.

Thus, urgent measures have already been taken to ease the adjustment process for African economies, especially for the least developed and most indebted countries. The summit meeting of June 1988 in Toronto approved a compromise scheme of external debt reorganization within the framework of the Paris Club. It was based on the so-called menu approach: official creditors were given the option to choose special interest rates with shorter terms of debt extension, select longer terms at market rates, or write off debt service commitments during a consolidation period. A combination of all three options is also possible.

A number of countries, including West Germany, Canada, Italy, and Japan, have already forgiven a considerable portion of "poorest country" debts, or have expressed their readiness to do so. Substantial concessions to African debtors have been made by the Soviet Union and other countries. In addition, the IMF plans, with the help of leading creditors, to expand the financing of the least developed and the most indebted African countries, mainly through special funds established to assist with structural adjustment. Finally, agreements have been reached on further rounds of replenishment of the International Development Association (IDA) and the African Development Fund (ADF), which grant loans to low-income countries at most favorable terms. Also, the capital of the African Development Bank (ADB) has been considerably increased.

All of this is expected to increase the ceiling of sub-Saharan Africa's external financing in 1988/89 by about $3 billion per year.[7] However, the actual needs of African economies are much greater. The UN consultative group on Africa's foreign financing estimates that even to ensure a 1 percent growth rate of imports and a debt service rate no higher than 25 percent, the countries south of the Sahara will need not less than an additional $2 billion a year, and more if poor export prospects are taken into account. Yet another $3 billion should be added to substantially relax the debt crisis, to make the UN Priority Programme stable and dynamic, and to ensure annual growth rates of at least 3 or 4 percent.

EXTERNAL DEBT AND DEVELOPMENT: A STRATEGY FOR THE FUTURE AND THE POTENTIAL FOR JOINT SOVIET–U.S. ACTION

Speaking in Los Angeles at an annual session of the Western Economic Association dedicated to "Mikhail Gorbachev's perestroika," Michael D. Intriligator emphasized the particular importance of cooperation in the solution of global problems, including the international debt crisis and economic underdevelopment. Indeed, the dramatic aggravation of this problem is the result of a combination of internal and external factors that evade effective control by debtor countries, suppress incentives for accumulation and growth, and restrain the "metabolism" of the world economy. There is really no reliable alternative to a clear understanding of the necessity for collective efforts on the part of both donor and debtor countries.

A collective approach to the African debt crisis should be based on the following criteria: (1) broad assistance directed toward the restoration of a stable economic growth and (2) the improvement of African debt management capabilities, particularly in countries with a very low domestic potential for development. What dimensions should the debt strategy possess?

First, broader opportunities should be pursued to provide African economies undergoing structural adjustment with an influx of bilateral aid at terms acceptable to borrower countries. Stress should be laid on satisfying the urgent needs of the least developed states. Simultaneously, strenuous efforts should be made to facilitate the cooperation of international and regional finance institutions with African countries. Structural adjustment financing for the most debt-burdened states should be further extended within the framework of the IMF and the World Bank. The resources of the IDA and the ADF should also be replenished as a means of expanding the most favorable credit terms to the poorest countries in the region. Equally important are less rigid preconditions for access to IMF credits.

Second, restoration of the net inflow of external financing must go hand in hand with a broader spectrum of measures facilitating debt management. A number of formulas for debt reorganization are far ahead of current methods. An UNCTAD initiative proposes a 30 percent reduction of commercial indebtedness for a group of countries that have accumulated the largest debts (Nigeria, Ivory Coast, and Morocco, among others). Of considerable significance are the proposals of Nordic countries to establish interest rate subsidies and to refinance the debt with the aid of preferential resources, permitting debt held on market terms by the least developed countries to be turned into loans on IDA's softer terms.

Third, the financial instruments of the debt strategy must be supported by measures conducive to the restoration of the influx of private investments. The most promising path to this goal appears to lie in the stimulation of various forms of joint enterprise in ways that allow national firms to offset part of their financial burden and to reduce the risk of operations in new, less developed zones of capital accumulation, such as agrobusiness and the industrial processing of raw materials. On the basis of expanding co-operative links, the firms of different nationalities should be encouraged to be more active in the field of contractual ("tied") financing. Equally important is support (in the form of guarantees and other incentives) to foreign companies operating in conjunction with bank consortiums or other financial alliances under the auspices of the World Bank and the ADB.

Fourth, a key element in the debt strategy should be inclusion of measures to facilitate the access of African exports to the markets of donor countries. Coordinated policy in this sphere should be aimed at containing currency-trade imbalances that encourage protectionism.

Fifth, all characteristics of the debt strategy detailed above must be coordinated with African structural adjustment policies. This strategy should take into account the differences in the countries' conditions. Some countries in the region, such as the states of northern Africa, have already achieved a relatively advanced level of development; most of the others are still listed among the more underdeveloped countries of the world. Far different still are national sociocultural heritages and political traditions. It is necessary to eliminate the market bias in adjustment policies, which sometimes poorly suit sub-Saharan Africa. Finally, state sector reforms should be promoted through technical and expert assistance.

Such a strategy must include measures to stimulate internal reform in donor countries themselves, for example, raising the rates and effectiveness of economic restructuring in the USSR and stabilizing the U.S. budget deficit. Equally important is the rectification of imbalances (removal of discriminatory restrictions in particular) in the structure of trade relations among the partners in development. Any approach to solving the debt problem should tap the potential for integrated world development, with due regard for the interests of creditors, debtors, Africa, and other zones of the Third World.

NOTES

1. *Development Forum* (October 1987): 10–11.
2. *Financial Times*, 7 September 1987.

3. *Financing Africa's Recovery: Report and Recommendations of the Advisory Group on Financial Flows for Africa* (New York: United Nations, February 1988).

4. *Africa Recovery* (March 1988): 23–24.

5. Ibid., 23.

6. Ibid., 20.

7. Gerald K. Helleiner, "The Question of Conditionality," in *African Debt and Financing,* ed. Carol Lancaster and John Williamson (Washington, D.C.: Institute for International Economics, 1986), 76.

10

Debt and Development in Sub-Saharan Africa

CALLISTO MADAVO

The external debt of sub-Saharan Africa grew from less than $6 billion in 1970 to an estimated $129 billion in 1987.[1] This debt is small by world standards: it represents about a tenth of the developing world's debt, and a fourth of Latin America's. Brazil alone owes almost as much. Still, the debt of sub-Saharan African countries is very large in relation to their economies. It is about 90 percent of GDP and about 300 percent of exports, or about $285 of debt per person compared to GDP per person of approximately $310.

This magnitude of debt can be traced to various factors. One was the sharp increase in oil prices in 1972/73, which led many of the oil-importing countries in the region to increase external borrowing in order to cushion the impact on their economies. Another key event was a boom in the prices of export commodities such as cocoa, coffee, and tea in the late 1970s. This encouraged governments in many oil-importing countries to expand expenditures, just as the oil-exporting countries were doing. At the same time, easy access to international finance at low interest rates enabled many countries to supplement domestic resources with large foreign loans to finance increased expenditures.

Many of the investments financed with foreign loans were not very productive. This was due partly to bad project selection and implementation and partly to inappropriate macroeconomic policies and regulations that tended to stifle efficient production incentives. Whereas the investment-to-GDP ratio in 1970–1981 was 6 percent higher than in 1960–1970, average GDP growth was lower. Export growth also fell. Hence, by 1980 the external debt of sub-Saharan Africa had increased almost tenfold, without a corresponding increase in the region's debt service ability. As the market for the region's export commodities turned soft in the 1980s, access to international finance tightened and interest rates rose, leaving African economies very vulnerable indeed.

Earnings from exports of goods and services in 1987, compared with 1980 earnings, were down by $24 billion, or nearly half. About $21 billion of that decline was in petroleum revenues, mainly because of a fall in the price of petroleum. But petroleum was not the only export commodity to suffer price decline. Prices for cocoa, sugar, sisal, wood, palm kernels, and phosphate all fell dramatically. The index of all export prices declined 18 percent from 1980 to 1987, while that of imports rose 2 percent. Excluding Nigeria, the largest petroleum exporter in the region, these rises in prices are estimated to have cost around $2.9 billion a year.

Service on long-term debt (maturities of over one year) alone increased from $548 million in 1970 to $9.4 billion in 1984, before falling gradually to $6.4 billion in 1987. Actual repayment obligations were much higher than the amounts paid, since arrears increased from $1 billion in 1980 to around $11 billion in 1987. Unfortunately for the countries in the region, disbursements from long-term external loans did not rise as fast as their payment obligations. In fact, they started falling after 1982, only to stabilize in 1986/87 at around $9 billion, compared to $11 billion in 1980. Many countries obtained some relief from short-term IMF "purchases" (loans), but by 1986 repayments to the IMF had also exceeded new inflows.

Rising external debt service, falling export revenues, decreasing levels of disbursements, and the disruptive effects of arrears accumulating on trade credit all combined to force drastic cuts in imports. In current dollar terms, goods imported in 1987 were 30 percent less than in 1980 (about 35 percent less in real terms).

The African region is heavily dependent upon imports for capital and intermediate goods, and also on the import duties as the greatest source of government tax revenues. The effects of import compression are therefore severe. Capital stock and physical infrastructure have deteriorated for lack of adequate maintenance, and productive enterprises have been forced to operate at very low capacities for lack of imported inputs, thus further eroding the tax base for governments, as well as investment. These conditions, together with certain misplaced policies, have reduced GDP growth and contributed to high inflation rates. Trying to make up for the shortfall in taxes by borrowing from their Central Banks has not helped. By 1987 real GDP per person was about 12 percent less than in 1980.

THE CRISIS IN LOW-INCOME AFRICA

The choke-hold of debt on economic development is particularly acute in the subset of sub-Saharan countries that the World Bank classifies as low-income (i.e., GNP per person of $425 or less in 1986). This group includes 30 of the 44 countries in sub-Saharan Africa. Fully 27 of these countries are debt-distressed (i.e., each has debt service obligations before rescheduling and increase in arrears that exceed 30 percent of its exports of goods and services).

Almost 80 percent of the debt of the low-income countries is owed to official agencies. Since these loans normally carry fixed interest rates, these countries have to some extent been protected from the sharp rises in interest rates in the 1980s. However, the terms on official loans hardened over the first half of the 1980s, reflecting the worldwide trend, and interest rates rose and maturities shortened, thus reducing the grant element in these loans. Of particular concern is the large share of multilateral debt, about a third of the total, which cannot be rescheduled.

THE OUTLOOK FOR THE FUTURE

To revive Africa's recovery from the downward spiral of the 1980s will require significant reforms. Correcting of distortions in product and factor markets are needed to encourage efficient production and to foster exports; and factor markers are needed to encourage efficient production. To slow down domestic inflation and encourage savings, fiscal discipline is required, and inefficiencies in state enterprises and in the public sector as a whole must be reduced.

About twenty-five low-income African countries, along with four others not so classified, are currently engaged in important reform programs with support from the World Bank or the IMF, or both. It is a slow and difficult process. In many instances the initial impact of such programs seems to lower consumption levels. This is made even more painful by the reductions that occurred during the 1980s at already very low income levels. If the courageous efforts of these countries—and the tremendous political risks being taken by their leaders—are to bear fruit, ways must be found to give them relief from the stifling effects of debt, and to provide them with concessional resources to help them rebuild their productive infrastructure.

INITIATIVES TO PROVIDE DEBT RELIEF AND CONCESSIONAL RESOURCES: IMPROVED PARIS CLUB RESCHEDULING TERMS OF 1987

To be sure, there have already been a number of significant innovations by creditors to help ease the burden. The Paris Club has adopted multiyear rescheduling and has extended rescheduling periods from a standard five years of grace followed by five years to repay to ten years of grace and ten years of repayment. It has also permitted arrears and previously rescheduled debt to be rescheduled again. Mozambique, Somalia, Guinea-Bissau, Malawi, and a few others have benefited from these new generous terms since 1987.

As welcome as these improved terms are, rescheduling for many of these countries merely postpones the problem; and successive rescheduling and nonconcessional rates actually worsen it. Because of the legal, statutory, accounting, and budgetary complexities involved, it has usually not been possible to reschedule bilateral export credits, which have accounted for about half of scheduled debt service, on concessional terms. Twenty-one sub-Saharan countries have rescheduled debt through the Paris Club a total of sixty-six times since 1975, and capitalized interest from such rescheduling now represents an estimated 20 percent of their total nonconcessional long-term debt.

For some of the countries, even rescheduling on concessional terms may not be enough to normalize relations with creditors and at the same time finance long-term development programs that ensure positive real growth in consumption per capita. Such is the case, for example, of Sudan.

Preliminary World Bank estimates indicate that even concessional rescheduling is not a viable financial option, even on optimistic assumptions about export growth and conservative estimates regarding imports, with new financial flows projected using recent trends. Thus, if all arrears as of June 1988 and all scheduled payments for the five years starting from June 1988 are rescheduled (except those of the multilaterals), at the improved Paris Club terms plus a concessional interest rate of 2 percent, debt service will still absorb about 40 percent of Sudan's exports up to 1998 and then climb rapidly to around 90 percent by the year 2004. The situation is almost as bleak in Somalia and Zambia.

OTHER INITIATIVES

The seriousness of the debt problem in low-income Africa is now generally recognized. As a consequence, initiatives have been launched to provide new funds at more generous terms, to provide more concessional re-scheduling, and in some cases to forgive debt.

The Special Program of Assistance

In December 1987 the World Bank launched, along with bilateral donors, the European Commission, the IMF, and the ADB, a three-year (1988–1990) Special Program of Assistance (SPA) for low-income, debt-distressed sub-Saharan African countries undertaking economic reform.[2] The main elements of the program are:

Additional IDA funding. About half of the $2.4 billion available under IDA-8 replenishment for 1988–1990 will go to sub-Saharan Africa. Some two-thirds of this amount, more than half of which will will be quick-disbursing, has been earmarked for the debt-distressed countries. This program should enable IDA to increase its disbursements to these countries by about 50 percent compared with much lower levels during the previous three

years. During fiscal 1988, 77 percent of IDA lending in the region went to
these countries.

Adjustment cofinancing. Eighteen bilateral donors and multilateral
agencies have pledged $4 billion in highly concessional, quick-disbursing aid
to help cofinance IDA operations in support of adjustment programs. About
half of this sum was in addition to aid already planned by donors for these
countries. By the end of June 1988, donors had indicated commitments of
about $3 billion, which may be expected to result in actual disbursements of
some $2.4 billion during 1988–1990.

Concessional rescheduling. The SPA calls for conversion of some
Official Development Assistance (ODA) loans to the status of grants (i.e.,
loan forgiveness) and for new approaches to rescheduling nonconcessional
debt. During 1978–1986 bilateral creditors, including France, West
Germany, the United Kingdom, the Netherlands, and the Scandinavian
countries, wrote off (in other words, forgave) $1.8 billion in sub-Saharan
debt. In addition, the grant component in new development assistance from
bilateral donors has increased. However, the scope for further relief through
forgiveness of concessional ODA debt is limited, since its share of scheduled
payments is relatively small.

IDA reflows. A number of countries, such as Kenya, whose economies
were doing well in the 1970s and therefore were able to borrow from the
World Bank on International Bank for Reconstruction and Development
(IBRD) terms (higher interest rates compared to IDA), have since fallen on
hard times. To ease the burden, the World Bank will provide them with
additional IDA resources to be financed from payments received from earlier
IDA loans.

The Enhanced Structural Adjustment Facility (ESAF) set up by the IMF
will provide $8.4 billion in ten-year credits at interest rates of 0.5 percent, to
low-income countries, most of them in sub-Saharan Africa. In July 1988
Malawi became the first country to benefit from this assistance.

The Toronto Initiatives

With regard to bilateral nonconcessional debt, the head of the seven leading
industrial countries agreed at their economic summit meeting in Toronto in
June 1988 that individual countries would, "within a framework of compar-
ability," choose among partial forgiveness, lower interest rates on rescheduled debt, and even longer rescheduling maturities as means of easing
the debt burden on debt-distressed low-income African countries pursuing a
program of adjustment. In October 1988 the Paris Club agreed on new
rescheduling terms under the Toronto framework.

Partial write-off. Forgiveness of one-third of debt service and
rescheduling of the remainder at market rates with a fourteen-year maturity,
including nine years of grace.

Lower interest rates. Rescheduling of debt service at concessional interest rates (either 3.5 percentage points below or one-half of market rates, whichever gives the smallest reduction), with a fourteen-year maturity, including nine years of grace.

Longer terms. Rescheduling of debt service at market interest rates, but with a twenty-five-year maturity, including fourteen years of grace.

Mali and Madagascar took advantage of these new terms in October 1988.

EXTERNAL RESOURCE REQUIREMENTS FOR DEVELOPMENT (1988–1992)

Taking into account the help that will come from the SPA and from rescheduling on Paris Club terms of 1987, World Bank staff have estimated that those debt-distressed low-income African countries implementing adjustment programs will have enough resources to take care of their external payments obligations and achieve positive growth in both real GDP and consumption per person over the period 1988–1992. For the rest of sub-Saharan Africa, there is an uncovered gap of over $2 billion a year over the same period. The UN report of the Advisory Group on Financing Africa's Recovery (the Wass Report) has, independently, arrived at similar numbers and conclusions.[3] A significant part of the $2 billion might be absorbed by debt-distressed low-income countries such as Sudan, Somalia, and Zambia, which have not yet begun implementing adjustment programs. These three, as well as other debt-distressed countries not yet implementing adjustment programs, must be encouraged to do so. If they act, more debt relief and new concessional flows will be needed to close the $2 billion gap. Thus, while the new Toronto Initiatives will help, it is unlikely to be enough.

THE SITUATION IN THE HORN OF AFRICA

There is special interest in the Horn of Africa in what the World Bank is doing in Ethiopia, Somalia, and Sudan to help solve the debt and development problem and to suggest how Soviet–U.S. cooperation might help. I should first point out, however, that all three countries face hostile climatic conditions, including recurrent droughts, and sometimes floods. Each of these countries is also in the midst of a civil war. These problems combine with the debt burden and inappropriate policies to hamper economic growth.

Ethiopia. Projected payments on existing debt for the next five years (1988–1992) are estimated to be around 30 percent of projected exports. Ethiopia's debt problem is not as acute as that of Somalia and Sudan. But rigid economic controls, in addition to the recurrent droughts and the destablization caused by the prolonged civil war, are hampering the country's economic development. The World Bank has been providing agricultural inputs to help increase agricultural output and minimize the potential impact of future droughts. However, in order for these efforts to bear fruit, production incentives to farmers must be improved through relaxation of the controls. The Bank is discussing with the authorities the best ways to bring this about.

Somalia. Projected annual debt service for the next five years is around 122 percent of exports of goods and services. Total external debt at the end of 1987 was approximately $1.7 billion, about 20 percent of which was in arrears. It is estimated that around $90 million of the arrears are owed to the United States and about $20 million to Eastern European countries, including Bulgaria, the German Democratic Republic, Romania, and Yugoslavia. The World Bank and the IMF have been discussing with the Somali authorities policy measures that if adopted would constitute an adjustment program that would help boost production and exports and qualify the country for assistance from the various initiatives launched for the debt-distressed countries.

Sudan. Total external debt at the end of 1987 was about $1 billion, of which about $.4 billion were arrears. Scheduled debt service on existing debt for each of the next five years is about 80 percent of exports of goods and services. In addition, the $.4 billion arrears represent almost 400 percent of exports of goods and services. Arrears to the United States are estimated to be about $30 million, and to other Eastern European countries (mainly Yugoslavia and Romania) about $158 million. The World Bank and the IMF have had extensive discussions with the Sudanese authorities on an adjustment program that will stimulate exports, provide the basis for approaching creditors for substantial debt relief, and furnish new concessional financing.

With the situation in these countries in mind, Soviet–U.S. cooperation should begin with two specific steps. Both Soviet and U.S. participants in this project should urge their own national authorities to encourage these countries to adopt adjustment programs that will provide greater incentives for efficient production and for exports in both the private and public sectors. They should further be urged to provide debt relief (e.g., through partial or full write-off of arrears) and new concessional financing to help smooth the path of adjustment.

NOTES

1. Sub-Saharan Africa comprises all of the countries south of the Sahara excluding South Africa.

2. The program began with Burundi, Central African Republic, Ghana, Guinea, Guinea-Bissau, Madagascar, Malawi, Mauritania, Mozambique, Niger, São Tomé and

Principe, Senegal, Tanzania, Togo, Uganda, and Zaire. Kenya and Mali were later added.

3. *Financing Africa's Recovery: Report and Recommendations of the Advisory Group on Financial Flows for Africa* (New York: United Nations, February 1988).

11

The Debt of Low-Income Africa: Profile, Problems, Prospects

CAROL LANCASTER

The external debt of sub-Saharan Africa is the focus of much discussion and concern, not only for Africans but foreign development and financial experts as well. It has been increasingly recognized over the past several years that the burden of debt for much of Africa is as heavy or heavier than the debt burdens of the larger debtors of Latin America and, together with other economic afflictions, represents an obstacle to economic recovery and growth in the region. It has also been increasingly recognized that the debt of much of sub-Saharan Africa is different from the debt of Latin America, because the external debt of low-income Africa[1] is nearly all (90 percent) owed to official lenders—foreign governments and international financial institutions. The complications of developing debt relief or debt restructuring initiatives are significantly eased where public rather than private institutions (whose objective is to make money and who must answer to their shareholders when they do not) are the principal creditors.

Further, the economies of low-income Africa are distinct from the economies of middle-income developing country debtors. These countries are typically producers and exporters largely of primary products and have relatively little industry. Their existing export markets are generally weak and, in the case of most primary products, are projected to remain weak for the foreseeable future. Thus, the option of these countries working out of their debt burden through expanding traditional exports is a limited one. Also, in contrast to middle-income developing countries, few low-income African countries have the option in the short term of generating substantial increases in their export earnings through expanding the production and export of nontraditional goods and services. Their economies are narrowly based and rigid in comparison to the more diversified economies of middle-income countries.

Finally, the relative debt burden of low-income African countries is heavier than the debt burdens of other low-income developing countries, of

95

middle-income oil-importing countries, and even of the highly indebted developing countries, as the following comparison[2] shows:

	Debt/GNP (%)	Debt/Exports (%)
Low-income Africa	102	509
Low-income Asia	18	159
Highly indebted countries	63	357

The debt of low-income Africa is especially onerous because these countries are among the poorest in the world, have suffered a dramatic deterioration in economic conditions during the past decade, and are least able to service their debts while promoting economic recovery and growth. Because debt relief initiatives for these countries would be less difficult to implement than such initiatives for middle-income countries with large concentrations of private debts, there has been some movement recently on developing a menu of concessional debt relief proposals for low-income African countries. Before examining the implications and adequacy of this menu, we first examine in more detail the debt profile of the countries in question, the problems and limitations in existing approaches to managing the debt burden of these countries, and the variety of objectives further debt relief initiatives might serve.

THE DEBT PROFILE OF LOW-INCOME AFRICA

As of 1988, low-income African countries owed $70 billion in external debt.[3] Of this total, $49 billion was owed to official creditors, with $19 billion owed to multilateral institutions (mainly the IBRD, the IDA, and the ADB and ADF), $30 billion owed to bilateral creditors (just over half in the form of concessional loans and just under half in the form of nonconcessional export credits), $7 billion owed to private creditors, $5 billion to the IMF, and $6 billion in short-term debt.[4] The scheduled servicing of this debt exceeded 30 percent of annual export earnings for many low-income countries; for a handful of countries, debt servicing exceeded 100 percent of export earnings. Actual debt arrears and reschedulings amounted to 20 percent of export earnings, still a hefty drain on foreign exchange earnings.[5] It is worth remembering that not all low-income African countries are equally encumbered by debt. The World Bank has identified twenty-two countries that are especially debt-distressed.[6] These are countries that have *ex ante* debt service ratios of more than 30 percent during 1988–1990, well above a level of debt servicing consistent with what these countries are likely to pay or with their establishing the preconditions for renewed growth, in the view of the World Bank.

THE BROADER DIMENSION OF THE DEBT PROBLEM

The debt of low-income Africa has broader implications than simply absorbing scarce foreign exchange. It is a part of a general problem of constrained resources. The deterioration in the terms of trade of primary producers, the drying up of commercial credit for those few low-income countries that had been able to borrow commercially, the stagnation in foreign aid at the beginning of the 1980s, and the burden of debt servicing all combined to reduce substantially the foreign exchange available for these countries to finance their imports of consumer goods, intermediate goods, and investment goods.[7] With substantially increased inflows of financial resources, the problem of debt servicing could be eased. While resource flows have risen over recent years to low-income African countries with stabilization and adjustment programs, these increases remain modest, with both the World Bank and the United Nations warning that additional assistance of between $1.5 and $2 billion is still needed if these countries are to recover and create the preconditions for renewed growth.

The debt servicing burdens of low-income African countries have been relieved through the reschedulings of debt payments. Typically, a debtor country must have in place a standby program with the IMF before its creditors will negotiate a rescheduling agreement, either at the Paris Club (for public creditors) or the London Club (for private creditors). Rescheduling arrangements involve agreement on an overall framework on the types of debt to be rescheduled (i.e., capital or capital plus interest payments), on the consolidation period (the period of time during which all debts due for payment are combined for rescheduling), on the grace period (during which no payments are required), on the repayment period, and on the interest rates applied to the rescheduled debts. Rescheduling arrangements for low-income Africa normally include interest and capital (and sometimes interest and capital on previously rescheduled debts), a consolidation period of twelve to eighteen months but rarely more, a maximum grace period of ten years, a maximum repayment period of ten years more, and a market rate of interest on rescheduled debts. These rescheduling agreements cover only the debtors of bilateral public and commercial creditors. The debts of "preferred lenders" such as the IMF and the World Bank are not rescheduled. Once a framework for rescheduling is negotiated between the creditors and the debtor government, then negotiations between the debtor and each creditor separately take place to implement the framework.

Twenty-four African countries have negotiated debt reschedulings since 1980, several repeatedly. (Zaire holds the world record with eleven debt reschedulings to date.) The current system of dealing with the debt problems through periodic reschedulings carries a number of problems. First, it is extremely time consuming, especially for that small number of top-level economic managers in African countries. The ministers of finance and the governors of the Central Banks of rescheduling countries must spend a great deal of their time preparing for and negotiating reschedulings. It is often the case that these individuals are very able and experienced economic managers, but they are typically among the limited number of such individuals in low-income Africa. When they are negotiating debt reschedulings they are not managing their economies. Second, the need to negotiate frequent reschedulings can inject a degree of uncertainty into economic planning in low-income countries and increase the costs of their imports. Arrears on unpaid debts typically build up while negotiations are planned and under way. Such arrears can lead to a cutoff of short-term trade financing and result in exporters charging premium prices to African importers. Third, the way debts have been rescheduled has greatly increased the stock of debt. Unpaid interest has been combined with unpaid capital to create a new, much larger loan to the rescheduling country, which is then charged market rates of interest. The capitalization of interest payments has added more to the stock of African debt than new borrowing in recent years and has increased future debt servicing burdens.

The existing stock of debt represents a heavy mortgage on the future of many low-income African countries. Indeed, in a number of such countries, it is already so large that no one realistically expects that it can ever be fully paid. It likely acts as a disincentive to voluntary capital transfers (including private investment, which is key to the success of structural adjustment programs), and to officials to undertake and sustain the difficult policy reforms necessary to restore their countries to growth. Why suffer the pain and risk of such changes today if much of the gain from growth tomorrow will simply go to service a virtually limitless debt?

THE OBJECTIVES OF DEBT RELIEF

There is little dispute that the debt burden of low-income Africa is a problem in need of a solution. There are, however, differences on what the objectives of any debt initiatives for these countries should be. There is the immediate cash flow problem facing Africans—the burden of giving up substantial amounts of scarce foreign exchange to service their debts. Some proposals aim at reducing this burden to manageable levels. There is the problem of the large stock of debt, much of which is unlikely ever to be paid. Some proposals would reduce or eliminate the stock of debt and the debt servicing burden by canceling some or all of the debt. There is the problem of increasing the stock of debt through the capitalization of interest rates in debt rescheduling agreements. Several recent proposals aim at eliminating this problem. There is the problem of the drain on scarce human resources caused by frequent reschedulings.

If there are a variety of objectives to be considered in examining the debt problem of low-income Africa, there are also constraints and costs of various relief measures. Debts result from loans that a government, individual, or institution agreed to receive. Debts create an obligation to repay, no matter how well or foolishly the money was used or what pressures the lender brought to bear on the borrower to take the money. This principle may not be just—lenders, public and private, can take advantage of the ignorance or venality of borrowers—but it is generally recognized as critical if financial relations are to remain orderly. And it seems unlikely to change in the near future. Creditors are reluctant to break with this principle except when faced with losing any prospect of repayment or when they have other, more important interests threatened by demanding continuing repayment. Not even the recent UN report, sympathetic to the debt and financing needs of Africa, favored overall debt cancellation.

Any debt relief measures raise problems of equity, precedent, or "contamination" and moral hazard. Equity problems affect both creditors and debtors. Individual creditors are reluctant to provide more concessional relief than their colleagues for fear of transferring resources to those colleagues. Where one creditor provides highly concessional debt relief, that relief can simply facilitate the servicing of debtors to other creditors. Equity must be a concern with debtors also. Global debt relief schemes will affect different debtors in different ways, depending on their debt profile. Any debt relief for low-income Africa will likely draw cries of protest from middle African countries, such as Nigeria, which will feel unfairly slighted if they receive no relief.

The issue of precedent is related to the issue of equity. The debt and development problems of low-income countries may be more intractable than those of middle-income countries, but debt relief measures for the former will likely provoke pressures from the latter for relief for their debts. The problem of precedent is not confined to international debt problems. In the United States, for example, debt relief for low-income Africa could well provoke further pressures from farmers, students, and others who owe the U.S. government money for similar relief. (In fact, they have received substantial relief already but debt relief for foreign countries could well encourage yet more pressures.) And these pressures could prove politically potent.

Finally, there is the inevitability of conditionality. Debt relief measures thus far have been conditioned on policy reform programs under IMF auspices on the part of debtors. Any future relief measures will be similarly conditioned. The possibility of some sort of global debt relief scheme applied to debtors regardless of their economic policies seems extremely unlikely.

DEBT RELIEF FOR LOW-INCOME AFRICA THUS FAR

In recent years, a number of modest changes have been made in the way the debt problems of low-income Africa have been managed. A few creditors have turned concessional loans into grants, in effect canceling debts. The grace and repayment periods in debt rescheduling negotiations have been lengthened. The IMF has sought to ease the problems of low-income countries associated with their repurchase (i.e., repayment) of IMF loans through, first, the Structural Adjustment Facility (SAF) and, most recently, through the Enhanced Structural Adjustment Facility (ESAF). These lending programs provide concessional loans to "prolonged users" of IMF credits at .5 percent interest, to be repaid over ten years. The ESAF and SAF total $12 billion, sufficient to cover most of the reflows to the IMF over the next three years from low-income countries. These programs are essentially refinancing programs for IMF repurchases.

The World Bank has initiated its own refinancing program, using IDA reflows (concessional money) to refinance the IBRD debts (on hard terms) of low-income countries. A number of countries in Africa have dropped from being eligible to borrow on harder terms from the IBRD to being eligible to borrow from IDA as a result of the deterioration in their per capita income levels and other economic troubles.

The 1988 Toronto Summit endorsed a menu approach to debt relief for export credits owned by low-income African countries. In the context of debt reschedulings, creditors can now agree to one or more of the following arrangements: canceling one-third of the stock and debt service payments owed (France's proposal); providing subsidies on the interest rates charged on rescheduled debts (the United Kingdom's proposal); and lengthening the repayment periods of twenty-five years (the United States' proposal). Seven countries have recently rescheduled their debts under this new regime. This scheme will prevent the stock of debt from continuing to expand with each debt rescheduling. It will not provide significant debt relief in the short run.

OTHER APPROACHES TO DEBT RELIEF

There are a number of other debt relief proposals on the international agenda. The ADB has proposed a "securitization" of all African debt, public and private (except that to multilateral institutions). Creditors would be offered twenty-year, single-premium bonds at agreed interest rates. The debtor would make annual payments into a "redemption fund," which would be managed by creditors and international financial institutions. These same institutions would review periodically the economic performance of the debtor. At the end of the twenty-year period, the funds in the redemption fund would pay off the debt. It was originally proposed that the pilot for this proposal be Zaire, an unfortunate choice since so much of the proposal rests on confidence in the debtor. The ADB hopes that Madagascar may be a possible alternative pilot, but the United States and possibly other creditors are strongly opposed to the idea. Its future does not look promising.

Legislation was recently passed by the U.S. Congress enabling the president to accept payment of debts of development loans to the United States in local currencies of low-income debtor countries that have an IMF program in place or waive such payments altogether. The administration, as of this writing, has yet to cancel any debts, although most agencies within the administration, including the Treasury, are prepared to support debt cancellation under this legislation.

There is already a menu of voluntary debt relief measures for middle-income countries, including debt-equity swaps, debt for conservation, the sale of debt in secondary markets, and so on. Few of these measures offer much relief to low-income Africa since a degree of private sector interest in the debtor country is implied by many of them and that interest is largely absent in low-income countries.

There is no lack of proposals to deal with the very special problem of debt of low-income Africa. There is only a lack of political will. It can only be hoped that this, too, will change in the near future.

NOTES

1. Low-income Africa, following the World Bank's classification, includes the following countries:

Benin	Guinea	São Tomé/Principe
Burkina Faso	Guinea-Bissau	Senegal
Burundi	Kenya	Sierra Leone
Central African Republic	Lesotho	Somalia
Chad	Madagascar	Sudan
Comoros	Malawi	Tanzania
Equatorial Guinea	Mali	Togo
Ethiopia	Mauritania	Uganda
Gambia	Niger	Zaire
Ghana	Rwanda	Zambia

2. Drawn from World Bank, *World Debt Tables, 1988–9, Volume 1* (Washington, D.C.: World Bank, 1988).

3. All statistics on debt used in this chapter are drawn from the World Bank's *World Debt Tables,* unless otherwise indicated.

4. For a brief background on how this debt was acquired, see Edward Brau, "African Debt: Facts and Figures on the Current Situation," in *African Debt and Financing,* ed. Carol Lancaster and John Williamson (Washington, D.C.: Institute for International Economics, 1986).

5. It should be remembered that export earnings are not the only source of import financing for low-income African countries. Many rely heavily on foreign aid and export credits to finance their imports. Thus, debt servicing as a proportion of export earnings overstates the impact of debt payments on import capacity.

6. As of the publication of the 1987–1988 volume of the *World Debt Tables,* these were Benin, Comoros, Equatorial Guinea, the Gambia, Ghana, Guinea-Bissau, Liberia, Madagascar, Mali, Mauritania, Mozambique, Niger, São Tomé and Principe, Senegal, Sierra Leone, Somalia, Sudan, Tanzania, Togo, Uganda, Zaire, and Zambia. Rumor has it that several additional countries have since been added to this list.

7. For a recent overview of the resource problem, see the United Nations, *Financing Africa's Recovery,* also known as the Wass Report (New York: United Nations, 1988).

Table 11.1
Debt Profile of Low-Income Sub-Saharan Africa

	World Bank Classification	Debt Service-to-Exports (%)		to GNP (1986)
		Ex Post (1986)	Ex Ante (1988–1990)	
Benin	D	9.2	90.0	54.2
Burkina Faso		14.8	14.0	41.8
Burundi	E	19.0	38.0	44.2
Cape Verde		—	20.0	68.7
Central African Republic	D,E	9.4	26.0	39.8
Chad		21.2	25.0	7.5
Comoros	D	6.4	60.0	96.3
Djibouti		—	—	—
Equatorial Guinea	D	—	46.0	—
Ethiopia		21.5	25.0	35.7
Gambia	D,E	11.3	64.0	132.0
Ghana	D,E	10.8	35.0	25.1
Guinea	D,E	21.0	41.0	—
Guinea-Bissau	D,E	54.1	224.0	181.9
Kenya	E	23.2	35.0	51.6
Lesotho		4.2	40.0	29.2
Liberia	D	6.0	81.0	99.0
Madagascar	D,E	29.9	84.0	105.6
Malawi	D,E	40.0	35.0	71.5
Mali	D,E	14.2	40.0	95.7
Mauritania	D,E	17.0	40.0	218.1
Mozambique	D,E	—	233.0	—
Niger	D,E	24.8	50.0	51.0
Rwanda		7.6	23.0	22.4
São Tomé and Principe	D,E	36.9	141.0	171.8
Senegal	D,E	10.9	34.0	69.2
Sierra Leone	D	8.4	46.0	40.4
Somalia	D	44.4	146.0	75.3
Sudan	D	7.7	165.0	96.9
Tanzania	D,E	15.1	102.0	85.3
Togo	D,E	32.3	41.0	92.9
Uganda	D,E	6.5	40.0	—
Zaire	D	18.2	53.0	96.8
Zambia	D	7.6	00.0	240.5

Source: Drawn from World Bank material
Key: D: Debt distressed
         E: Adjustment program in place

PART 4

Mineral Resources and Development

Several African countries with rich endowments of mineral resources and petroleum have, paradoxically, achieved less by way of economic development than African states without such wealth. In the African mineral economies there is less diversification of production, less investment, higher foreign debt, greater unemployment, and weaker overall productive growth than in many countries lacking these resources. The causes of this poor economic performance involve both external factors, such as declining prices of primary commodity products; and internal factors, such as the rent-seeking activities of politically powerful groups, which give their support to governmental leaders in return for access to wealth—these groups tend not to invest the wealth thus acquired in any productive manner.

The availability of large windfalls of mineral wealth early in the post-independence era exacerbated this tendency in mineral-producing countries, allowing privileged elites to entrench their power within the state. Inevitably, the mineral industries, which depend on timely investments and good management, decline. Thus, African governments must resort to heavy borrowing, the negative consequences of which were examined in the preceding section.

The Soviet Union and the United States favor political stability and rapid economic development in the mineral-exporting countries. Neither is highly dependent on mineral imports from Africa; they are therefore in a good position to assist these countries by way of cooperative programs. Such joint Soviet–U.S. programs might include:

• Creating a trilateral study commission composed of economists, metallurgists, mining engineers, managers, and others to make applied studies and formulate recommendations to competent organizations in African countries, the Soviet Union, and the United States.

• Performing studies, under the guidance of this commission, relating to the prospect of creating industries that are associated with ferrous metallurgy and other basic industries. These studies would examine current and future requirements in priority economic sectors such as agriculture and food production and distribution, and the manufacture of metal products for metal-working, engineering, and other industries.

• Training specialists, in accordance with national and regional needs, in activities related to minerals production and its developmental uses. These specialists would include geologists, metallurgists, mining engineers, economists, and general managers, among others.

• Transferring appropriate technology, based on consideration of the needs of African countries. Along with this transfer would come assistance in its use, such as in prospecting for raw materials.

• Acting jointly in support of multilateral price stabilization programs, such as the UN Common Fund for Commodities, which would be more effective than separate efforts directed toward that goal.

•. Helping to support economic diversification and industrialization, including joint research and development, technical assistance, demonstration projects, and other such projects relating to geological exploration, mining, and metals production.

• Assisting in geological cartography using remote sensing from space by Soviet and U.S. experts, including geological and hydrogeological surveys to compile national mining inventories.

12

Solving Africa's Priority Problems Through the Development of Mineral Resources and Industry

LEONID N. AKSIUK

This chapter pursues three main objectives:

- To show the urgent need to establish in developing African countries, on a step-by-step basis, industries that can play a role in sastisfying the continent's most acute material wants;
- To identify the role of mineral resources in the realization of this goal; and
- To identify priority problems beyond the means of most African countries to resolve, but without whose solution it will be impossible to attain many vital objectives.

While Soviet–U.S. cooperation for Africa is the underlying idea of our joint project, it is necessary to take the maximum possible account of African countries' official stand on all of these issues. Therefore, this chapter draws on the most important intergovernmental African program-setting documents, and particularly on those of the ECA.

In the Monrovia Declaration and in the preamble of the Lagos Plan of Action, African heads of state expressed a great deal of concern about the excessive dependence of the continent's economies on exports of primary commodities and minerals, and the absence of integration of commodity-exporting industries into the general economies of African countries. The thrust of these and other documents, such as the African Priority Programme for Economic Recovery, 1986–1990, is toward the speediest achievement of self-reliance and independent development consistent with economic growth. This chapter takes those documents as a point of departure in discussing Africa's use of its mineral resources.

Africa's economic crises, especially external debt and hunger, have diverted the attention of many researchers from issues relating to the development of African industry. Of those analysts who have focused on industrialization in Africa, many write of it in a negative way. In so doing, they call into question one of the main conclusions of the Lagos Plan (the most important of the economic documents), that is, the urgent need to implement plans of collective self-reliance through the industrial development of Africa. The anti-industrial stance of these analysts is not new; indeed, the Lagos Plan, in anticipatory fashion, explicitly notes the negative attitude of developed nations toward measures taken by African states to speed up industrial development in the region. It should be added that writers who spurn industrial investment as a viable option for achieving rapid development are especially disapproving of import-substituting industrialization, which seeks to do away with Africa's dependence on imports of all types of manufactures and even simple tools, instruments, and other metal-using items from industrialized countries.

The Priority Programme adopted at the Assembly of the Heads of State of the OAU in July 1985 pays considerable attention to the agricultural sector, particularly with respect to food production. On the other hand, this document promotes implementation of the Lagos Plan's goals, stressing the integrated economic and social development of Africa through creation in every member state of an industrial base from which to develop other economic sectors and satisfy the basic needs of the population.

The emphasis in these blueprints for development created by African heads of state is not only on industrial growth, but on a kind of industrialization that is self-sustaining and that meets the needs of African populations. To this end, it was considered necessary to create an industrial production structure capable of adapting to changing internal needs, particularly for food, construction materials, and clothing. This was to be achieved via an integrated program of industrial development based on the extraction and processing of natural resources and the formation of ties between various industries, as well as between industry and other sectors. Among these nonindustrial sectors, all the planning documents referred to lay heavy emphasis on agricultural production, both for the inputs it could supply to local industry and as a market for manufactured items.

The Priority Programme, for instance, stresses that a major task will be to give new impetus to agricultural productivity through the application of modern agricultural technology; more extensive application of fertilizers and pesticides; improvement and expansion of storage facilities and distribution and marketing systems; and an increase in the number of facilities for repairs of agricultural machinery. The section of the Priority Programme that discusses linkages between industry and agriculture provides first and foremost for the development of industries that produce agricultural tools, spare parts, and equipment for small-scale irrigation systems; and for assembly and repair operations, including a capacity for the overhaul and repair of state-owned means of transport, machines, and equipment.

Therefore, the Priority Programme, an extension of the Lagos Plan, more specifically develops and updates the latter's objectives, such as the production in sufficient quantity of basic agricultural inputs. It is only through the establishment of industry, which helps the development of agriculture and other economic sectors, that it will be possible to integrate an economy into a single complex. The result will be effective vertical (i.e., intraindustry) and horizontal (between industry and the agricultural, transport, natural resources, and energy sectors) production ties.

A locally produced industrial supply of basic inputs would promote higher productivity of labor and increase agricultural output overall. It would reorient industry toward meeting the basic needs of the population, especially in the countryside, expand the flow of goods between town and village, and gradually lead to the universal spread of commodity-money relations and to the erosion of subsistence economies, which impede socioeconomic development in many African countries. It would lead to the formation of a single economic complex.

Following adoption in July 1985 of the Priority Programme, the importance of heavy industry's potential for development was reaffirmed at the December 1985 meeting of African experts held under the auspices of the United Nations Industrial Development Organization (UNIDO). Creation of a basis for stage-by-stage development of heavy industry as a critical step for self-reliance, especially in the production of intermediate goods, was declared a task for the very early stage of implementation of the Lagos Plan. In this regard, the document emphasizes the need for studies to determine what branches of heavy industry could be developed in the near future at the national and subregional levels, and what branches should be developed in the longer term, requiring cooperation at the subregional or regional levels.

The Lagos Plan suggests studying and determining the order in which the following branches of heavy industry should be created: those related to food production and rural industry, metallurgy, engineering, electrical equipment and electronics, chemistry, the timber industry, and energy. The plan also emphasizes that attention should be focused on the use of local raw materials in industry and reducing today's excessive dependence on imports of industrial inputs. In particular, it proposes that special attention be paid to minerals, because of their strategic importance as inputs for basic industries producing such intermediate products as pig iron and steel, aluminum and major nonferrous metals, petrochemical products, fertilizers, cement, and so on.

The Lagos Plan stresses above all the need to improve the forecasting of demand and of studying rational management of known mineral resources. To identify approaches to these two interrelated branches of research, we need first to determine the extent to which the mentioned industrial activities are related to meeting the basic needs of broad sections of the population and ensuring agricultural development, of addressing, that is, the priority tasks set forth in the Lagos Plan and the Priority Programme.

Many branches of the chemical industry respond directly to the needs of agriculture, health care, and the consumer goods sector. They supply the fertilizers, pesticides, and insecticides needed to raise productivity and cut losses of agricultural produce. They produce chemicals for waste treatment and the purification of drinking water, thereby protecting human and animal populations from diseases. The petrochemicals industry supplies various fuels and vital goods such as automobile tires.

Enhancement of fertilizer production will make it possible to make productive use locally of African minerals such as phosphates, potassium salts, natural gas, oil, coal, sulfur-containing minerals, limestone, and others. Production of pesticides will draw into the African economy the most widely used phosphorous-containing materials, copper oxides, oil, chalk, talc, and caoline. In addition, many chemical production processes, being energy intensive, would be able to draw on Africa's mineral fuel resources. Fuel production and oil processing are directly linked to the sphere of consumption, to the satisfaction, in other words, of the basic needs of the African population. Of special importance to rural dwellers are fuel for cooking and kerosene for lighting. One of the tasks set in the Priority Programme is to conduct research toward the development of small gas, coal, or oil-burning kitchen stoves suitable for rural communities. This will increase the use of local reserves of oil, and especially gas (though a substantial share of these needs may be met by biogas tanks), as well as ferrous metals. The more widespread and inexpensive availability of mineral fuels, which will remove a major reason for the cutting of trees by rural inhabitants, will be a considerable contribution to the struggle against desertification, primarily in the Sahel region.

There is no need to prove the importance of construction to all economic sectors and social life in general. Among other things, the food and agriculture section of the Lagos Plan sets as a priority task the radical reduction (by 50 percent) of food losses, mostly by building appropriate food storage and processing facilities, thus improving the standard of living in rural areas. African states, as the Lagos Plan stresses, plan above all to do everything in their power to achieve self-reliance in food production, construction materials, clothing, and energy.

African countries use to a varying degree the following construction materials: rough stone, plant fibers, timber, clay, adobe bricks, clay bricks, lime, cement and cement-based items (including asbestos cement sheets and pipes), corrugated iron, aluminum sheets, rolled steel and aluminum, sheet glass, and ceramics. The choice of materials depends on specific conditions of use (such as whether they are for use in a rural, suburban, or urban environment), functional considerations, availability, cost, and equipment. Cement and cement items are becoming the most widely used construction materials, replacing stone, clay, bricks, and other traditional local materials. The use of cement has also resulted in the use of rolled steel instead of traditional wooden reinforcing materials. Cement's obvious advantages have resulted in such high demand that most African countries are forced to import it, lacking adequate domestic production capacity. If small local deposits are developed, miniplants can be built with due consideration given to limited supplies of fuel, water, and other materials, and to narrow local markets whose situation is compounded by underdeveloped transport and communication networks.

Modern construction cannot do without steel, and rolled steel is increasingly being used in African countries (including rural areas), mostly in industrial, municipal, and road construction. Most African steel consumption is direct and primary, as in these uses. However the use of such commodities as wire, sheet metal, pipes, simple tools, spare parts, basic manufacturing equipment (primarily in agriculture and the food industry), and other metal items (such as containers), will increase the consumption of iron and steel for machine tools manufacture, repairs, and engineering.

The orientation of the Lagos Plan toward the development of industries producing intermediate goods and on the use of local raw materials in industry envisages in the long run the creation at the national and subregional level of metallurgical complexes, and on this basis, of metal-working plants, engineering works, and repair shops. It is possible, for instance, to set up several miniplants, with an annual capacity of 300,000 tons of rolled stock, which would make direct use of the widespread small deposits of iron ores whose size makes them unsuitable for export.

Given the universal importance of ferrous metals and ferrous metallurgy even for countries, such as African ones, with low levels of economic development, and the variety of barriers to their application in integrated national development, it is particularly urgent to study a number of problems related to the creation of African ferrous metallurgy and other basic industries. These are:

- The volume and structure of current and future demand in the agricultural sector, especially in food production, for products of iron and steel-using industries;
- The minimal necessary complex of small metal-working and engineering plants that can put out a certain range of necessary products in sufficient quantities; and
- The calculation of demand for metal from specified enterprises in the agroindustrial complex, construction, and other sectors.

The entire set of studies is designed to research, in any given country or subregion, the market for and potential uses of ferrous metals and to determine the appropriateness of setting up ferrous metallurgical, metal-working, and engineering plants, taking into account prospective exports to neighboring countries. The need for assistance in such studies has been indicated by the secretariat of the ECA, in noting that industrial or planning ministries of African countries had no data on the number (though very small) of metal-working enterprises in their countries. These problems should be approached as case studies in the most promising countries. Studies ought to be oriented toward production and focus, for instance, on the fuel and energy and raw materials requirements of a plant, including the possibilities for and costs of prospecting for deposits of specific minerals. Attention should be given to small-scale extraction that would correspond to local needs or, if necessary, the needs of interested African countries.

The Lagos Plan stresses that the main problem confronting African countries in the exploitation of natural resources is the lack of data on vast and unknown areas. One of the main causes of this situation is African countries' weak geological and mining services. The Lagos Plan considers that expansion of information-gathering capabilities on mineral resources in Africa is one of the main objectives of a strategy for developing mineral resources. But few African countries were able after independence to set up geological and mining services capable of independent prospecting or of industrial and commercial valuation, development, and exploitation of deposits. That is why the Lagos Plan recommends enhancement of the capability of national institutions to conduct geological surveys and exploitation of mineral deposits. It follows that African countries need, above all, assistance in carrying out purposeful geological surveys and prospecting, compiling national mining inventories, and creating and strengthening geological and mining services. This would be the first and most important stage of assistance in the formation of the fuel/raw materials base of plants that supply intermediate products for sectors tied to production of food and nonfood agricultural commodities.

So, production of consumer goods and equipment in Africa requires simultaneous development of the metal-using intermediate goods industry. This depends, in turn, on the development and exploitation of the continent's rich mineral deposits. At the initial and subsequent stages of the program, the African countries need assistance in carrying out a wide range of applied economic, technical, geological, and prospecting studies, including preinvestment studies for specific projects.

13

Mineral Industries and Development in Sub-Saharan Africa

RICHARD L. SKLAR & GEOFFREY BERGEN

A fundamental problem for those who practice the arts of development in Africa today is an insufficiency of capital needed to pursue their stated goals.[1] More than a dozen African states possess proven endowments of mineral wealth that should easily have furnished the necessary revenues for sustained development.[2] Strange to say, nearly all of them have actually experienced lower degrees of developmental achievement than many of those African states with substantially inferior natural endowments.

As a source of income for allocation to developmental purposes, minerals give the favored states financial capabilities that are superior to those provided by nonmineral resources, such as good agricultural land, which represent equivalent amounts of wealth. Mines produce income that is more easily measured and acquired by states than agricultural income. Agricultural wealth is often controlled by domestic producers with the political influence required to evade significant levels of taxation. By way of contrast, the proceeds of mineral enterprises in developing countries are rarely subject to local private ownership and are much more easily acquired by the state. What is more, mineral resources may serve as inputs for resource-based industries, giving mineral economies a natural competitive edge over those industrializing countries that need to import nearly all such resources.

A paradoxical characteristic of mineral-exporting states throughout the Third World is that, in general, they do less well than non-mineral economies as measured by a number of standard indicators of national development: mineral economies have experienced weaker productive growth overall, agricultural production is lower, industrial manufacturing is lower as a percentage of GDP, unemployment is significantly higher, indebtedness is higher, and there is less diversification of production.[3]

These findings for the mineral-exporting developing countries generally are consistent with the recorded performance of sub-Saharan Africa's mineral economies. Although, on a comparative basis, these results are no worse than those for a number of African nonmineral economies, the important question concerns why they are not substantially *better* given this great initial advantage.[4] The major exception to this trend, Botswana, provides revealing clues toward explaining this paradoxical record of economic performance. We return to consideration of this special case below.

Two fundamental sets of reasons have been offered to explain this poor development record: those that place much of the blame on the conditions of African statehood, and those that point to the structure of international power and interests in control of mineral resources. While there is merit in both arguments, we will argue for a third approach that is now emerging, one that incorporates the valid lessons offered by the first two but that also provides a more hopeful scenario for future development.

THE STATE AND UNDERDEVELOPMENT IN AFRICA'S MINERAL ECONOMIES

The first set of explanations for the connection between minerals and underdevelopment revolves around the question of irresponsible investment. Simply stated, African states have seized and reallocated the enormous revenues forthcoming from mineral wealth in such a way as to make sustainable development unlikely when the source of revenues exhausts itself, as it must.[5]

The nature and conditions of African statehood are principal factors in the misuse of national wealth by state managers, whose primary goals are political rather than economic. Mineral rents, because they are so easily seized and redistributed by officials of the state, exacerbate the problem. Nigeria, black Africa's economic giant, has long suffered from this abuse. When the price of Nigeria's oil nearly quadrupled in the six months from November 1973 through April 1974, the huge windfall of revenue served to intensify the activities and greatly increase the rewards of rent seekers. The results with respect to national productivity are summarized by Sayre Schatz:

> For the most vigorous, capable, resourceful, well-connected, and "lucky" entrepreneurs (including politicians, civil servants, and army officers), productive economic activity . . . has faded in appeal. Access to and manipulation of the government spending process has become the golden gateway to fortune.[6]

Many of those who might have invested their time and energies in productive activities have sought instead to acquire rents through the agency of the state. In turn, those who manage the state cater to the interests of rent seekers, for political reasons, in ways that betray the public interest. To cite one well-known example, in 1974/75 the military regime then in power sought to consolidate its hold by using oil revenues as the basis for vast increases in salaries for civil servants.

The results of this situation form an exaggerated version of a chain of economic and social calamities that occurred elsewhere in Africa. Rural producers, neglected by the state and attracted to cities by the (often illusory) promise of work on public projects, left the agricultural sector, and the result was shortages of rural labor and shortfalls of production.[7] Furthermore, the rapid influx of petroleum revenues and increased federal spending, stimulating internal demand for nontraded goods, resulted in inflation and appreciation of the real exchange rate. Because an overvalued exchange rate allowed cheap imports of food and luxuries for politically important urban groups, as well as a source of speculative profits for some, there were pressures against currency reform by the state. The political control of oil rents in Nigeria led, finally, to a massive increase in recurrent state expenditures and indebtedness, whose financing, since oil revenues were not productively invested, would be dependent on future oil returns. Yet the 1980s have been a time of declining oil prices, with great hardship for Nigeria the result.

A similar process has occurred in other mineral-producing states. In Zambia and Zaire, nationalization of multinational corporate assets in mining industries actually made developmental conditions worse.[8] As in Nigeria, the cause is the state's inability to invest resources seized in any fashion other than as rents to politically powerful groups.

MINERALS AND INTERNATIONAL INTERESTS

The second set of explanations linking Third World minerals with underdevelopment emphasizes the interests of outside actors in controlling both access to, and profits from, those minerals. These arguments frequently point to the way in which mining enterprises were established as "enclave" operations in the colonial period, providing few benefits to the economy at large. It is further argued that in the postindependence era, even following nationalizations, the continued presence of multinational corporations (MNCs) under management and supply contracts allowed external actors to continue manipulating the situation.[9]

Here the question is one of power, conceived for this discussion as the ability of one party to impose its will on another. In response to the assertion of continued MNC power, it has been argued that given the capital-intensive nature of mining enterprises, once initial investments have been made by MNCs, the vulnerability of assets to seizure gives a large measure of negotiating leverage to host country governments.[10] The accuracy of this perceived shift of power is reflected in the clamoring of Europe's mining companies for support from the EC in their dealings with African mineral economies.[11] At the same time, other multinational investors in minerals have simply looked elsewhere to "safer" havens for investment.

To complicate matters further, international interests and bargaining power with respect to different sorts of minerals vary. A study of mining companies and exporters of bauxite, iron ore, and copper identified five factors likely to affect the division of benefits between the two trading sides: market concentration, the ability of one side to inflict losses on the other, the share of raw material in final product price, the type of market in which the raw material buyer sells his product, and the very process of negotiation.[12] There is significant variation in bargaining leverage within each of these factors depending on the mineral involved. Exporters of copper, for example, have less bargaining power in a number of ways than exporters of the other two minerals. One reason is the substitutability of other metals for copper in industrial processes, which has resulted in the ability of foreign investors in Third World copper concerns not only to threaten to look elsewhere but actually to do so. In addition, because the cost of unrefined copper in the final product price is higher than for the other two minerals, buyers have a greater incentive to fight against price increases.[13]

Zaire and Zambia are both highly dependent on exports of copper; they sell this mineral to a relatively concentrated group of buyers (mostly in Europe) who have an interest in resisting attempts by the sellers to turn pricing decisions (e.g., in the form of cartelization) to their favor. These countries have found themselves in particularly weak bargaining positions. As an example, in the case of Zaire, European mining company pressure has been successfully exerted on the European Commission to impose strict conditions on compensatory financing for shortfalls in copper revenues. Zaire had little choice but to agree to these conditions. By way of contrast with Zaire, Guinea, which shares a number of Zaire's internal problems, has had a large measure of success in meeting its goals in negotiations with international mining companies, reflecting to some extent the structural conditions of bauxite markets.[14]

While international actors have in some cases impinged on the ability of African states to control the rate and direction of change within their borders, they cannot be said to be the sole or direct cause of underdevelopment even in cases where they exert greatest power. The Zairian state, like the Nigerian, has invested its rents from minerals in patronage and other forms of political control. When the flow of copper revenues diminished, economic conditions became worse than they would have been had there been no mineral wealth to begin with. Ironically, by not reinvesting the earlier rents in productive enterprise, Zaire has been forced to approach international actors for additional capital. Insofar as the available donors of investment capital to such countries invariably impose conditions of internal adjustment on them, state managers lose control of their own national institutions, a loss they have largely brought upon themselves.

A SEARCH FOR CAUSES, EFFECTS, AND REMEDIES

Thus far, this analysis may be thought to suggest some inherent tendency of a country's mineral wealth to cause political and economic distress over time. In this section, we shall argue to the contrary: that a deeper analysis of the evidence from Africa shows that mineral wealth itself is not the cause of irresponsible political or economic behavior. Rather it facilitates a process of deterioration that is entirely avoidable. The experience of Botswana shows that accountability in government is conducive to the productive use of resource windfalls.

In light of the poor performance of most mineral-exporting African countries, Botswana's success is intriguing. While rates of GDP growth for most of these economies were relatively stagnant, Botswana grew at an annual rate of 14.3 percent for the period 1965–1980, and 12.1 percent during 1981–1985. Annual per capita income has increased from $290 to $1,690 in the past decade.[15] The key to this success lies not in the character of diamonds—like any mineral, these are subject to slumps and upswings in world markets—but in prudent and well-implemented economic management. Whereas most mineral economies have dispersed sudden windfalls of income from mineral price booms as though there were no tomorrow, Botswana has established a workable policy of running up cash balances in good years for use in bad ones, thus managing to keep the economy on a stable course. As a result, it has been able to keep its debt down to a comfortably low margin of national income.[16]

Why has Botswana succeeded where others have failed? One highly suggestive difference between Botswana and these other countries lies in Botswana's firmly institutionalized and stable democracy.[17] One of the most fundamental principles of democratic government is that of accountability, by which we mean the rule that those who exercise power on a continuing basis shall be required to answer or account for their conduct to others who are entitled to judge it.[18] From this standpoint, economic development is directly related to the obligation of those who make and enforce decisions to account for their actions to the public. Resource windfalls are meant to be managed in the public interest, and not appropriated by the managers themselves. While the view that authoritarian forms of government are conducive to rapid economic development has many advocates, it is simply not relevant to Botswana's excellent record of economic achievement.

Moreover, there is significance in the observation that in the case of Botswana, a system of effective accountability for state managers preceded the large-scale exploitation of minerals. The question arising from this observation concerns whether it is even possible for many other countries to duplicate Botswana's political and economic achievement. A preliminary answer involves pointing out the extent to which political and economic insecurity are major obstacles to reform in Africa today. The international community has both the means and the responsibility to reduce the level of uncertainty that all African states now confront. African statesmen often encourage or acquiesce in rent-seeking behavior primarily as a result of their perceptions of insecurity in both the domestic and the international environments within which they must operate. The Soviet Union and the United States could help to reduce the level of insecurity by devising noninterventionary methods of assistance for the mineral-exporting African countries.

In fact, we find grounds for optimism in the evolving relationship between African mineral exporters and the rest of the world. We perceive an increasing convergence of interests between outside actors and the mineral-exporting states. A salient feature of the international mineral trade is uncertainty, so that a primary goal for each side in bargaining situations is the avoidance of risk. In the past, risk aversion was partially achieved by means of the oligopolistic structure of companies, which facilitated their control over pricing, marketing, and investment decisions. The corporate exploiters of mineral resources were then able to avoid the many market risks to which state enterprises have been susceptible more recently. The problem with this oligopolistic mechanism of risk avoidance was that it decreased uncertainty for only one side in the bargain; in fact, it signified the absence of bargaining.

So long as the mineral industries were owned by foreign oligopolies, the raison d'être for state participation in ownership was fairly clear.[19] Multinational firms could and did transfer rents abroad, rents that African leaders regarded as belonging rightfully under their control. However, nationalization of the mineral assets also transferred the risks of mineral production to African states (which lacked the oligopolistic benefits of international firms) without increasing the rewards. State-run mineral production has proven less profitable than corporate-run production.[20] The mineral-exporting states, lacking sufficient technical and marketing capability, had little choice but to offer the former corporate owners profitable management and sales contracts, which drained a good deal of the hoped-for rents. At the same time, as potential investors looked elsewhere (especially in the case of copper), African mineral producers were forced to turn to debt, rather than equity, financing. This method of financing bears greater risks for the borrower than direct finance, since it is normally tied to specific performance goals, decreasing the ability of state managers to redeploy resources in response to market conditions. Nationalization also increased the risk to African mineral exporters of price fluctuations in international markets. The loss of protection previously provided by oligopolistic firm structure increased the vulnerability of nationalizing states to sudden downturns in price, while the very act of nationalization in a number of places at roughly the same time had the likely effect of provoking price increases.[21]

Mineral exporters and mineral importers alike pursue the elusive goal of risk reduction, but neither side has been notably successful. The quest by mineral importers in the industrial countries for risk-free market conditions is now seen to have been illusory. Their once-confident expectation of relatively easy access to raw materials was shattered by the successful cartelization of petroleum exporters and widespread nationalizations of mineral enterprises in the 1970s. The EC—75 percent dependent on imports of vital minerals—has attempted to limit the extent of its vulnerability to stoppages of supply by entering into the so-called SYSMIN agreement (System for the Promotion of Mineral Production and Exports) under the Lomé accords. While this agreement is designed to stabilize mineral prices, it does so in return for the maintenance of existing mineral-export relationships between Third World producers and the EC.[22]

Perhaps the best source of optimism about the future lies with the growing evidence that state-controlled mineral enterprises, with the benefit of time and experience, are able to operate on a profitable basis. Evidence from state-owned mineral corporations in Brazil, Chile, and Indonesia indicates that although state firms do not normally operate as efficiently as private firms, they do approach a degree of operational effectiveness similar to that of oligopolistic international firms. While the risk-diminishing mechanisms of international firms may be gone, the increasing number of "arms-length" bargaining transactions themselves may have a stabilizing impact on prices.

Out of a rapid flux of factors affecting the mineral markets, new combinations of private and public, national and international interests are clearly emerging.[23] There are good reasons for states to claim the rents derived from exhaustible resources for use in national development; and there are sound reasons for private investment groups to aid public corporations in Africa, given the importance of continued access to mineral resources. For example, although the nature of international investment in the Zambian mining industry has undergone alteration, external actors are still present and contributing to the extraction of Zambia's wealth on terms much more favorable to Zambia's ability to set and achieve its own internal goals than in the past.[24]

For both sellers and buyers of Africa's minerals, avoidance of uncertainty is critical. With the passage of time, given the increasing experience of both sides with the changed situation and with each other, and their increasing awareness of converging interests, this security may be obtainable. Africa and its international partners are slowly creating mechanisms that will enhance the ability of each to pursue its goals with confidence. This represents a maturing of the ability of societies to work within the limitations, and to perceive the opportunities, that are inherent in the geographical distribution of resources. This gradual maturation on both sides of the so-called North-South economic equation lends hope to the belief that Africa will be able to use its natural endowments in a way that enhances, rather than detracts from, its development.

A RECOMMENDATION TO BEGIN JOINT ACTION

What can or should the Soviet Union and the United States do to contribute to the development of Africa's mineral-producing states? In responding to this question, we emphasize at the outset that any such assistance must be noninterventionary in principle. The primary responsibility for reform lies, unquestionably, with the African governments themselves. However, to the extent that ill-conceived policies can be attributed to justifiable fears and uncertainties relating to the external environment, there could be a joint role for the two global powers of the current era, whose actions are critical in determining the overall conditions for world security or insecurity.

One major source of insecurity in the international context of African development is the excessive fluctuation of prices for commodities on which the African states depend for revenues. Insofar as reasonable certainty regarding revenues is a prerequisite for political reform, joint action in creating devices for stabilization of mineral commodity prices may well be a useful step. The virtue of Soviet–U.S. cooperation in this respect derives from the nonessential character of their respective trading relations with most of the African mineral producers. By contrast, the SYSMIN fund, a mechanism of the convention governing trade between the European Community and Africa, while it does provide compensation to African mineral producers for losses that result from shifts in world prices, also protects the parochial interests of the European states that rely so heavily on African minerals.

SYSMIN appears to discourage the diversification of African mineral economies by locking them into reliance on trade in specific commodities with the EC for essential revenues. While price stabilization devices may be intended to aid development, they may also produce the reverse effect by entrenching patterns of production and trade that do not serve the long-term interests of African countries. What is needed are means that both reduce the degree of uncertainty in international markets *and* provide for the investment of mineral profits in modestly planned industrial enterprises. Although there is little that any external actor can do to better the international market position of trading states with purposively overvalued currencies, there is much that can be done to improve the ability of African manufacturers to trade their goods without tariff or other barriers blocking the way into lucrative markets. The Soviet Union and the United States together could seek means to enhance market security for African mineral producers with fewer onerous conditions.

Finally, there is a potential for cooperation to prevent the deterioration of those mineral industries that are presently productive. One important target might be the huge potential for productive mineral extraction in an independent Namibia. While today's productive capabilities in Namibia remain high, it is vital to ensure that South Africa's prospective political withdrawal will not result in lasting damage to the country's principal source of income. The Soviet Union and the United States could collaborate to preserve and strengthen the mining industry and consult on the provision of material support in the event of a disruptive political transition.

In several countries, structural impediments to mineral-led development—particularly deteriorated infrastructure, plant, and equipment —and the negative effects of ill-conceived policies that serve the interests of powerful groups will be difficult to overcome.[25] The dual goals of enhancing mineral production and supporting reforms that would be conducive to the most productive use of earnings from the mineral sector can be addressed only through intensive studies of means and ends. That would appear to be a worthy aim of cooperation of African, U.S., and Soviet scholars and specialists in this field.

NOTES

1. In his contribution to this book, Leonid Aksiuk identifies their primary goal as reduced dependence for revenues on exports of unprocessed commodities and growing self-reliance through the integration of economic sectors within countries.

2. The "mineral economies" discussed here are defined as those sub-Saharan states (excluding South Africa) whose mining enterprises constitute at least 10 percent of GDP or 40 percent of merchandise export trade, as indicated by World Bank statistics.

3. Pierre Noël Giraud, *Géopolitique des Ressources Minières* (Paris: Economica, 1983), 652–653.

4. The issue is all the more perplexing in view of the significantly better performance of some African economies with far lower endowments of natural wealth. Kenya and Côte d'Ivoire, for example, had average annual rates of GDP growth in the period of 1970–1979 of 6.5 and 6.0 percent, respectively. Mineral-rich Zambia and Guinea had rates of 1.5 percent and 3.6 percent, while Zaire had a *negative* rate of GDP growth for the same period.

5. Gobind Nankani, *Development Problems of Mineral-Exporting Countries,* World Bank Staff Working Paper No. 354 (Washington, D.C.: World Bank, 1979).

6. Sayre P. Schatz, "Pirate Capitalism and the Inert Economy of Nigeria," *The Journal of Modern African Studies* 22, no. 1 (1984): 55.

7. Rural-urban migration in Nigeria rose from about 0.5 percent annually prior to the 1974 oil shock to 1.0 percent afterwards. In the absence of sufficient federal attention to the needs of rural producers (particularly price reform), agricultural output barely maintained food availability per head in rural areas and was entirely unable to meet urban needs.

8. Michael Shafer, "Capturing the Mineral Multinationals: Advantage or Disadvantage," *International Organization* 37, no. 1 (1983): 93–120.

9. See, for example, Oye Ogunbadejo, *The International Politics of Africa's Strategic Minerals* (London: Frances Pinter, 1985), 25–29.

10. This relationship has been defined by Raymond Vernon as the "obsolescing bargain"; see his *Sovereignty at Bay: The Multinational Spread of U.S. Enterprises* (New York: Basic Books, 1971).

11. See John Ravenhill, *Collective Clientelism: The Lomé Convention and North-South Relations* (New York: Columbia University Press, 1985), chapter 3.

12. Marian Radetzki, "Market Structure and Bargaining Power," in *Mining for Development in the Third World: Multinational Corporations, State Enterprises and the International Economy,* ed. S. Sideri and S. Johns (New York: Pergamon, 1980), 123–142.

13. The attempt by CIPEC, the ill-fated copper producers' cartel, to set prices has been well documented. See Raymond F. Mikesell, *The World Copper Industry* (Baltimore: Johns Hopkins University Press, 1979).

14. See Giraud, *Géopolitique des Ressources Minières,* 677–699.

15. Sheila Rule, "In Botswana, Diamonds Add Some Glitter to Flat Economy," *New York Times,* 19 June 1988.

16. Stephen Lewis, "Botswana: Diamonds, Drought, Development, and Democracy," *CSIS Africa Notes,* no. 47 (11 September 1985).

17. The most satisfactory account to date of Botswana's political institutions is given by John D. Holm, "Botswana," in *Democracy in Developing Countries, Volume 2: Africa,* ed. Seymour Martin Lipset, Juan Linz, and John D. Holm (Boulder, Colo.: Lynne Rienner Publishers, 1988).

18. Richard L. Sklar, "Development Democracy," *Comparative Studies in Society and History* 29, no. 4 (1987): 686-714.

19. Richard L. Sklar, *Corporate Power in an African State: The Political Impact of Multinational Mining Companies in Zambia* (Berkeley: University of California Press, 1975).

20. For reasons described by Marian Radetzki in *State Mineral Enterprises: An Investigation into Their Impact on International Mineral Markets* (Baltimore: Johns Hopkins University Press, 1985).

21. This both because a large number of independent sellers, each seeking to maximize profits, will generally cause an oversupply in international markets; and because if substitutes are available, as in the case of copper, demand for the mineral may drop.

22. See Ravenhill, *Collective Clientelism,* 129–149.

23. For a fuller treatment of this thesis, see David G. Becker, Jeff Frieden, Sayre P. Schatz, and Richard L. Sklar, *Postimperalism: International Capitalism and Development in the Late Twentieth Century* (Boulder, Colo.: Lynne Rienner Publishers, 1987).

24. Radetzki, *State Mineral Enterprises.*

25. For a comprehensive and thorough study, see Bureau of Mines, *Mineral Industries of Africa* (Washington, D.C.: United States Department of the Interior, 1984).

14

The Role of Industrial Minerals in the Economy of a Developing Country: The Case of Zimbabwe

ROBERT M. TINDWA

Industrial (nonmetallic) minerals are usually regarded as high-volume–low-price commodities. This notion is quickly fading, however, as various minerals become key components of high-technology and high-performance materials. While the notion of high-volume–low-price commodities still lingers on, it must be noted that developing countries that do not have them or that have not invested in research and development are paying dearly in precious foreign currency when they must be imported. Most of the developing countries in Africa have reserves of one or more industrial minerals; however, in most countries such reserves lie dormant, for a variety of reasons:

- The value of the industrial mineral(s) may not be recognized.
- Even when the value of mineral resources is realized, there may be a lack of expertise for developing small scale mining enterprises.
- Most industrial minerals as mined are not pure or readily available for direct use but may require some physical and chemical beneficiation prior to being used. This process is commonly referred to as "adding value" to the mineral. The process of "adding value" usually requires some expertise in chemistry or engineering. Lack of trained manpower may prevent the beneficiation of industrial minerals.
- Some of the beneficiation ("adding value") process may require sophisticated equipment, e.g., rotary kilns, air classifiers, filter-presses, gas suspension calciners, etc.; and such equipment is generally very expensive. As most developing countries do not manufacture such equipment, they have to import it with precious foreign currency. This usually strains scarce cash reserves of foreign currency. Faced with this problem, some countries and governments become discouraged and abandon the project. The results may be a disastrous drain on the country's foreign currency reserves.
- The domestic market may not be large enough to justify the capital investment required to produce a desired product from the industrial mineral and therefore manufacturing for export may be the only viable option. If the option to process the industrial minerals for international export is taken,

then the problem of international competition arises. It may be very difficult to enter the international market, and if it is highly penetrated and high standards must be maintained, quality control must ensure clients of an uninterrupted supply of the product. Cases have been known in which a developing country's ability to keep customers supplied has fallen short for lack of spare parts or because of shortages of foreign currency for the purchase of imported equipment.

• In some cases security may be such a serious problem that it is also too risky to develop a mining enterprise in a particular area (e.g., some parts of Mozambique). In cases like these the mineral reserves usually lie dormant.

UTILIZATION OF INDUSTRIAL MINERAL RESOURCES IN A DEVELOPING COUNTRY

The nonmetallic industrial minerals that play key roles in technological developments include lime and limestones, clay minerals, phosphates, various forms of silica and silicates, graphite, and alumino-silicates. These minerals form part of the backbone of the chemicals industry. They find applications in the paint and coatings industry as pigments and extenders; the plastics industry, as fillers; the soap industry, as fillers and for bleaching animal fat before it is used for soap; the pottery, refractory, and ceramics industries; the abrasives industry; the cement and the construction industries; and the pharmaceuticals industry. (This list of applications is not exhaustive.)

A trend typical of most African countries is that they actually *have* reserves of some of the industrial minerals that could be used in local industries, but they import these materials from developed countries nonetheless. An example of this phenomenon will be discussed in the following sections.

THE CASE OF ZIMBABWE

Zimbabwe, which may be described as an "advanced developing country," has a fairly sophisticated intellectual and industrial infrastructure. The country's consumption of industrial minerals, and chemicals derived from them, is very high. What is very distressing is that most of the industrial minerals that are consumed by local industry are imported. The chemicals and some of the products derived from these industrial minerals are also imported.

Under sponsorship from UNIDO, the Zimbabwe Mining Development Corporation (ZMDC) has conducted a study to determine the kind and extent of the reserves of industrial minerals in the country. The study revealed that

Zimbabwe is endowed with an abundance of industrial minerals. At the time the study was completed, the ZMDC established a research and development laboratory and the author was recruited as its manager. Faced with the perennial problem of shortages of foreign currency, a vigorous research program was initiated to develop import substitutes from locally available industrial minerals. This program was instituted in close liaison with local industries (including multinationals). Market surveys were conducted to determine the nature of the chemicals and industrial minerals that are imported, and the costs and benefits of replacing these imports through local production.

Research projects geared toward eventually supplying local manufacturers with "homemade" products from industrial minerals were initiated. Furthermore, other consumer chemicals that can be made from locally mined industrial minerals were also identified. Production cost estimates were made. In the cases where it was clear that the projects were economically viable, research work aimed at eventual production was initiated. This approach has had immediate positive benefits:

- A thorough knowledge of the needs of the private sector has led us to generate new ideas on possible import substitutes based on local mineral resources. We now have too many possible potential projects to work on with no adequate financing.
- Employment has been created for our local high school and university graduates.
- A unique research laboratory, which has the potential of greatly enhancing the economic development of the country and the SADCC region, has been established. Products developed from this laboratory will soon save Zimbabwe millions of dollars in foreign currency expenditures and will also earn the country foreign currency.
- A training ground for future research scientists has been established.
- A resource and consultative center (think tank) for local industry has been created.
- Potential opportunities for research collaboration with other advanced international laboratories exist.

POSITIVE RESULTS OF INVESTING IN RESEARCH AND DEVELOPMENT ON INDUSTRIAL MINERALS IN ZIMBABWE

Once the needs of local industry were identified we set out to work very hard on projects aimed at beneficiation of our industrial minerals. Projects on the manufacture of chemicals have also been initiated based on locally available mineral raw materials. Successful projects are summarized below:

• *Mining and beneficiation of diatomaceous earth.* Diatomaceous earth is an industrial mineral used in a variety of industries: brewing, for filtration of beer; plastics, as a filler and extender; paints and pigments, as a flatting agent and an extender; chemicals manufacture, as a solid carrier for certain pesticides; and fertilizers, as an anticaking agent in ammonium nitrate fertilizers. We have established, through our research and development work, that the local deposits can be upgraded and beneficiated to the same level as varieties that are being imported currently at a price of Z$2,000 per tonne. Production commenced on 1 July 1988. The project will save the country Z$5 million per year in foreign currency expenditure.

• *Chemical activation of local clay minerals for bleaching of fats and oils.* Zimbabwe has a fairly extensive industrial sector engaged in the manufacture of soaps and oils. One of the key steps in the manufacture of soaps and oils is the removal of undesired colors (bleaching). Clay minerals, which Zimbabwe has always imported in spite of their local presence, are used for this process. At the time of this writing, initial pilot plant tests were being carried out. Savings in foreign currency expenditure could reach Z$3 million.

• *Synthesis of dental-grade calcium from locally mined limestone.* High purity calcium carbonate is the abrasive in some varieties of toothpastes. This chemical is currently being imported because it cannot be purchased locally. We have been successful in synthesizing dental-grade calcium carbonate from locally mined limestones. This material is also used as a filler and extender in paints and as a filler and binder in the production of medicinal or pharmaceutical tablets. This project is at a very advanced stage and production was scheduled to begin in late 1989. Savings in foreign currency expenditure will exceed Z$10 million per year.

• *Production of consumer chemicals from phosphates and limestones.* Our laboratory is currently doing some applied research work on the eventual production of the following phosphate-based chemicals: sodium acid phyrophosphate, the active ingredient in baking powders; sodium tripolyphosphate, a detergent booster; dicalcium phosphate, a dental abrasive; and monocalcium phosphate, a leavening agent in baking powders. Our process economic studies show that all these compounds can be produced at an attractive profit margin. Commercialization of these projects will save Zimbabwe in excess of Z$20 million in foreign currency expenditures.

THE IMPACT ON ECONOMIC DEVELOPMENT

One of the most pressing problems faced by any developing country is the availability of foreign currency for allocation to various sectors of the economy. Development of local mineral resources for domestic use will save the country precious foreign currency, which no longer would be absorbed by imports containing these materials. If export markets can be secured, the products derived from the industrial minerals will actually earn the country foreign exchange.

Unemployment is also a key problem in most developing countries. Development of products from industrial minerals will result in the creation of new industries and hence new jobs for people with a variety of skills.

PROBLEMS IN THE DEVELOPMENT OF INDUSTRIAL MINERALS: HOW SOVIET–U.S. COOPERATION CAN HELP

Development of the industrial minerals sector requires personnel with specialized skills, such as geologists, mining engineers, metallurgists, chemical engineers, research chemists, market analysts, economists, and technicians. In Africa the problems encountered in developing the minerals industry are:

- Inadequate skilled manpower resources;
- Lack of research and development facilities;
- Lack of finances to take a project from the laboratory to pilot plant and eventually to full production;
- Small markets that discourage investment;
- Fear of risk-taking in such entrepreneurial ventures by governments and other potential investors; and
- Lack of appreciation—largely due to ignorance—of what impact such projects will have on the country's economy.

Our own solutions to these problems have included providing in-house and on-the-job training to university and high school graduates; collaborating closely with other international laboratories, e.g., the British Geological Survey; and encouraging our staff to do their own market and economic analysis, since we do not have people trained in these disciplines. However, there are a number of ways in which the Soviet Union and the United States could be of help in the efforts of Zimbabwe and other African states to develop their mineral resources.

The Soviet Union and the United States could train African geologists, mining engineers, metallurgists, chemists, and mineral economists to develop mineral resources for the creation of viable industries. Soviet and U.S. corporations could offer opportunities to African chemists and engineers to do internships in these corporations for the purpose of acquiring technical and managerial skills. There is no substitute for experience. U.S. and Soviet laboratories could also help in training African graduates in the various aspects of technical research.

Most African countries lack proper research facilities and this has hampered efforts in research and development. Money that is spent in the form of military aid could better be used in building laboratories. Nonmilitary aid could be used in financing projects in the mining sector with the goal of developing mineral-based industries. The Soviet Union and the United States could also assist by providing African countries with modern methods of mineral exploration, including acquisition of data via satellites and other remote-sensing techniques. More dialogue and technical communication among African, U.S., and Soviet scientists should be encouraged through more conferences on the development of mineral resources.

The Soviet Union and the United States could work together to promote regional peace, as they have done in Angola and Namibia. This should be extended to other strife-torn areas such as Mozambique. The conflict in Mozambique has hindered the development of Mozambique's mineral resources.

The Soviet Union and the United States could also give assistance through technology transfer. Most African countries have the raw materials but lack the necessary technology to process these materials on a commercial scale. Rather than channeling aid in this area to governments, it would be more efficient to channel aid to emergent entrepreneurs who show promise and potential. These emergent entrepreneurs could be assisted by Soviet and U.S. industrialists and consultants.

Industrial minerals can play a key role in the economy of a developing country. The country can become self-sufficient in the production of certain essential commodities derived from industrial minerals. Opportunities for saving foreign currency expenditures can be created. Also the development of commodities derived from industrial minerals can earn the country precious foreign currency if export markets are secured. Most important of all, establishing new industries based on industrial minerals will result in the creation of much-needed employment. The two global powers have the potential of making great positive contributions in the area of utilization of mineral resources.

PART 5

Communications

Telecommunications is a vital tool for economic development. Access to instantaneous, interactive communication can enhance such diverse development activities as agriculture, industry, shipping, education, health, and social services. To have untapped telecommunications *capacity* is even more beneficial, because telecommunications has an economic multiplier effect. That is, returns—in the form of production, employment, earnings of foreign exchange, and so on—are generated at an exponential rate.

Africa is seriously deficient in both telecommunications access and capacity. Several areas require urgent action to remedy the situation. Among these are management and control, financial regulations, planning, financial results, investment and growth, staff and training, equipment and maintenance, supply and demand, service to rural areas, and international service. To create an enabling environment, prompt and effective material assistance, knowledge and skills transfer, and stepped-up trade, investments and monetary aid are needed. Efficient and profitable operation, demand maintenance, acquisition and utilization of appropriate technology, and attainment of universal access are realistic goals. To satisfy these needs, the following steps should be taken through African–Soviet–U.S. action:

• Press forward with the SatelLife "space-for-health" project, a joint Soviet–U.S. space project now being planned under the sponsorship of the International Physicians for the Prevention of Nuclear War and the Soviet Academy of Sciences. The goal of this innovative project, in which Africa is a key focus, is improving access to health information in developing countries by linking health professionals around the world with one another and with information resources.

• Collaborate on expanding and accelerating African remote-sensing programs for application in agriculture, forestry, geology and nonrenewable resources, water resources, oceanography and mineral resources, and land use and the environment. The Soviet Union and the United States, with advanced capabilities in data collection from space, could cooperate to Africa's benefit, perhaps in conjunction with the UN Committee on the Peaceful Uses of Outer Space. A top priority would be to encourage the development of local capabilities by jointly assisting in education, research, and training activities for regional remote-sensing programs and centers. In addition, the Soviet Union and the United States could take the lead in forming an international "users' club" with other interested nations to ensure continued cost-effective access to remote-sensing data.

- Study and examine ways to utilize disarmed strategic missiles for peaceful telecommunications purposes.
- Carefully explore possible applications of land-mobile satellite communications, as recently demonstrated in tests of the Standard-C data communications system conducted throughout Eastern Europe and the Soviet Union by the International Maritime Satellite Organization (INMARSAT). Examine the merits of Radio Determination Satellite System (RDSS) technology, which can reportedly overcome infrastructural difficulties in rural areas at low costs, with a view toward determining applications in Africa.
- Advance proposals for aiding development and implementation in Africa of mobile communications technologies, such as cellular telephone systems for both rural and urban areas. Study the ways in which Very Small Aperture Terminals (VSATs) could be utilized, possibly in conjunction with mobile cellular systems, for establishing paging and messaging networks. Assess the suitability of high-frequency radio and telephone systems for rural areas in Africa, again marking complementary usages in Eastern Europe or the Soviet Union.
- Study the results of the highly successful program of the U.S. Agency for International Development (USAID), Satellites for Rural Development, noting particularly the role of videoconferencing in health and educational development. Explore the means by which VSATs could be used in tandem with videoconferencing for such purposes in Africa.
- Make the liberalization of information exchange—especially through databases—a foremost priority both bilaterally and internationally, given that unimpeded exchange of information for developmental aims lies at the heart of cooperative efforts for Africa.
- Study the feasibility of establishing an international "donors' club" to fund small-scale projects for repairing and maintaining existing equipment, purchasing spare parts, and establishing research centers throughout Africa.
- Support regionally based African consulting organizations, either through existing multilateral channels or through innovations such as donors' or users' clubs, and jointly support the buildup of African organizations.
- Explore the incentives and disincentives for future Soviet–U.S. joint ventures in African telecommunications/informatics industries.
- Organize Soviet–U.S. cooperation through or with the assistance of international and regional African organizations with the goals of achieving economies of scale and promoting African participation. In particular, Soviet–U.S. cooperation on the proposed regional African satellite system, RASCOM, and the Pan-African telecommunications system, PANAFATEL, should be organized on this basis.

15

African Communications in an Information Age: What Role for a Joint Soviet–U.S. Development Program?

RAYMOND U. AKWULE

"Today *is* the information age, and telecommunications comprises its chief transportation system."[1] This assertion is based on the remarkable pace at which microtechnology has been developing over the past decade or so, and in particular on the outcome of the merger of the technologies of communications and the computer. Vast amounts of information can be processed and transmitted across the world instantaneously; and the uses for communications facilities multiply constantly. In advanced societies, the impact of the new technologies is felt everyday: in industry, public administration, the service sector, the community, and even the family. Yet, for those in the poor regions of the world who wrestle daily with problems of poverty, disease, hunger, and lack of formal education, the achievements of the information age are of little significance. They have no hope, except in the longer term, of enjoying the fruits of the information society. As is well known, these countries do not possess communications systems capable of offering even rudimentary service. Furthermore, the rate and patterns of technological progress worldwide fosters rather than diminishes the communications gap between the developing societies on the one hand and the industrialized countries on the other.

In the recent past, international attention has been increasingly focused on the communications development problems of those poor regions. Africa is perhaps the most vivid example of a communications-poor environment in an age of abundant communications and information. This chapter will briefly review the state of communications in Africa. It will describe ongoing efforts to address the problems of communications development in the region and will offer some recommendations for appropriate joint Soviet–U.S. assistance in developing Africa's communications technology.

BACKGROUND

The work of the Independent Commission for Worldwide Telecommunications Development (1983–1985)[2], established by the International Tele-

129

communications Union (ITU) to study the problems of communications development (especially among developing nations), is a good starting point for gaining an appreciation of the current global communications situation. The commission's report painted a most poignant picture of the potential role of communications in the development process and also of the existing disparities between the world's advanced nations and the developing societies in terms of communications technology.

Not surprisingly, the commission's work paid significant attention to Africa, since that region has the least available communications technology of any region in the world. Telephone availability, for example, averages 0.7 per 100 population on the African continent as compared to 2.8 per 100 inhabitants in Asia, 5.3 per 100 in Latin America, and 50 or more per 100 in many industrialized nations of Europe and North America. It has been said that there are more telephones in Tokyo than in all of Africa put together. If indeed the world has advanced into an information age in which telecommunications is the chief vehicle, then obviously Africa as a continent is at an extreme disadvantage. Any attempt to assist in redressing the situation first requires an understanding of the scope of the problem.

COMMUNICATIONS DEVELOPMENT IN AFRICA

Historically, modern communications were introduced into Africa by the colonial administrators who governed most of the continent for over a century. Accordingly, African communications systems reflected, in structure and availability, the needs of colonial governments. After independence in the late 1950s and early 1960s, leaders of the new African nations recognized the inadequacy of the inherited communications networks for the development tasks ahead. Particularly worrisome to African leaders were the following concerns: (1) that the available communications technology was concentrated mostly in the capitals and the major urban centers, with little or none available to rural populations; and (2) that the inherited networks were such that information transmission between any two African states had to include transit centers in Europe.

In an effort to redress these problems, the nations reached agreement in the 1960s to give priority to the development of communications facilities, especially public telecommunications and sound broadcasting, at both the national and continental levels. A plan for the Pan-African Telecommunications (PANAFTEL) network was initiated, which would first interconnect the national networks and later enhance the entire public telecommunications network down to the subscriber level. Regional organizations, such as the Pan-African Telecommunications Union (PATU), were created to oversee and foster the integrated development of various aspects of telecommunications on the continent. Under the PANAFTEL project, Africa has allocated much of its limited resources to the establishment of an extensive telecommunications network that will eventually link all African states by microwave radio relay systems, satellite circuits, and land or submarine cable systems.

For its part, the United Nations, in recognition of the severity of the communications problem on the continent, proclaimed 1978–1988 the United Nations Transport and Communications Decade in Africa (UNTACDA). The purpose of UNTACDA was that the UN would encourage, through its various agencies, the formation of efficient and reliable transport and communications links among all African countries. Among other goals, a target of 1 percent telephone density in Africa by the year 1988 was set as part of the UNTACDA program. And, consistent with the UN program, the ITU, as the specialized UN agency charged with responsibility for the development of telecommunications in remote areas of the world, has focused much of its activities on Africa. The ITU has been partly responsible for the PANAFTEL project, but despite remarkable progress in the implementation of the project, the continent is far from attaining the set target of 1 percent telephone density by 1988. Moreover, there is still a great disparity in telecommunications presence within Africa itself. For example, South Africa alone has more than half the total number of telephones in the continent, and the North African countries of Egypt, Libya, Algeria, and Morocco have average telephone densities that far exceed that of their neighbors to the south, except South Africa.

Obstacles to Telecommunications Development in Africa

During the implementation of the PANAFTEL project, it was found that the major factors hampering telecommunications development and services in Africa were as follows:

- Telecommunications not being accorded adequate priority in some countries
- Absence of uniform technical standards
- Related power supply problems
- Use of equipment not adapted to the African environment and local requirements
- Lack of telecommunications operations agreements between national administrations
- Unharmonized tariff rates
- Fast-changing technology
- Inadequate high-level manpower for technical and administrative management

- Scarcity of financial resources
- Lack of industrial and manufacturing capability

Although these obstacles remain and have caused African leaders to reevaluate the options available to arrive at an optimal solution to their communications development problems, the leaders seem to be more resolved than ever to seek solutions to those problems. The reevaluation has resulted in a more comprehensive communications development project that goes by the name of Regional African Satellite Communication System for the Development of Africa (RASCOM).

The RASCOM Project

The feasibility study for RASCOM is a total telecommunications network study for Africa that aims to ascertain the long-term telecommunications requirements and provide the necessary information for the establishment of efficient and well-managed communications infrastructural facilities for the continent as a whole. The RASCOM project is intended to build on existing facilities and to supplement the accomplishments of the PANAFTEL project. But it is perhaps not surprising that RASCOM (Africa's latest and most comprehensive communications program to date) emphasizes a prominent role for satellite communications, for satellites have been touted as viable solutions to the communications problems—especially the rural communications problems—of developing nations. Many African countries have already embraced the satellite solution by utilizing the International Telecommunications Satellite Organization Network (INTELSAT) to provide for their domestic or international telecommunications traffic, or both. A majority of nations have acquired membership in INTELSAT by purchasing shares of the organization. The emphasis on satellite communications within the RASCOM project is therefore a reaffirmation of faith in the potential of satellite communications for African development.

History. Since the mid-1970s, a number of African leaders have expressed the desire to utilize the potential of satellite and other appropriate telecommunications technologies to improve the telecommunications services within the African continent, with special emphasis on the rural areas. Beginning in 1980 at least three different prefeasibility studies were carried out to consider a regional African satellite communications system.

The first study (1980–1984) was conducted under the direction of UAPT (Union Africaine des Postes et Télécommunications), an organization that consists of thirteen French-speaking African countries and that was financed by France and the European Development Fund (EDF). The second study was carried out in 1981 by PATU, a specialized OAU agency. The third study, completed in 1981, was directed by the ITU and financed by the

Federal Republic of Germany. The studies investigated the possibilities of using satellites for communication in Africa, especially in the rural areas. The practicality of setting up the space segment and the earth stations required for an Africawide system was also studied. The early studies resulted in an unnecessary duplication of effort by various organizations that did not necessarily consult with one another.

Consequently, an Inter-Agency Coordination Committee (IACC)[3] was set up in 1983 to harmonize and integrate all the prefeasibility studies into a single study, as well as to supervise and monitor the implementation of the study. The IACC has thus been responsible for producing the drafts and also—after comments by all the African states and visits to forty-nine countries by teams of consultants—the final version of the terms of reference of the single feasibility study that is now called RASCOM.

Objectives. The specific objectives of the RASCOM feasibility study are as follows:

• Carry out a country study to identify the needs for satellite communications, including the requirements for transmission of sound and television broadcasting and community TV reception by satellite with a view to providing services at the national level—in particular to rural and remote areas—and at the regional level. This will include submitting proposals for efficient and economical services using a regional African satellite communications system, complemented where necessary by other appropriate technologies that shall be properly integrated into the existing and/or planned infrastructures.

• Undertake technical and economic studies for the design, launching, and operation of a regional, dedicated satellite system for the African region that provides efficient and economical telecommunications and the following: (a) intra-African connections; (b) interurban connections within countries; and (c) links in rural and remote areas of participating countries.

• Cover all the aspects relating to the integration of a space component into the existing or planned network, particularly the interfaces and any adaptations needed for the smooth functioning of the two components.

• Identify and prepare a broad outline of specifications for the design (and local production where possible) of all types of equipment and systems (that may be required individually or collectively) for the integrated regional system. These specifications shall be designed to respond to the African economic, social, technical, and physical environment.

Funding. One of the main tasks facing the IACC is the search for funds to finance the RASCOM study. Resolution ECA/UNTACDA/Res.83/26, which established the IACC, also called on bilateral and multilateral financing agencies to collaborate with the IACC with a view toward harmonizing their financial and technical contribution for the welfare of the whole of Africa. Funding for the RASCOM feasibility study has thus far been provided by the OAU, the United Nations Development Programme (UNDP), ITU, and UNESCO organizations, as well as by Italy and the Federal Republic of Germany; and a technical assistance loan from the ADB has been guaranteed by a few African countries. The national studies were completed at the end of 1988 and the final feasibility study report is expected in 1990.

International cooperation. Judging from the enthusiasm of the African countries, the support from the ITU and other multilateral agencies, and the financial and technical assistance from a few countries outside of Africa, one can predict a bright future for RASCOM. The point should be made, however, that the RASCOM project—from feasibility study to implementation of whatever combination of systems is agreed upon by the African ministers of Planning Transport and Communication—is a gigantic project by any measure. The immensity of the challenge of RASCOM becomes even more striking when matched against the available financial, personnel, and technical resources on the continent. It is reasonable to assert that because of the scarcity of resources in the region, the eventual implementation of a communications network (which might include the option of an African-owned and dedicated satellite network) will be possible only through sustained international cooperation that will only include support from countries outside of Africa. The potential roles of giant nations with advanced space programs, such as the United States and the USSR, is incalculable. The IACC is positioned to receive assistance through the RASCOM office that was set up in 1987 at the ITU in Geneva. Assistance should not be viewed as charity, but rather as the creation of further opportunities for mutually beneficial international partnerships between African nations and the rest of the world.

CONCLUSION

The problems of communications development in Africa are enormous, but efforts are under way at various levels to rectify those problems. While new ideas will continually be sought, the conclusion of this paper is that any new initiatives directed at the problems of communications development on the continent should best be integrated into, or have some strong relationship to, existing programs that have been devised through years of discussion and planning and that involve African leadership at every level.

The RASCOM project is the most comprehensive approach yet to seeking a solution to the communications development problem in Africa. It is expected that the project will have resulted in an efficient, reliable, and economical means of telecommunications—including sound and television broadcasting, community reception by satellite, and data communication service—using a regional African satellite communications system and complemented where necessary by other appropriate technologies for the development of the continent. This is the African aspiration. But the odds of implementing RASCOM are very small if the continent is to rely only on its limited resources. The full support of the international community will be needed to make the aspiration a reality.

NOTES

1. National Telecommunications and Information Administration, *NTIA TELECOM 2000: Charting the Course for a New Century* (Washington, D.C.: U.S. Department of Commerce, October 1988), 3.

2. See Donald Maitland, *The Missing Link: Report of the Independent Commission for Worldwide Telecommunciations Development* (Geneva: International Telecommunications Union, December 1984).

3. The IACC is composed of the following organizations: OAU, chairman; ECA, vice-chairman, ADB; AFCAC; ITU; PATU; UAPT; UNDP; UNESCO; and URTNA.

16

The Modernizing Link: Cooperation in Telecommunications Development in Africa

GERALD J. BENDER & CRAIG A. JOHNSON

STRATEGIC ISSUES IN AFRICAN TELECOMMUNICATIONS

The strategic importance of telecommunications for African development has been widely acknowledged for over a decade. A benchmark of African awareness and involvement was signaled during the Plenipotentiary Conference of the ITU when the "fundamental importance of communications infrastructures as an all essential element in the economic and social development of all countries" was recognized.[1] The Declaration of Yamoussoukro, issued at a meeting, "Informatics and Sovereignty: A Contribution to the Lagos Plan of Action," held in the Ivory Coast, 27–29 March 1985, directly positions "information" as central to the development process:

> Information is an economic resource. It is a basic raw material of which unfortunately Africa currently has the least. The importance that must be given to every form of informatics—data, text, image, sound and knowledge processing and pattern recognition—stems from the economic importance of information itself.

The report of the Independent Commission for Worldwide Telecommunications Development (the Maitland Commission), entitled "The Missing Link," published in January 1985, resonated strongly in Africa. Its conclusions that "no development plan was likely to be effective unless it allotted telecommunications an appropriate role" and its proposal for a joint international effort "to bring the whole of mankind within easy reach of a telephone by the early part of the next century" were endorsed, along with the broad thrust of the commission's recommendations at the World Telecommunications Development Conference in Arusha, Tanzania (May 1985). This conference was attended by delegates from ninety-three countries and international and regional organizations.

The African dilemma is extreme. Africa has the lowest average number of direct exchange lines (DELs)—six per 1,000 people—among developing areas. Moreover, in 1986, less than a quarter of African countries were growing at rates high enough to increase telephone penetration by even 1 percent in ten years, and another fourth were experiencing negative real growth (i.e., below population growth).[2] Currently, 40 percent of the continent's telecommunications lines have fewer than 10,000 users.[3] If a conservative goal of one telephone per 100 inhabitants within ten years is adopted, 4 million new lines will be required to supplement the existing 3.3 million lines, representing a growth rate of 8 percent and an investment of between $8 and $20 billion. The ITU estimates that it will cost $50 billion to expand existing telephone subscriber lines to achieve a more ambitious target ratio of three telephones per 100 people by the year 2000.

The African pattern of telecommunications development has revealed a chronic set of organizational/managerial difficulties at all levels. These include: underutilization of existing equipment and services (corresponding with severe network congestion); dire need for extensive and intensive human resource development to raise skill and maintenance levels; and utilization of equipment, procedures, and services that are suited to African conditions. The continent remains at shockingly low levels of infrastructural development, as measured by the speed, accessibility, and interactive capabilities that make decisive differences in ways data and communication resources are shared and used. These deficiencies are visible in the large numbers of applicants waiting for service; the emergence of a huge hidden demand, resulting in congestion when service provision accelerates; a virtual absence of services in rural or remote areas; and a largely nonexistent supply of advanced services, a virtual requirement in modern sectors.

A succession of studies has identified the tremendous range of benefits that could be realized through improved telecommunications. One of these, undertaken by Communication Studies and Planning International, and recently published by the ITU, assesses the contribution made by telecommunications to trade and to the enhancement of foreign exchange earnings in other sectors. The research measured the foreign exchange benefits that would arise from an improved telecommunications network for twenty export businesses in Kenya, representing agricultural, industrial, and service sectors, and accounting for 17.7 percent of total Kenyan export earnings. All three sectors "were shown to benefit substantially," with increased foreign exchange and export earnings and reduced import needs. The potential benefits of improved telecommunications for business were grouped into two principal categories: export effects (improved operational efficiency, sales prices, sales expansions, and savings in manpower) and import effects (improved purchase prices, inventory levels, and savings in transport). The results of the project implied that the foreign exchange benefits of investing in a major project would exceed costs by a ratio of 3.6

to 1. The study concluded that "export companies require investment in the telecommunications network in order to function competitively." The study also identified "indirect" benefits to the country's foreign exchange position, spotlighting five companies that produce for the domestic market in order to displace essential imports. It estimated that "indirect" foreign exchange benefits to these five companies were equivalent to over 2 percent of their total foreign exchange contribution.[4]

This study, which echoes the findings of others, underscores the importance of basic services in Africa. Targeting, planning, and implementing the extension of universal service to all areas, and capitalizing on the substantial benefits to be gained from the expansion of business communications should be overriding priorities.

Soviet–U.S. cooperation for Africa must consider the needs and absorptive capacities represented by the significant modernization in the region. For example, twenty-five African countries have embarked upon digitalization plans or programs. Zimbabwe plans to spend $65 million over the next five years, primarily in upgrading its switching and transmission facilities as the first phase of a twenty-year development plan designed by the ITU. Somalia, Malawi, and Mozambique are also involved in establishing digital exchange networks.

Evidence continues to mount that African telecommunications administrations are leaping forward toward self-reliant operations, planning and management, and structural reforms. For example, Nigerian Telecommunications, Ltd (NITEL) was formed in 1985 with the premise that the organization would be a financially self-sustaining private limited company run like any profit-oriented venture. Thus far, investments have sustained the services offered, which include telephone, telegraphy, telex/gentex, private wire (voice) point-to-point, pay phones, broadcasting bearers (sound and television), and data transmission. NITEL has installed exchanges and lines, has extended International Direct Dialing (IDD) to parts of the country outside of Lagos, is planning to provide a new 5,000-trunk international telephone switching center for Lagos, and is building a third international gateway in Enugu. NITEL is also addressing the problems of network congestion, inadequate lines, and delayed dialing tones. Most importantly, perhaps, digitalization is progressing rapidly with plans for a business-oriented videophone network and a low-density satellite communications facility for rural and remote areas. There are also plans to expand the present domestic satellite network to accommodate communications with neighboring countries. NITEL's major problem has consistently been the import bill for equipment and spare parts. To reduce the impact of the cost of importing necessary materials, NITEL has established a manufacturing affiliate to produce spare parts. Its research and development unit is studying ways to do so with minimal foreign involvement. This venture, when it becomes operational, is expected to save the country at least 50 percent in foreign exchange. NITEL also plans to establish a telecommunications management training center.[5]

Another case of impressive modernization in telecommunications has occurred in Kenya. The Kenyan Post and Telecommunications Corporation (KP&TC), which is entering its second decade, is moving forward in its modernization efforts at a pace that could be considered breathtaking for an African country. Planned services include INTELSAT business services, which will allow the business community to transmit and receive data, facsimiles, and teleconference information using small earth stations. KP & TC also plans to improve maritime telecommunications through the use of a maritime satellite earth station located in Mombasa, and introduce packet-switching data services to Europe and the United States.[6]

An important case of rapid, self-directed advance in African telecommunications at the regional level is the SADCC, which has undertaken activities aimed at accelerating efforts to bypass the Republic of South Africa (RSA) network. Currently, because of the use of diverse satellite paths, including the Atlantic Primary Path and the Indian Primary Path, a large portion of satellite traffic among the SADCC countries must pass through either the RSA or Europe. The intra-African voice and telex traffic of Swaziland, Lesotho, and Botswana is particularly dependent upon RSA facilities. One of the larger projects is a program funded primarily by the Canadian International Development Agency (CIDA) to upgrade the intraregional satellite network. This "regional connectivity" project is oriented toward boosting Zambia's satellite capacity to divert transit traffic going through South Africa.[7]

COOPERATIVE AID AND INVESTMENT

These developments should be considered before developing plans for Soviet–U.S. cooperation. Increasingly, cooperation in Africa must assume the forms of cofinancing, technology agreements, grants and aid, and supplier financing. Supplier credits, technological and managerial contracts, and local assembly and manufacturing provisions are likely to be progressively required to do business in Africa. As trade and investment expand, both the United States and the USSR could learn from the examples set by European, Canadian, and Japanese development agencies. These include the Caisse Centrale de Coopération Economique (CCCE) of France, the EC, the European Investment Bank (EIB), CIDA, and the Japanese International Cooperation Agency (JICA). Grants, loans, education, and training are very much a part of the modus operandi of these organizations.

A recent instance of U.S. assistance denotes progress. A $30 million contract was awarded to the U.S. firm Telectron, an affiliate of AT&T, as part of a program to upgrade the microwave telecommunications network throughout Kenya. The company will be the first to benefit from Kenya's $20 million share of the $100 million export finance facility provided in 1987 by the U.S. Export-Import Bank (EXIMBANK) and the United Kingdom's Standard Chartered Export Finance. In addition, discussions are under way regarding a $5 million to $8 million credit line allocation directed toward expanding U.S. presence in Africa.[8]

Cooperative Soviet–U.S. initiatives are burgeoning in the areas of culture, news, and information exchanges. In 1987 the Soviets ceased jamming the Voice of America. The first in a series of U.S. Information Agency (USIA) Worldnet-Soviet TV video dialogues has taken place. In 1988 a series of satellite TV linkups between the USSR Supreme Soviet and the U.S. Congress was established. In cooperation with Stoner Broadcasting, phone-in satellite shows were organized between the two countries with live communication among citizens. More exchanges are planned. Soviet–U.S. cooperation of this kind may serve as a model for joint efforts on behalf of Africa.

A critical area of national telecommunications policy that requires the attention of U.S. decisionmakers is that of information exchanges involving on-line databases. On-line database services put the user in direct contact with the database through a terminal device connected to leased lines or a network. Africans can access several critical databases, such as the ITU's Teleinformatics Center for data transmission, which contains information on agriculture, health, utilization of natural resources, market prices, and technologies. EURONET and the European Space Agency's Earthnet may also be accessed. Enhanced access opportunities are desperately needed, but serious barriers exist for users in developing countries. These include telecommunications costs, lack of training and education, language difficulties, and limited access to full-text documents.

Regrettably, although the United States is the acknowledged leader in the supply of database services, "the U.S. government's export controls, which dictate what can be sold to Communist countries, . . . represent a . . . serious challenge" to the database industry.[9] The Soviets, on the other hand, have established a solid record of cooperation with their allies in the CMEA countries. A new international automatic information exchange system is being used to share intellectual resources in CMEA member countries. The new system also provides a means to organize international scientific televised conferences.

International organizations, particularly those in the UN system, have served as pioneers in information exchange. The Technological Information Pilot System (TIPS), a daily information service on technology and trade directed at 5,000 users in ten developing countries, is a three-year project for testing and designing a multisectoral development information network to promote technology transfer, industrial development, and technical and economic cooperation among developing countries. The African countries of Kenya and Zimbabwe have agreed to participate in this pilot project launched by the UNDP and DEVNET and funded by the United Nations Financing System for Science and Technology for Development (UNFSSTD).

SPACE: THE COOPERATIVE FRONTIER

A prominent vehicle of Soviet–U.S. cooperation in telecommunications is the Committee on the Peaceful Uses of Outer Space (COPUOS) of the UN Outer Space Affairs Division. The meeting of experts on space science and technology held in Lagos, 27 April to 1 May 1987, was hosted and co-sponsored by the Federal Military Government of Nigeria and was organized by the UN Outer Space Affairs Division and the Federal Ministry of Science and Technology of the government of Nigeria. The objective was to promote the growth of capabilities in space science and technology in order to achieve benefits in communications, weather forecasting, natural resource development, transportation, and other economic spheres. Data can now be received by small, inexpensive receiving stations, which most countries possess.

Remote-sensing data are being collected worldwide by the U.S. Landsat system, the French SPOT system, and the Soviet SOYUZ-KARTA system. These data are available to all countries at commercial prices. Such sensing techniques have been cost-effective when used to record changes in forest cover, land use, vegetation and rangeland mapping, maize and wheat forecasting, crop acreage, urban development, and human settlement. Applications of this technology are being further utilized in an advanced environmental monitoring system designed to give early warning of drought, crop failures, and insect plagues in Africa. The alert system is supported by several computerized databases and could save lives by enabling health and agricultural authorities to prepare for major food shortages before they strike. The system has backing from scientific establishments in Canada, EC member countries, and the United States. It could transform current patterns of emergency food assistance and contribute to long-term agricultural development planning in some of the poorest countries. Other current programs include drought monitoring in the Sahel zone, national analyses of changes in land use and the ecological consequence of those changes, and acid rain studies. Training programs in French and English are conducted for the benefit of a number of African countries. The COPUOS program, for example, has established regional training and user assistance centers in Africa at Ougadougou, Burkina Faso; Ile-Ife, Nigeria; and Nairobi, Kenya. A number of other training centers have been proposed.

The SatelLife project, the first in a series of Soviet–U.S. space projects, is sponsored by the International Physicians for the Prevention of Nuclear War and the Soviet Academy of Sciences. It is a collaborative space-for-health project to improve access to health information in developing countries by linking health professionals around the world with each other and with information sources. Representatives of the Soviet Space Research Institute, the Rockefeller Foundation, and the U.S. Amateur Radio Satellite Corporation are contributing. Several World Health Organization (WHO) programs have offered to establish electronic mail linkages. The USSR has offered to contribute and launch a satellite at no charge for the purpose of transmitting medical information from the industrial world to developing countries through organizations such as WHO and the International Red Cross. Africa is to be a key focus. Planning is under way for a project in East Africa linking remote clinics with central health organizations responsible for implementing an AIDS surveillance and training program. Support is to be provided to ministry of health operations in various countries of the African Region of WHO, especially in the areas of management, training, and health information.

International disaster communications provide fertile ground for future Soviet–U.S. cooperation. Satellites can be used for disaster prevention, preparedness, and relief. Global systems with broad coverage, including INTELSAT, INMARSAT, Cospas/Saract, and INTERSPUTNIK are perhaps the most important. Beyond these, new types of systems utilizing amateur radio frequencies or RDSS frequencies promise even more versatile coverage. Several existing plans include the Satellite Project, a proposed network of medium-altitude or geosynchronous satellites in the amateur radio band (which could also be used for tele-health and tele-education purposes), and LifeNet, proposed by the Foundation for Global Broadcasting. This demonstrates the advantages of "piggybacking" emergency communications on broadcasters' on-site or flown-in earth stations. Projects by Geostar and Omninet allow communications between satellite and hand-held "beepers." VSAT fly-away microterminals are highly mobile, easily storable, and can be set up almost anywhere for connection with global beam satellites of INTELSAT, INMARSAT, or INTERSPUTNIK. They provide voice and data service and, in some cases, 384 kilobit/second video service. Mediasat, a proposed commercial satellite equipped for high-resolution earth imaging, would provide images from space for news gathering and for rescue and disaster relief efforts.[10]

A milestone in cooperation was recently marked, with the launching of an extensive program of land-mobile satellite communications tests and demonstrations conducted throughout Eastern Europe and the USSR by INMARSAT. The program involved demonstrations of the use of satellite technology to provide reliable communications and position-reporting capabilities for road and rail transport industries in an extensive range of operational and geographic conditions. Approximately 500 government, telecommunications, and transport industry officials attended special demonstrations during the INMARSAT team's visits to Bulgaria, Czechoslovakia, the German Democratic Republic, Hungary, the USSR, and Yugoslavia. All countries relaxed border formalities for import and export of equipment and granted INMARSAT permission to transmit and receive messages. INMARSAT's planned land-mobile services are based on its Standard-C data communications system, which features inexpensive mobile terminal equipment about the size of a car radio. Officials in the countries visited expressed interest in Standard-C for road transport, railways, river transport, and remote area communications.[11]

U.S. COMMUNICATIONS ASSISTANCE AS A MODEL FOR COOPERATION

Several U.S. programs deserve mention as models of possible further collaboration. These are the United States Telecommunications Training Institute (USTTI), the U.S. Department of Commerce Definition Mission to Jamaica, and the USAID rural satellite program.

The USTTI describes itself as a joint venture between "the leaders of the U.S. telecommunications industry and ranking officials from the Federal Government." Established in 1982, it has provided "a comprehensive array of telecommunications and broadcast training courses" in the laboratories, training facilities, and factories of major U.S. corporations and government agencies. Eleven corporate sponsors provide free training at their corporate facilities, finance overhead costs, and serve on the board of directors. Twenty other U.S. companies support USTTI by providing free training or financial support. Key government leaders in telecommunications policy also serve on the board.

Since the spring of 1983, 164 diverse courses have been offered to more than 1,400 men and women graduates, including telecommunications and broadcast managers, engineers, and technical experts who operate telecommunications systems in 108 developing countries. The program had more than 1,900 applications for 451 training positions available in 1987 in such areas as frequency management, satellite design and satellite systems applications, single channel per carrier (SCPC) satellite system architecture for rural communications, computer operations and computer-aided techniques, management skill development, disaster communications management, digital carrier transmission, and policy questions and skills.[12] In Africa, USTTI coordinated a joint venture in 1986 with COMSAT, INTELSAT, USAID, the National Telecommunications and Information Administration (NTIA), and USIA, offering a training course in radio propagation measurements using radiometric methods. Two scientists each from Cameroon, Kenya, Chad, and Nigeria participated.

The NTIA and the International Trade Administration (ITA) Definition Mission to Jamaica (2–13 February 1986) participated in the Caribbean Telecommunications Infrastructure Development Project. A technical assessment team from the Department of Commerce and the U.S. private sector identified eleven projects to strengthen Jamaica's telecommunications infrastructure. Seven of the projects focused on domestic requirements and four on international requirements. The team concluded that the implementation of these projects would attract increased foreign investment. The seven projects to be considered by the domestic telecommunications carrier, Jamaica Telephone Company, are rural telephone feasibility, cellular radio for rural and urban applications, automation of directory assistance, improved public telephones, cable pressurization, management information, and construction efficiency. The four international projects recommended to the Jamaica Telecommunications, Ltd (JAMINTEL) were a management information system, a portable earth station, a portable microwave system, and a teleport.[13]

In 1980 USAID established the Rural Satellite Program (RSP) to investigate the possible use of satellite-based telecommunications to support rural development. The project's challenges were to identify and transfer appropriate telecommunications technologies to rural or remote areas of the Third World and to develop applications that support and strengthen the public institutions involved with development. The program addressed the following questions:

• Are modern two-way telecommunications technologies technically feasible within the severe operating constraints of developing nations, especially rural areas? How can these technologies be made more appropriate in terms of cost and operations? What procedures are required for technical management and operations?

• Can these technologies be used effectively to address major development problems? How can programs supporting agriculture, health, and education be developed?

• Do telecommunications technologies provide an affordable and cost-effective solution?

• Can these technologies be effectively exploited by rural institutions and indigenous personnel? What are their management requirements?

In collaboration with host government agencies, the RSP established pilot projects in Indonesia, six countries of the West Indies, and Peru. The primary goal in all three cases was to extend educational opportunities and support basic services using the telephone or teleconferencing. "At the heart of each project is a fully interactive, two-way communications network linking several sites. Each site can initiate a conference and communicate with all other sites."[14]

The programs described above have been highly successful and have received wide acclaim. They should be regarded as models of effective and appropriate telecommunications development assistance, both on a continued bilateral basis and through cooperative innovation.

In the face of widening disadvantage, Africans are assertively modernizing their telecommunications sectors. International cooperation must proceed with approaches that are demand- and needs-based. As the African Telecommunications Development Conference cautioned, "any cooperation, whatever its scope, cannot by itself solve Africa's problems." Africa must be guided by a commitment to correct past mistakes, set up strict management controls at all levels, adhere to priorities established for development projects, and ensure national manpower management and development.

NOTES

1. African Telecommunications Development Conference, Tunis, 12–16 January 1987, "Introduction," *Final Report,* 1.

2. William L. Guttman, "U.S. Telecommunications Policy in Sub-Saharan Africa: Determinants and Initiatives," in *A Report to the U.S. Agency for International Development* (Geneva: PPC/PPDR, August 1984).

3. *Africa Telecommunications Report* (December 1987).

4. International Telecommunications Union, *Contribution of Telecommunications to thte Earnings/Savings of Foreign Exchange in Developing Countries* (Geneva: ITU, 1988).

5. *Africa Telecommunications Report* (May 1988): 508.

6. *Africa Telecommunications Report* (January 1988): 2, 4.

7. *Telecommunications Development Report* (February 1987): 10–13.

8. *Africa Telecommunications Report* (July 1988): 7.

9. Russell Pipe, "The Information Traders," *Datamation* (1 July 1988): 48–6, 48–8.

10. Joseph N. Pelton, "In Orbit and on the Drawing Board: Satellite Resources for Emergency Communications," in *Internatitonal Disaster Communications: Initiatives for Greater Effectiveness in Mitigating Sudden Catastrophes.* Summaries of papers prepared for the International Disaster Communications Project, The Annenberg Washington Program. A presentation at the Annual Conference of the International Institute of Communications, 15 September 1988, Washington, D.C.

11. *Transnational Data Report* (Washington, D.C.: Transnational Data Reporting Service, October 1988).

12. U.S. Telecommunications Training Institute, *Course Catalog/Annual Report* (Washington, D.C.: USTTI, 1989).

13. U.S. Department of Commerce, *Caribbean Telecommunications Infrastructure Development Project, Definition Mission to Jamaica, February 2–13, 1986.* National Telecommunications and Information Administration, Office of

International Affairs and the International Trade Administration, International Economic Policy, Caribbean Basin Division. (Washington, D.C.: U.S. Department of Commerce, 1986).

14. United States Agency for International Development, *The AID Rural Satellite Program: An Overview* (Washington, D.C.: USAID, 1987).

PART 6

Health and Epidemics

Health problems represent a particularly severe crisis on the African continent. Inadequate health care for Africa's population stems from lack of resources, inadequate training of personnel and understanding of diseases, and the absence of cures in the African setting. African health problems can be viewed in the broader context of overall economic, social, and political stress. Lack of national resources for training and adequate compensation or employment opportunities for skilled medical personnel have led to an African biomedical brain drain. The financial troubles of African states also affect their ability to purchase necessary drugs, vaccines, and other supplies, many of which have to be imported at a high cost in foreign exchange. Health information and data collection systems in most African countries are also inadequate, constraining the ability to plan for and prevent outbreaks of epidemic diseases.

In another sense, the crisis is augmented by the actual availability of locally accessible and inexpensive remedies and techniques that have largely been ignored by medical authorities. Another problem concerns the increasingly widespread practice in Africa of health-damaging treatment of the physical environment. This includes the widespread use of pesticides, uncontrolled deposition of locally generated industrial waste, and the dumping in Africa of toxic and radioactive waste from abroad.

As an underlying reality, African–Soviet–U.S. cooperation in the area of health and epidemics will be helpful only if it increases long-term African self-sufficiency against the trend of African dependency on developed nations. Plans of action must be "Africa-friendly," including African participation at all stages in the development of an action plan. With this in mind, specific steps that might be taken include:

• Development in conjunction with the WHO of university-based tropical health research and training centers, run by Africans. The Soviet Union and United States could channel funds and expertise to these centers. An important goal of the centers would be to foster multidisciplinary expertise, which is essential in dealing with the many-faceted problems involved in the practice of tropical medicine. Financial incentives should be provided to physicians, scientists, and nurses who successfully compete for grant funds and who effectively implement research and training activities.

• Research that focuses on locally available knowledge of medicines, foodstuffs, and pesticides. Present knowledge should be incorporated into the curriculum and research program of the proposed tropical research and health training centers.

• Development of databases at these tropical health research and training centers on the short- and long-term adverse health effects of man-made and natural chemical substances with toxic potential. This locally available information should be put to use in advising African governments on appropriate courses of action concerning pesticide usage, industrial development, medicine usage, and environmental preservation.

• Development of local African data management expertise, along with simple and appropriate surveillance tools for identifying and preventing African epidemics.

17

Epidemic Diseases in Africa: Their Impact on Human Health and Productivity

OLADELE O. KALE

The health sector is a very fertile area for significant and productive cooperation between the superpowers; yet there are, to my knowledge, no extant health programs or projects in Africa in which the United States and the Soviet Union are collaborating.

The contributions by developed countries to health and health-related programs of developing countries are either direct or indirect, continuous or ad hoc. Direct contributions include the provision of relief materials at times of man-made or natural disasters such as regional military conflicts, drought, or famine. Favored African countries enjoy some measure of direct and continuous bilateral material and financial support from the superpowers for specific health programs such as family planning, and for health-related projects such as the construction of irrigation systems in the agricultural sector. Assistance in the training of health workers also belongs to this category. Much of the aid the superpowers provide is channeled indirectly to the health sectors of developing countries in Africa through statutory contributions to international bodies such as WHO and UNICEF.

THE CURRENT STATE OF HEALTH IN AFRICA

Most African countries are now at a stage of health development roughly similar to that of European countries before the Industrial Revolution. A notable characteristic of the preindustrial stage of development is the frequent and unmitigated occurrence of epidemics of communicable diseases, particularly those related to a poor physical and sanitary environment. This state of relative underdevelopment in health is further compounded by grinding poverty and a high prevalence of cultural and social practices that are inimical to healthful living.

What is more alarming for Africa is that while these "traditional," "ancient" epidemic diseases persist, a variety of "modern" epidemic health problems is being introduced. Among these are road traffic accidents, diseases associated with smoking, intemperate consumption of alcohol, and substance abuse. These diseases and health problems have already reached epidemic proportions in many African countries. If one adds the spreading impact of the human immunodeficiency virus (HIV) infection, which is taking a frightful toll on the most economically productive age group in these African countries, the overall health situation in Africa can be seen to be very grim indeed.

CATEGORIES OF EPIDEMIC DISEASES IN AFRICA

Diseases prone to epidemic outbreaks can be broadly classified into three groups on the basis of their mortality and morbidity rates and their propensity to spread.

In the first group are the internationally notifiable (quarantinable) diseases—cholera, plague, yellow fever, and (until its global eradication over a decade ago) smallpox—which from time to time occur as pandemics. To this group belongs the modern day pandemic due to the HIV virus, the cause of AIDS. The diseases in this group are universally dreaded and have attracted commensurable global attention and collaborative efforts aimed at their control.

The second group of diseases occurs in epidemics that are confined to special risk groups within defined national boundaries. These diseases have been largely controlled in industrialized societies through a combination of improvement in general standards of living and the development and application of effective prophylactic measures, notably immunization. Diseases in the group include measles, meningitis, and paralytic poliomyelitis. They are still very prevalent throughout tropical Africa and take a heavy toll on human life, particularly in childhood.

The third group is made up of the "invisible" and "neglected" epidemic diseases—invisible and neglected because, although they are often fatal, they tend to occur in and be confined to remote agrarian rural communities, whose residents—though they constitute approximately 75–80 percent of the population of Africa—have little or no access to even the most basic modern health facilities. Moreover, these communities do not possess the sort of political, economic, or social clout that could compel urban-based decision-makers and providers of medical care to undertake meaningful and effective interventions aimed at eliminating or controlling these diseases. The classical example of a disease that belongs to this group is *Dracunculiasis* (guineaworm infection), which will be used to illustrate the theme of this chapter.

INTERNATIONAL COOPERATION IN HEALTH

It is noteworthy that economic considerations were the primary motivation for the first major concerted international cooperative effort to deal with problems arising from the scourge of disease. In the nineteenth century, frequent and uncontrolled pandemics, notably of cholera, led many countries of Europe to introduce and impose, unilaterally and arbitrarily, wildly uninformed, draconian, and self-serving quarantine regulations, in a bid to keep dreaded diseases from their shores. The resultant threat of an imminent breakdown in international trade and commerce was averted only through the creation of a forum for international cooperation and collaboration.

An important landmark in this development was the drawing up of the International Sanitary Convention at the Venice Conference of 1892, although for some time after, quarantinable diseases continued to wreak considerable havoc, particularly in Europe.

For example, bubonic plague is estimated to have caused the death, in Europe alone, of 25 million people between 1346 and 1355. Plague is now largely confined to discrete foci in Southeast Asia and parts of Africa.

The ravages of smallpox over the centuries are too well known to need recounting at length here. The smallpox outbreak of 1691 is reported to have destroyed the entire population of several Russian towns. Notable among the victims of smallpox who survived are Queen Elizabeth I of England (in the sixteenth century) and President Abraham Lincoln of the United States, who was actually incubating the disease while delivering his famous Gettysburg Address (19 November 1863). The last recorded case of naturally acquired smallpox was one Ali Maow Maalin, a Somali cook who developed a rash on 26 October 1977 and recovered. He acquired the infection in Ethiopia, the only country in Africa that still had smallpox by December 1973.

Cholera and yellow fever are still very much with us. The former caused the death of over 1 million people in Russia during the protracted epidemic that lasted from 1847 to 1849. The disease is now endemic in many African countries and occurs on the continent in sporadic or epidemic forms from time to time. Among the draconian measures introduced by European countries to keep cholera at bay following catastrophic waves of pandemics in the eighteenth and nineteenth centuries were the destruction of entire cargos and the ships conveying them, and in the case of Spain, the imposition of the death penalty for anyone contravening quarantine regulations.

One of yellow fever's most celebrated devastations occurred with the loss of hundreds of thousands of laborers who were engaged in the construction of the Panama Canal. Africa has witnessed many outbreaks of yellow fever. One of the most recent began in eastern Nigeria in the latter half of 1986 and has been occurring sporadically ever since in different parts of the country.

The massive and almost unprecedented scale of mobilization of resources and international cooperation aimed at stemming the tide of the AIDS pandemic underscores the historically accurate axiom that nations do not pay sufficient attention to the health problems of their neighbors until they perceive a direct threat to themselves, or are engulfed by their neighbors' problems.

The lesson of AIDS is that cooperation between the United States and the USSR is desirable if problems on all fronts, social as well as economic, are not to engulf all and sundry.

The debt crisis of today is the economic equivalent of epidemics in the health sector, and its ultimate solution may well lie in the application of measures similar in concept to those that have been found effective in combating epidemic disease. One of these measures is improvement in the standard of living of affected societies, the other is cooperation among all concerned.

CAUSES OF AFRICA'S HEALTH PROBLEMS

Various factors predispose Africa to the occurrence of epidemics. Notable among these are:

- *Poverty*, which is aggravated by crushing debt burdens;
- *Population* growth rates, which outstrip the resources of the countries of Africa and their per capita growth rates;
- Uncoordinated and uncontrolled population *migration*, forced or unforced, which facilitates the spread of disease by exposing migrants to infections to which they have no immunity, and the hosts to communicable diseases imported by the migrants;
- Poor levels of *sanitation* coupled with poor and often inadequate supplies of wholesome water (over 80 percent of all diseases and health problems on the continent are associated with poor water supply and sanitation);
- Poor *nutrition*, due in part to ignorance and in part to lack of self sufficiency in food production, and problems related to food preservation and distribution, both of which contribute to the increased susceptibility of malnourished populations to infection;
- *Political and social instability* with consequential disruption of all aspects of life, making it impossible to build a durable system that can withstand and effectively combat the sort of challenges posed by epidemic diseases;
- Deficiencies in *managerial capacity* to cope with and sustain effective and efficient modern health services; and
- A poorly developed *health information system*, which makes effective disease surveillance, a sine qua non for control of epidemic disease, impossible.

Although by no means exhaustive, this list identifies some of the major constraints to growth and development in Africa's health sector.

DISEASE CONTROL AMONG AGRICULTURAL WORKERS: AN AREA OF POTENTIAL SOVIET–U.S.–COOPERATION

Pride of place at the African–Soviet–U.S. Cooperation conference was rightly given to agricultural production and distribution. The rest of this chapter will concentrate on this area of potential cooperation between the superpowers from the health perspective.

Much time and energy have been devoted to the technical aspects of the food crisis in the sub-Saharan region of Africa. While conceding that agricultural practices and related technoecological issues are important points worthy of consideration in any attempt aimed at reversing the downward trend in food production, it is of equal if not greater importance that attention should be paid to the labor force, that is, to the human beings who are primarily responsible for food production.

Contemporary African farmers are ravaged by myriad diseases that severely reduce their productivity. If this disease burden could be lifted, a commensurate improvement in productivity would be expected to result. It is therefore worthwhile and desirable to identify the health problems that adversely affect the productive capacity of African farmers and to design ways and means of effectively tackling these problems if there is to be a positive and durable transformation of the agrarian sector in Africa.

The spectrum of health problems prevalent in farming communities in most of Africa is similar. Preeminent among these are bites from disease-transmitting vectors and venomous insects and reptiles; attacks by wild animals; and physical injuries, often involving farming tools, which may lead to complications with infections such as tetanus. In recent times farmers have become increasingly exposed to toxic doses of chemical agents, such as pesticides and fertilizers. In at least seventeen countries of sub-Saharan Africa, there exists an additional and unique health problem. Guineaworm disease (*Dracunculiasis*) has a deleterious, well-documented socioeconomic impact on agriculture, education, and child survival. An overview of the impact of this disease in these countries will illustrate the importance of personal health in any agrarian revolution and suggest what great potential exists for Soviet–U.S. cooperation in the health sector.

Guineaworm Disease

Guineaworm is a disease of those whose sources of drinking water, especially stagnant ponds, are polluted. Many rural farming communities in Africa fall into this category.

The agent of guineaworm disease is the threadlike parasitic round worm, *Dracunculus medinensis*. The fully grown female of the parasite measures about 70 centimeters long by 0.2 centimeters wide and normally dwells under the skin of the mammalian host. Man becomes infected when he swallows water containing infected *cyclops*, the small (barely visible to the naked eye) crustacean intermediate host in which the larvae of the parasite develop. The *cyclops* in its turn becomes infected when it ingests guineaworm larvae that have been shed by gravid female worms, through an ulcer on the skin of the infected host while the host is wading in water.

Guineaworm is the only disease of man that is transmitted exclusively by way of water and that therefore can be completely eradicated through the provision of wholesome drinking water to affected communities. It is for this reason that the reduction in incidence of the disease was chosen as a sensitive indicator for measuring the progress of the Water Decade (1981–1990).

The relevance of guineaworm to my presentation and this discussion lies in its potential as an area of African–Soviet–U.S. cooperation, particularly within the context of the project's overall objectives for African development. To put things in proper perspective, however, it is necessary to point out that guineaworm is not the only endemic parasitic disease in Africa with demonstrable adverse effects on agricultural productivity. Schistosomiasis falls into the same category. Some of the salient differences between guineaworm and other debilitating diseases that are prevalent in farming communities in Africa and elsewhere are that:

- The global eradication of guineaworm is achievable using relatively simple and, in most cases, inexpensive methods;
- The peak prevalence of the disease coincides with the period of highest agricultural labor input demand, i.e., planting and harvesting, and by decimating the labor force at a most crucial time the disease exerts the maximum negative effect on productivity; and
- The disease is largely local and very rarely spreads from community to community.

Disease. About 8–10 million persons are estimated to suffer from guineaworm worldwide every year. The population at risk of infection numbers about 140 million.

In endemic communities guineaworm is a major health problem. Since it does not confer protective immunity, reinfection of the same individual year after year is not uncommon. Secondary bacterial infection of guineaworm ulcers occurs in about 50 percent of cases, and many farmers are too incapacitated to work for up to three months, some for longer. Some are permanently disabled.

The disease is most prevalent among the sixteen- to forty-five-year-old age group, which supplies the bulk of the agricultural labor force. Thus the disease is a major cause of lost productivity in agriculture. What is more, there is no pool of surplus, uninfected labor on which to draw.

Socioeconomic impact. A few examples will suffice to illustrate the impact of guineaworm disease on the socioeconomic status of affected communities.

In Togo, with a national population of 2,747,000, the estimated number of lost workdays per annum is 40 million. In Nigeria, with a population of about 100 million, about 120 million workdays are lost, 50 percent of them to agriculture alone.

The World Bank has estimated the value of the global loss of marketable goods attributable to guineaworm as high as $1 billion. In Burkina Faso as much as 10 percent of per capita income may be lost because of guineaworm disease. Between $56 million and $277 million in wages are lost globally every year as a result of guineaworm. A UNICEF-sponsored study in a part of Nigeria with a population of 1.6 million suggests that the annual losses in rice production profits alone are of the order of $20 million. If this loss is extrapolated to the rest of the areas of the country susceptible to guineaworm infestation, taking into account other crops, the total annual agricultural loss caused by guineaworm in Nigeria, where about 2 million cases occur in all the states of the federation, is on the order of three-quarters of a billion dollars.

Treatment of guineaworm disease varies from $17 for an uncomplicated case, to $147 for a very complicated case.

Guineaworm is the major cause of school absenteeism in endemic areas. This leads to a stifling of the educational potential of the affected children. At the height of the guineaworm season up to 60 percent of school children, as well as their teachers, may be forced to stay away from school for up to three months.

Guineaworm has also been shown to have a detrimental effect on child survival. Mothers suffering from the disease are unable to provide adequately for their families; their infants are likely to be weaned prematurely, with the attendant increased susceptibility of the children to infections and of their mothers to a lowering of the "natural resistance" to further pregnancy provided by breastfeeding.

It has been suggested that there is a causal relationship between labor losses resulting from guineaworm-related incapacitation, production of inadequate staple food supplies, and seasonal chronic malnutrition. There is also a distinct correlation between year-to-year fluctuations in seasonal rainfall and the incidence of guineaworm, as well as between rainfall and agricultural productivity. In endemic areas farming and the incidence of guineaworm both increase sharply after a season of relative drought or drastic reduction in precipitation.

Significantly, it has been shown that, in areas where guineaworm has been eradicated, farmers have benefited by way of an increase in agricultural yield from their farms. In summary, it can be concluded that the eradication of guineaworm would lead to increased availability of labor in the agricultural sector and that this would result in improved crop yields, which, over time, would be reflected in improved nutritional status. Thus, the eradication of guineaworm disease would go a long way to fulfilling one of the cardinal objectives of this project: the development of the agrarian sector.

Soviet and U.S. experience in eradicating guineaworm. Guineaworm disease has been present in both the USSR and the United States. Although human infections were apparently eradicated in the USSR by 1932 and are virtually unheard of in the United States, the disease persists in a variety of animal populations in both countries.

In the case of the Soviet Union, credit for unraveling the mode of transmission of the disease goes to a Russian researcher, Aleksej Pavlovic Fedchenko (1844–1973). His research on guineaworm opened the way for other scientists to establish the role of other agents, such as mosquitoes, ticks, lice, fleas, and blackflies, in disease transmission. It was another Russian scientist, Leonid Mihajlovic Issav, who, while director of the Tropical Institute founded in Bukhara in 1924, resolved a dispute about how guineaworm embryos gain entry into *cyclops*, i.e., by ingestion, and also carried out a number of experiments on guineaworm-carrying dogs.

The major contributions of the United States are more contemporary and are related to efforts at controlling the disease. The First International Conference on *Dracunculiasis* was held under the auspices of the Board on Science and Technology for International Develop-ment, Office of International Affairs of the National Research Council, 16–19 June 1982. The Center for Disease Control in Atlanta has been designated the WHO collaborating and reference center for the disease.

Eradication of guineaworm disease was the subject of a hearing of the Select Committee on Hunger of the U.S. House of Representatives in April 1987. The committee recognized the important benefits that would result from eradication of guineaworm disease and made recommendations to strengthen the U.S. response to the problem. The first among these recommendations was that "the U.S. Government should commit itself to exercising leadership in a coordinated international campaign to eradicate guineaworm disease." A positive boost to that recommendation could be achieved if this project on Soviet–U.S. cooperation for Africa were to devote particular attention to the guineaworm problem.

Also notable among U.S. contributions toward the goal of eradicating guineaworm is the effort of Global 2000 of the Carter Foundation, with the financial support of the Bank of Credit and Commerce International (BCCI). Global 2000/BCCI is active in the campaign against the guineaworm in Pakistan, Ghana, and Nigeria. In Ghana, Global 2000's guineaworm program, aimed at improving production of food grains, began in 1986 with forty farmers and was expected to involve 18,000 in 1988. Other bodies, such as the Hunger Project and Water and Sanitation for Health (WASH), are also contributing.

Both the Soviet Union and the United States are party to the objectives of the Water Decade and subscribe to the resolutions of the Interlaken meeting in Switzerland. Both are also party to the WHO resolution calling for the eradication of guineaworm by 1995. By providing cooperative leadership in international efforts they can play a vital role in the global eradication of the disease.

18

Health and Epidemics in Africa: Lessons from Environmentally Triggered Paralysis

VALERIE S. PALMER & PETER S. SPENCER

The major health problems of tropical communities—infections and malnutrition—are related to and inseparable from socioeconomic underdevelopment. Long-term solutions must be sought by the governments of tropical countries to ameliorate the quality of human life through health education and control of the habitat. So said G. Lobe Monekosso in an invaluable essay, which discusses training, service, and research needs to improve tropical health in black Africa.[1]

How can developed countries best assist African governments to improve health and reduce epidemics? We offer possible responses to this question by examining the problem of environmentally induced paralysis. We illustrate the theme with four subjects pertinent to Monekosso's central theme of infections and malnutrition: lathyrism, cassava toxicity, retrovirus-associated paralysis, and schistosomiasis. Like poliomyelitis, all are causes of irreversible and sometimes progressive crippling disease. Unlike poliomyelitis, however, there is no method to immunize individuals against these disorders, and other methods of prevention must be sought.

SCHISTOSOMIASIS AND ENDOD

Schistosomiasis, or bilharzia, a debilitating and fatal parasitic disease, is a constant threat to as many as 600 million people of seventy-four developing countries, including much of Africa.[2] Children are especially vulnerable to the water-borne organisms. While the children are at work or play, the parasites penetrate the skin, circulate in the blood stream, and develop into long worms that infect the liver, spleen, intestine, bladder, and nervous system. Chills, headache, eye pain, loss of appetite, leg weakness, and death may follow. Eggs that pass out of the child's body into water seek out and infect snails, in which the parasite is able to complete its life cycle. One method of schistosomiasis control, therefore, is to eliminate the snail.

During a 1964 study to determine the distribution of bilharzia-transmitting snails in a small stream in northern Ethiopia, research scientist

Akilulu Lemma observed large numbers of dead snails immediately downstream from where local people washed their clothing with berries of the African soapberry plant (*Phyotolacca dodecandra*) known as Endod, a natural detergent. Areas upstream and further downstream from the laundry site were rich in live snails. This simple observation led to research on the snail-killing property of the soapberry plant. Further investigation reveals that Endod is at least as effective as the leading synthetic molluscicide, which few developing countries are able to afford. The high cost in hard currency, coupled with declining foreign exchange, has resulted in the stoppage of bilharzia-control programs at a time when the prevalence of the disease is increasing. Endod is a possible substitute since it can be grown locally for use both as a molluscicide and a detergent.

In 1986 an international panel of experts acknowledged the potential benefits of Endod but cautioned that a carefully performed, Western-style toxicity study must be undertaken before the compound is registered as a pesticide. The U.S. National Center for Toxicological Research, in cooperation with the Third World Medical Research Foundation, has agreed to conduct these million-dollar studies if part of the cost is underwritten by public donation. A donor agency has yet to come forward. Meanwhile, a small amount of field work continues in Ethiopia, Zambia, Swaziland, and Zimbabwe, and interest in Endod for the control of schistosomiasis remains high.

RETROVIRUS-ASSOCIATED PARALYSIS

From urgently needed million-dollar assistance from developed countries, we turn to a mere $25,000 study that dramatically resolved the likely underlying cause of a mysterious type of paralysis that was first reported in the Seychelles Islands off the east coast of Africa. In adults this chronic disease begins with back pain and foot discomfort, is followed by weakness and the appearance of a spastic gait, and eventually results in the afflicted becoming bedridden and incontinent. While relatively few people within the Seychelles population were affected, the prevalence of the disease was very high and an epidemic was feared. The government of the Seychelles cooperated in assembling a multidisciplinary, international team of developed-country scientists and physicians who worked with local experts in tackling the problem. The suggestion of food-borne toxicity was rapidly rejected and, with the cooperation of the U.S. National Institutes of Health, it was possible for the team to demonstrate in serum antibodies the Human T-cell Lymphotropic Virus Type-1 (HTLV-1).[3]

This rapidly performed and inexpensive study demonstrated for the first time in Africa a link between HTLV-1 infection and crippling disease, which is now widely recognized. Subsequent studies by other groups have confirmed the relationship in parts of West Africa, including the Ivory Coast, where signs of infection may be found in 1–2 percent of the population. The disorder is also know in Colombia, South America, and the Caribbean islands of Martinique and Jamaica. The link has also been established in longtime residents of North America. Thus, here is an example of how low-budget applied research in developing countries benefits not only the target population but also impacts human health globally. As the worldwide AIDS epidemic shows, we are all potentially prey to infective agents irrespective of our race or location.

CASSAVA TOXICITY

The root of the cassava plant is an extraordinarily reliable and useful source of energy for tens of millions of Africans. Its ease of cultivation, drought resistance, abundance, good storage potential, taste, and social acceptability all combine to ensure that cassava will continue to play an important role in feeding the rural poor of Africa. But cassava root contains toxic elements that must be removed before the material is eaten. Sometimes, the information fails to reach the consumer and the root is eaten raw. At other times, as in the Mozambique drought of 1981, water may be too precious to be used to leach out the chemical toxins from the cassava root. The consequence: an epidemic of irreversible paralysis, mostly among children and young women.[4] Speech, vision, and hearing were also affected. Similar outbreaks have occurred elsewhere in Africa, including Zaire and Tanzania, and earlier studies from Nigeria raise the possibility that neurological change may develop slowly in cassava-consuming people and only appear late in life.

Despite widespread professional recognition that cassava root releases an appreciable quantity of cyanide, there is no explanation for cassava's apparent ability to damage the nervous system and cause paralysis. Even more troubling is that, although the enormous population of cassava consumers in Africa and beyond is still growing, research to address the problem has yet to begin. Here is another opportunity to bring scientists together from developed and developing countries for the mutual benefit of all.

GRASS PEA AND LATHYRISM

The fourth and final illustration concerns seed of another toxic plant, which causes crippling disease when consumed in excess. The grass pea (*Lathyrus sativus*) is also resistant to drought and to water-logged soils; unlike cassava, however, it is rich in protein, fixes nitrogen, and is resistant to many pests. Once widely eaten throughout Europe and the western part of the Soviet Union, the grass pea is now heavily consumed only in the poorest of countries, such as Bangladesh, India, and Ethiopia. Small amounts have no known adverse health effects, but those who must consume larger amounts on a regular basis develop lathyrism—another type of irreversible spasticity. Unlike the situation with cassava root, the neurotoxic agent in the grass pea has been isolated and characterized. This has opened the possibility of developing safe, low-toxin strains of the grass pea for use not only in Ethiopia, but also in other rainfed areas of Africa. This hardy legume might also serve as a backup insurance crop for cassava, which is presently threatened by the voracious appetite of certain pests.

The Third World Medical Research Foundation has developed an international network of scientists and physicians from ten developing and developed countries to address this problem. The largest study of the International Network for the Improvement of Lathyrus Sativus and the Eradication of Lathyrism (INILSEL) is under way in Ethiopia in a collaborative, multidisciplinary effort involving leading universities and medical schools, as well as agricultural and nutritional institutes.[5] If support continues to be forthcoming for this important project, it should be possible to develop in Africa a stable, low-toxin strain of the grass pea to prevent epidemic lathyrism, to provide safe food and fodder for those reliant on rainfed crops, and to contribute to the alleviation of protein-calorie malnutrition in drought-stricken regions of Africa.

RESEARCH AND TRAINING PRIORITIES

Several important conclusions can be drawn from these four examples of African epidemics of crippling disease related to infection and nutrition. First and foremost, the diseases are *not* specific to Africa: lathyrism afflicts the poor of Ethiopia and a number of other countries; schistosomiasis is a worldwide health problem essentially out of control; cassava root is enthusiastically promoted as a foodstuff in many parts of the world; and retrovirus-associated spasticity affects a broad worldwide belt of tropical and subtropical countries. Assisting Africa to research and resolve these problems will, therefore, impact humankind worldwide. Second, possible solutions to African health problems may sometimes be available locally: for example, Endod to combat schistosomiasis, and low-toxin strains of the grass pea to prevent paralysis and promote nutrition. Third, the exploitation of current scientific knowledge may open up new vistas for health improvement in Africa. The latter requires the active promotion of research and training in Africa.

As Monekosso has pointed out, medical research in Africa should fall into three broad interrelated categories: biomedical, laboratory-based research; clinical, hospital-based research; and sociomedical, community-based research. Medical research is at present undertaken in universities and medical faculties, as well as in research institutes, which are often established to address a single disease or a group of diseases. Research workers are few in number, are often isolated, function in an uncoordinated manner, and, in recent years, have been attracted abroad by more lucrative positions.

The strengthening of medical research by Africans in Africa is of paramount importance to the improvement of health and the reduction of epidemics. Medical research priorities in Africa include malnutrition, tropical infective diseases (notably malaria, filiaris, and schistosomiasis), maternal and child health, operational problems in the delivery of health services, medicinal plants, and African traditional medical practices.[6] Toxic chemicals in food, industrial waste, and the dumping practices of developed countries should be added to the list. Resolving critically important problems, such as malnutrition and infective diseases, will require a multipronged attack involving health teams composed of laboratory- and field-based scientists of many disciplines, working in conjunction with physicians, nurses, and community health care specialists.

Strenuous efforts to train and retain African personnel in Africa are urgently needed to replace lost personnel and to build the army of specialists needed to improve health and reduce epidemics on the African continent. Integrated, multiprofessional health sciences research and training centers should be established regionally, nationally, and locally. Research should be based in the laboratory, the hospital, and the community. Adequate technical facilities should be provided for the practical teaching of biomedical, clinical, and sociomedical disciplines. Continuing education should be provided to maintain modern standards. In short, the development and training of African personnel is the top priority for the improvement of health and reduction of epidemics in Africa. Let this also be the priority of benevolent superpowers bent on assisting Africa to help itself.

> International cooperation is an imperative necessity of our times. Action programmes at the national level should be strengthened by carefully designed exchanges between Third World countries themselves, and between them and the developed countries. The final objective of such cooperation should be mutual respect and understanding.[7]

NOTES

1. G. L. Monekosso, "The View from the Third World," in *Tropical Medicine: From Romance to Reality* (London: Academic Press, 1978).

2. K. E. Mott, "Schistosomiasis, New Goals," *World Health* (December 1984).

3. G. C. Roman, P. S. Spencer, B. S. Schoenberg, J. Hugon, A. Ludolph, P. Rodgers-Johnson, K. O. Osuntokun, and C. F. Shamlaye, "Tropical Spastic Paraparesis in the Seychelles Islands: A Clinic and Case-Control Neuroepidemiologic Study," *Neurology* 37: 1323–1328.

4. Ministry of Health, Mozambique, "Mantkassa: An Epidemic of Spastic Paraparesis Associated with Chronic Cassava Intoxication in a Cassava-Staple Area of Mozambique," *Bulletin World Health Organization* 62 (1984): 477–484.

5. A. K. Kaul and D. Combes, *Lathyrus and Lathyrism* (New York: Third World Medical Research Foundation, 1986).

6. Monekosso, "The View from the Third World."

7. Ibid.

PART 7

Nuclear Nonproliferation

The principles embodied in the NPT and the strengthening of the non-proliferation regime internationally, including Africa, serves international peace and security. Nonproliferation is an area of common interest between the United States and the USSR in which the two countries have a good record of cooperation. To further the goal of nonproliferation, in Africa, the Soviet Union and United States could take the following cooperative steps:

• Bring the NPT into effect for all African countries, especially South Africa. Because of the advanced level of the RSA's nuclear program and the security threat that it poses to other African states, a special effort should be made by the Soviet Union and United States, using the resources and means at their disposal, to ensure unequivocal South African adherence to the NPT, with all its attendant obligations and responsibilities.

• Establish a nuclear-free zone in Africa, which would assist the goal of nuclear nonproliferation on the continent. Such a zone is highly desirable and corresponds to the views expressed by African states on numerous occasions at the United Nations and at the OAU. Since 1974, both the Soviet Union and United States have endorsed proposals at the United Nations calling for all states "to refrain from testing, manufacturing, deploying, transporting, storing, using, or threatening to use nuclear weapons on the African continent." The creation of such a nuclear-free zone in Africa should strengthen the international nonproliferation regime and the security of all African states. Although such a zone should ideally include the entire African continent, a first step in that direction could be a sub-Saharan nuclear-free zone. In order for any African nuclear-free zone to have meaning, however, it should include South Africa.

• Promote the resolution of conflicts in Africa, the existence of which may give rise to aspirations to acquire and make use of nuclear weapons.

• Provide technical and economic assistance to Africa for the development of non-nuclear energy sources.

• Strengthen the IAEA and, especially, its international safeguards program. Additional national and multilateral efforts should be undertaken to reduce the risk that sensitive nuclear material and technology might be diverted to military use.

• Strengthen the missile technology control regime in order to deny access to nuclear capable delivery systems to aspiring nuclear weapons states.

• Reduce the worldwide stockpile of nuclear arms in pursuit of their NPT Article VI obligations.

19

Africa and Nuclear Nonproliferation

OYE OGUNBADEJO

Scholars seem divided over whether nonproliferation is a positive agent of global peace. Kenneth Waltz, for example, argues that nuclear spread is to be welcomed rather than feared, but George Quester thinks otherwise. To Quester, there is a direct link between the number of nuclear powers in the world and the probability of nuclear war. This latter viewpoint is also shared by numerous international peace movements, which consider nuclear proliferation to be highly dangerous for humankind and have, therefore, warmly endorsed the virtue of nuclear weapons-free zones, an idea that was developed at the United Nations' first special session on disarmament.

From Africa's standpoint, it can be argued that given the harsh realities of the various social and economic problems that confront the continent, nuclear nonproliferation is in itself a desirable goal. Besides, with the well-publicized nuclear reactor accidents in the technologically-advanced United States, (at Three Mile Island in 1979) and in the USSR (at Chernobyl in 1986), it can be further contended that the relatively technologically backward African states ought to refrain from becoming nuclearized.

Yet, Africa is being squeezed from both the north and south by the nuclear activities of Israel and South Africa.[1] In situating Africa's nuclear equation in the context of nonproliferation, this chapter not only will analyze the major challenges that confront, or are likely to confront, African states, but it will also conclude by offering policy recommendations for managing nuclear nonproliferation in the continent.

TOWARD THE DOMESTICITY OF NUCLEAR WEAPONS

An important challenge that confronts Africa is how the continent can live peacefully with the reality of the nuclear status of Israel and South Africa. It is an open secret that the two states have benefited from their close nuclear collaboration. Both states have nuclear devices as well as suitable delivery systems. True, Israel has not openly announced its nuclear war capability.

All the same, recent evidence indicates that its nuclear arsenal may well contain up to 200 weapons, deliverable by aircraft and missiles. Israel, therefore, ranks as the sixth nuclear power, in terms of its weapons arsenal.

South Africa, for its part, reportedly has as many as forty nuclear weapons. For delivery purposes, the RSA can use either aircraft or artillery. And to facilitate the use of the latter, a tactical battlefield mininuclear device has been specially developed for the country's popular long-range 155mm G5 howitzer. In August 1988 South Africa openly admitted that it could, indeed, manufacture nuclear weapons.

It should be mentioned that Israel and South Africa have also collaborated on the production of a neutron bomb. Nor must we forget to mention, too, that Israel's advance in nuclear technology has since moved into a second-strike capability. The nuclear strides of Israel and South Africa have spurred the nuclear interest of some Arab and black African states. While Egypt and Libya possess advanced nuclear programs, Nigeria has embarked modestly on its development of nuclear energy.

Moreover, and no doubt in competition with Israel's own range of missiles, each of the two Arab African states has acquired a thriving arsenal of missile systems (see Table 19.1).

Table 19.1
Missile Proliferation in Arab Africa

Country	Missles	Range (km)
Egypt	Frog-7	70
	Sakr-80	80
	Scud-B	270
	Bader 2000	770
Libya	Frog-7	70
	Scud-B	270
	MB/EE	970
	OTRAG	?

Source: Washington Institute for Near East Policy.

Since Egypt and Libya are generally considered part of the Middle East, it may be helpful, if only for comparative analysis, to have an idea of the missile buildup in the other affected states in the region as well, including Israel itself (see Table 19.2).

Admittedly, from Arab Africa's standpoint, some of these missiles carry conventional warheads. All the same, it is relevant to point out that they can be armed with chemical or even nuclear warheads. It appears, however, that for as long as Israel does not use its own range of missiles, the two Arab African states are not likely to threaten the Jewish state by deploying missiles. Even if we argue for a moment that such a possibility really exists, especially under a war situation, Israel has quietly signed an agreement with

Table 19.2
Missile Proliferation in Other Parts of the Middle East

Country	Missiles	Range (km)
Iran	Oghab	40
	In development	130
	Scud-B	270
Iraq	Frog-7	70
	SS-21	100
	Scud-B	270
	al-Hussein	630
	al-Abbas	870
	SS-12	900
Israel	MAR-290	30
	Lance	110
	Jericho	970
Saudi Arabia	DF-3A	3,000
Syria	Frog-7	70
	SS-21	100
	Scud-B	270
	M-9	600

Source: Washington Institute for Near East Policy.

the United States for a joint development of a new antimissile system, called the Arrow, and for "tactical solutions in the realm of intelligence."[2]

The nuclear arms race poses a serious threat to Africa. The question then arises: Can nuclear weapons be domesticated on the continent? On the present showing, it seems that to the degree that there are, as yet, no other known nuclear weapons states in Africa, and since, too, South Africa and Israel have been producing and developing nuclear weapons for use against their neighbors only when, as Benjamin Beit-Hallahmi has pointed out, the two isolated states have no other alternative, the prospects for domesticity of nuclear weapons seem good, at least in the short, and perhaps medium, term. The more so, as the black African states, except in the case of South Africa, do not have the capability, nuclear or conventional, to launch the "total onslaught" that Pretoria fears. Essentially then, nuclear weapons in Africa, for now, have the value of deterrence.

THE INTERNATIONAL NUCLEAR NONPROLIFERATION REGIME RECONSIDERED

Theoretically, to the degree that members of the international system have devised a series of rules and procedures that are designed to check the spread of nuclear weapons, the domesticity of these weapons should not constitute a major problem. After all, the centerpiece of relevant rules and procedures, the NPT, bans the transfer of nuclear weapons and technology outside the original five weapons states and further commits these states to negotiations that would halt the arms race. Moreover, the non-nuclear signatories, on their part, commit themselves not to manufacture nuclear arms and, where nuclear facilities exist, to accept all necessary safeguard measures such as inspections, audits, and inventory controls. Indeed, to ensure that the fuel and waste from the nuclear power plants of these countries are not diverted to the making of nuclear devices, the NPT makes use of the IAEA, whose inspectors check the power plants to keep track of fissionable material.

On paper, the provisions of the NPT seem adequate and acceptable to several states. Thus, by October 1987 a total of 137 states had ratified the treaty. In reality, however, problems abound, especially over key regional powers that possess "unsafeguarded" facilities but have not ratified the treaty. These regional powers—notably Israel, India, Pakistan, South Africa, Argentina, and Brazil—pose the foremost threats to the international nuclear nonproliferation regime. To further complicate issues, although some states have signed the NPT, their behavior, as can be seen through the clandestine nuclear programs that they run, show that they are not committed to honoring the spirit of it. States in this category include Iran, Iraq, and at least one African state, Libya.

Arguably, the rules and procedures embodied in the NPT have had some impact on the pace of nuclear proliferation; the momentum of nuclear spread has been relatively slow. Still, every new or suspected weapons state has cheated one way or another, particularly in the clandestine use of heavy water and enriched uranium. We should quickly add that the phenomenon of cheating is not an exclusive feature of the proliferators alone. Some of the nuclear suppliers tend to turn a blind eye to what their clients do with nuclear imports.

Theoretically, all NPT signatories agree to require safeguards on all of their nuclear exports. In practical terms, this is easier said than done. In 1981 South Africa bought sixty pounds of enriched uranium from the German firm Rohstoff Einfuhr, part of Alfred Hempel. The Hempel company has tended to specialize in buying nuclear materials and in secretly reselling them to countries that do not adhere to the NPT. The enriched uranium that it sold to South Africa, for example, came from China. And the diverted material has been used, for several years, to triple the output of South Africa's pilot enrichment plant at Valindaba. Needless to add, it has also significantly boosted the amount of weapons-trade material available to the RSA.

Nuclear commerce, as conducted by Hempel's company, has caused such industrial countries as Norway, the Soviet Union, West Germany, and Switzerland to violate parts of the NPT. Nor is the Hempel company alone in its shady dealings. In January 1988 the West German environment minister, Klap Toepfer, announced that Nukem, a nuclear fuel manufacturer based near Frankfurt, had been suspected of delivering weapons-grade uranium, which could be used to make atom bombs, to Libya and Pakistan. Granted, export-oriented countries like West Germany and Switzerland formally accept the NPT. Nevertheless, these countries have not created the domestic regulatory structure to live up to their international commitments on nuclear nonproliferation. To the degree that their national frameworks do not fit into the larger framework of the NPT, weaknesses exist in the implementation of the international body of rules that have been designed to stop unsafeguarded trade in nuclear materials.

Given the publicity that has, in recent years, surrounded detected illicit diversions of nuclear supplies, some vital challenges have arisen. First, non-nuclear African states, especially those that already have or plan to obtain nuclear power plants, ought not to emulate the illicit practices of others. One way of achieving this objective is for these states to adhere strictly to the relevant rules and procedures laid down in the NPT. To this end, the IAEA needs to play a more vigorous role in devising safeguards, utilizing surveillance and containment techniques of a nonintrusive nature, and monitoring mothballed warheads and weapons systems and other forms of cheating.

Second, it is equally essential for the exporters of nuclear supplies to tighten safeguard clauses both for enriched uranium and heavy water. For instance, there is no requirement to account for transfers of heavy water within, or between, states that have signed the NPT. Here, all inventories could, whenever they are moved, be logged in and out, as is done with some types of natural uranium.

Third, and closely linked to the previous point, is the challenge of devising, and indeed having, better international law enforcement cooperation to track materials and monitor nuclear dealers. As modest as it may seem, it is significant that the recent controversies over heavy water have caused Norway to tighten its controls somewhat; and prospects for some reform in West Germany are good.

Fourth is the challenge for the superpowers to prevail on themselves as well as on their respective allies in the North to positively and effectively encourage strict adherence to the international nuclear nonproliferation regime. This particular challenge is important if we bear in mind that the Reagan administration, unlike the Carter regime before it, permitted certain exports to several states that have yet to agree to the full scope of NPT safeguards. These include Argentina, Brazil, India, and South Africa. In addition, the Reagan administration, as Warren Donnelly has pointed out, "did not stop an American firm from arranging the supply of enriched uranium to South Africa from European sources."[3]

Fifth, since some newly industrialized states in the South now engage in international nuclear commerce in their own right, African states could use the nonaligned movement, as an important platform, not only to campaign for the elimination of nuclear weapons at both the systemic and subsystemic level, but also to resist the temptation of nuclear nationalism by sealing off the transfer of nuclear supplies, be it enriched uranium or heavy water, to aspiring nuclear states in Africa.

The last challenge that we can identify under this topic is the need for nuclear engineers and scientists all over the world to conduct research into new types of "safe" reactors that may not necessarily use items that can be diverted for surreptitious production of nuclear weapons. Such reactors can be utilized by African states that may want to embark on the nuclear power option, as a genuine economic move to diversify available energy sources.

NON-NUCLEAR SOURCES OF ENERGY

Save for countries such as South Africa, Egypt, and Libya, which may have military and strategic reasons for going nuclear, most of the other African states that have nuclear programs often advance the need to diversify energy sources. Their programs, they insist, are for "peaceful" purposes alone. Given the numerous hazards that surround nuclear power reactors, including the risk of accidents with the obvious attendant dangers, a major challenge to African states is to seek alternative and renewable sources to nuclear energy.

Two alternatives that readily spring to mind are wind power and solar energy. Let us take a brief look at the latter. The sun is an abundant potential source of energy in Africa. While it is true that there is an African Regional Centre for Solar Energy, located in Burundi, many states have not so far embraced the idea. Yet, it could be useful for many developmental needs, including agricultural processing, cooling systems, lighting, and pumping of water.

In any case, solar power should be of immense interest to African states for several reasons. First, many areas of the continent receive up to 3,600 hours of sunshine every year. Second, the technology of solar power can be mastered relatively quickly by Africans themselves, with minimum recourse to foreign technical support. Third, solar power has several advantages for a continent as large as Africa, with its several thousands of remote villages. In this regard, the solar option stands to be a solution to the problem of electrification and could bring energy to those villages that the national electricity grid would never reach economically.

A major challenge to the superpowers in the years ahead will be to provide generous aid to enable African countries to embark on this peaceful way of harnessing energy. For now, a number of international development agencies have risen to the challenge and have expressed an interest in funding three major solar energy projects in Africa. Under the sixth European Development Fund Regional Programme, one of the projects aims at using solar-powered pumps and local power supply systems, ranging from

40 watts to 3.9 kilowatts, to combat desertification in the Sahel. Another project costing $2.2 million is to be built in Bamako, Mali, over the next two or three years, using imported components for an initial production capacity of 150 kilowatts of solar photovoltaic cell (PV) devices annually, rising to double the capacity after two years.

A third project, funded by the EC, will be located in Sierra Leone, where Britain's BP Solar International recently won a contract to convert eleven diesel-powered radio stations to PV power. The project is expected to cost $1.5 million.

THE NUCLEAR OPTION VERSUS ECONOMIC DEVELOPMENT

African states that emphasize the peaceful nature of their nuclear programs also point to other potential contributions. They contend that aside from the issue of energy, other known advantages span the field of medicine (isotopes) and agriculture (food irradiation). On the other hand, given the deplorable state of the economies of several African countries, it is questionable whether nuclear programs of any kind are the best use of scarce resources for investment. The funds allocated to nuclear programs could be used more efficiently to tackle more pressing economic difficulties.

In any case, the consequences of nuclear spending for an African state's capacity for productive investment is crucial in terms of its long-term effect on socioeconomic development, most notably in preempting commensurate spending on education and health. Although it is true that the relationship between economic growth and spending to acquire nuclear capability is far more complex than just a trade-off between bomb and butter, it is arguable that, in the African context at least, an increase in nuclear spending does lead to a decrease in economic growth.

THE SUPERPOWERS AND THE TASK OF CONFLICT RESOLUTION IN AFRICA

Whatever may be the economic payoffs for not going nuclear, some African states are bound to embark upon, or consolidate, their nuclear programs for political reasons. In this regard, the conflicts in the Middle East and southern Africa tend to accentuate the yearning for nuclear weapons. Qaddafi's quest for the "Islamic Bomb," for example, is not unconnected with the Arab-Israeli conflict; just as Israel's nuclear capability reflects its strategic calculations in that endemic conflict.

Similarly, the complex conflict in southern Africa, notably South Africa's perceptions of a hostile environment, constitutes an important reason behind the RSA's development of a nuclear capability. And it is precisely because of the militancy of some key black African states on the issue of southern Africa that these countries feel threatened by the RSA. Certainly, Shagari's Nigeria advanced the southern African situation as a major motivation for nursing the nuclear ambition.

It seems then that the resolution of the major conflicts in Africa may slow down the nuclear arms race in, or around, the continent. Herein lies a major challenge for the superpowers. Their ability to meaningfully engage in conflict resolution can be an antidote to nuclear proliferation.

Specifically, for southern Africa, the points need to be made that no lasting resolution of conflict can be attained while the policy of apartheid remains deeply entrenched in the RSA even if there are occasional cosmetic changes in the underlying principle of separate racial development; the National Union for the Total Independence of Angola (UNITA) forces of Jonas Savimbi continue to be armed by the United States and South Africa; and Pretoria still promotes regional destabilization, particularly in the other frontline states.

It should perhaps be further stated that in the task of conflict resolution, it is important for the two superpowers to recognize the peculiar African characteristics of major conflicts in the continent. They should, accordingly, address their energies toward understanding those peculiarities rather than approach every conflict from the globalist standpoint, which, because of ideological considerations, often distorts situations and events. In any case, the superpowers, if they are to be effective conciliating powers, need to be objective in analyzing situations, in identifying the most suitable time to seek resolution, and, just as important, in carrying out the task with utmost skill.

CONCLUSIONS

Given the nuclear collaboration between Israel and South Africa, and given, too, the growing nuclear arsenals of these two regional powers and the nuclear programs of some Arab African states (notably Libya and Egypt), the quest for making Africa a nuclear weapons-free zone seems to be a herculean task. Although, black Africa may lack nuclear devices for now, the militant states in the region see themselves as the potential target for Pretoria's nuclear weapons.

Simply put then, no particular area of the continent can be totally insulated from the abrasive nuclear pressures of the other areas. Nuclear weapons in one region would naturally stimulate the security consciousness of the other regions, which, in turn, may aspire to broaden their military preparedness with the bomb. It is hardly surprising, therefore, that nuclear nationalism manifests itself in every region of the continent. It can even be argued that nuclear nationalism has always been the motivating factor in South Africa and Israel, at least in protecting white power in the RSA and the Jews in the Jewish state. With such an extent of nuclear nationalism, several major challenges emerge, the greatest of which is the need to domesticate nuclear weapons.

An equally important challenge is the need to tighten the international nuclear nonproliferation regime. In circumstances where the nuclear path cannot be blocked altogether, emphasis should be on strictly peaceful uses, especially in the fields of medicine and agriculture, which, in any case, are useful in the development process. To achieve this objective, suppliers of sensitive nuclear materials in the north and south alike need to enforce their safeguard clauses whenever they part with supplies like heavy water or enriched uranium.

Since nuclear power plants can easily be abused, particularly by countries with unsafeguarded facilities, there should, as a matter of urgency, be concerted research efforts into the production of "safe" reactors. These reactors would not use uranium, nor would their spent fuel be used to breach the international nuclear nonproliferation regime. In this regard, my argument about the usefulness of thorium elsewhere can be gainfully pursued.[4]

Closely tied to the idea of making the nuclear power option "safe," is the challenge to seek alternative and renewable sources of energy that will not only be "safe" from the weapons production standpoint, but will also not constitute environmental health hazards. While both the wind power and solar energy options deserve close study for adoption, the latter stands to be a more viable alternative.

Inasmuch as the major conflicts in the Middle East and southern Africa propel the nuclear arms race, we need to restate our earlier challenge; namely, the two superpowers need to collaborate effectively in the task of conflict resolution. A significant success in that realm by both the Soviet Union and the United States could serve as an antidote to nuclear proliferation.

For African states, the challenge ahead is not simply over the nuclear option per se. Among the many other challenges, the rational priority is, arguably, not the acquisition of the nuclear capability, whether for prestige or national self-image, deterrence, security, or aggressive intention. Instead, priority ought to be accorded to economic development by African governments. Funds that have been earmarked for undertaking, or consolidating nuclear programs could profitably be transferred to the productive sectors of the local economies to stimulate economic recovery and growth in real terms.

The counterpoint is clear: going nuclear is essentially a political decision; politics, in that context, can be bad economics. Be that as it may, the case for nuclear nonproliferation is, in the African milieu, and bearing our various arguments in mind, an overwhelming one. Whatever may be the political and strategic payoffs cannot, at least in my opinion, derail the weight of the economic argument.

To translate into reality the challenges identified in this chapter require cooperation among African states and the active support of the two giants of contemporary international relations, the United States and the Soviet Union, along with that of the other industrial countries of the north and the newly industrialized countries of the south. Moreover, the momentum of the apparent trend toward results-oriented arms talks and negotiations between Washington and Moscow, as evidenced by the 1987 Intermediate-Range Nuclear Forces (INF) Treaty, needs to be sustained. After all, there is a useful lesson for African states in a clear demonstration, through major all-round nuclear arms reductions, that even the world's foremost nuclear powers themselves doubt the utility of nuclear weapons.

NOTES

1. For background on Africa's nuclear enterprise, see Oye Ogunbadejo, *The International Politics of Africa's Strategic Minerals* (Westport, Conn.: Greenwood Press, 1985), especially chapters 5–7; "Nuclear Capability and Nigeria's Foreign Policy," in *Africa Contemporary Record, 1983–84,* ed. Colin Legum (New York: Africana, 1985), A136–A151; "Africa's Nuclear Capability," *The Journal of Modern African Studies* 22, no. 1 (March 1984): 19–43; and Robert S. Jaster, "Politics and the 'Africaner Bomb'," *Orbis* 27, no. 4 (Winter 1984): 825–851.

2. *The Christian Science Monitor* (weekly edition), 25–31 July 1988, 7.

3. Warren H. Donnelly, "Nonproliferation Policy of the United States in the 1980s," *SAIS Review* (Summer–Fall 1987): 175.

4. Oye Ogunbadejo, *War and Peace in Our Time: On the Politics of Nuclear Systems* (Ile-Ife, Nigeria: Obafemi Awolowo University Press, forthcoming).

20

Cooperation for Nonproliferation in Africa

WILLIAM C. POTTER

The United States and the Soviet Union have been ideological adversaries and military rivals. It is not surprising, therefore, that most comparisons of the two countries emphasize areas of disagreement and divergence. It is nevertheless important not to lose sight of significant similarities and areas of common interest. One such area in the domain of foreign policy is nuclear nonproliferation.

As the paramount nuclear states, the Soviet Union and the United States share an interest in restricting entry into the nuclear weapons club. This common interest is reflected in U.S. and Soviet cooperation for nonproliferation in numerous bilateral and international forums, and has continued across both Democratic and Republican administrations and during periods of détente and international tension. Elsewhere I have detailed the major parallels (as well as areas of divergence) in U.S. and Soviet perspectives on nonproliferation and the correspondence in the evolution of their respective nuclear export policies.[1] Here the focus is on the more specific topic of the potential for U.S.–Soviet cooperation in one geographical region—Africa.

THE PRIOR RECORD OF COOPERATION

Since 1974 the United States and the Soviet Union have often worked closely together to tighten nuclear export restraints and to gain greater adherence to the NPT.[2] At the meeting of the London Suppliers Group, for example, the Soviet Union regularly aligned itself with the supplier state proponents of strict nuclear export controls, a group usually including the United States, Canada, and Great Britain. The Nuclear Exporters' (or Zangger) Committee, set up in 1970 to interpret the safeguards clause (Article III) of the NPT, also has served as an important forum for U.S.–Soviet consultations on nonproliferation. The United States has often found it easier to gain support from the Soviet Union than from its Western allies for its efforts to tighten export controls. The Soviets, for example, supported the U.S. initiative in 1982 to plug gaps related to gas centrifuge technology in the existing 1974 and 1978 "trigger lists" (that is, those items whose export would trigger the application of IAEA safeguards to the facility for which items were supplied). More recently the Soviet Union has backed a similar U.S. effort to develop more precise definitions for reprocessing technology and its components.

Important U.S.–Soviet consultations on nonproliferation also take place at the annual IAEA General Conference and in biannual meetings between the U.S. ambassador for nonproliferation (Richard Kennedy), other senior U.S. nonproliferation specialists, and their Soviet counterparts from the Foreign Ministry and the State Committee for the Utilization of Atomic Energy. For the most part, these bilateral consultations (which alternate between Moscow and Washington) have been without polemics when the discussions focused on technical issues such as IAEA safeguards. Much less progress, however, has been made on the politically sensitive issues of "problem" countries.

Probably the most unusual example of Soviet cooperation with the United States on nonproliferation measures occurred in the summer of 1977 when the Soviets shared intelligence information with the United States that indicated the possibility that South Africa had constructed a nuclear test site in the Kalahari Desert. The Soviet Union also subsequently respected U.S. requests for behavior in the United Nations that would not jeopardize a U.S. initiative to gain South African adherence to the NPT and international safeguards.

STATUS OF THE PROLIFERATION THREAT IN AFRICA

There are very real and compelling reasons to be concerned about nuclear weapons proliferation in the future. The failure of past prophecies to materialize, however, highlights the need to avoid deterministic thinking about proliferation and the mistake of equating proliferation of nuclear capabilities with the decision to exercise those capabilities. Stated somewhat differently, it is useful when discussing the threat of nuclear proliferation to distinguish between *technical capabilities* (e.g., the availability of fissile material and bomb design know-how) and the *political will* to pursue a nuclear weapons program. Nonproliferation strategies may attempt to influence both capabilities and political incentives and disincentives.

Table 20.1 summarizes the capabilities of African countries with nuclear technology and materials. It also indicates the NPT status of those countries. As is evident from the table, very few African countries possess nuclear technology, and only one, South Africa, has developed a range of sensitive fuel cycle technologies usually associated with development of a nuclear weapons program.[3] Because South Africa is not a party to the NPT, it is not required to have its nuclear facilities under IAEA safeguards. The Vlindaba uranium enrichment plant and the fuel fabrication facility at Pelindaba, in fact, are not safeguarded. The hot cell reprocessing complex at Pelindaba is under IAEA safeguards only when safeguarded fuel is present.[4]

Table 20.1
African Countries with Nuclear Technology in Operation or Under Construction

	Research Reactor	Spent Fuel Reprocessing	Uranium Enrichment	Fuel Fabrication	Power Reactors	NP Party
Egypt	1 (2,000 kw)					yes
Libya	1 (10,000 kw)					yes
Morocco	1 (100 kw)[a]					yes
South Africa	1 (20,000 kw)[b]	yes[a]	yes	yes	yes	no
Algeria	[c]					no

Sources: Nuclear Research Reactors: Status and Trends (Vienna: IAEA, 1986); The Nuclear Fuel Cycle System (Vienna: IAEA, 1987); Leonard S. Spector, Going Nuclear (Cambridge, Mass.: Ballinger, 1987); "World Survey," Nuclear Engineering International (June 1987), 26.

[a] Under construction.

[b] A second 0 power reactor (Pelinduna Zero) is now decommissioned.

[c] Algeria is reported to have ordered a small research reactor from Argentina, although the status of the deal is unclear. See Nuclear Engineering International (June 1986).

It remains unclear whether or not South Africa has actually produced nuclear weapons. A recent study, however, estimates that since 1981 South Africa has had the ability to produce approximately 50 kilograms a year of highly enriched uranium at its Vlindaba plant.[5]

If one shifts attention from capabilities to the balance of incentives and disincentives "to go nuclear," the list of African states usually identified as seeking a nuclear weapons capability is also small. South Africa and Libya generally head the list, with Nigeria and Egypt occasionally noted as potential proliferators.[6]

Neither Nigeria nor Egypt has significant nuclear technology capabilities and there are few indications that either state today seriously contemplates a nuclear weapons program. Both countries are also parties to the NPT. Libya is also a party to the NPT, having ratified the treaty on 26 May 1975, nearly seven years after it signed the treaty and despite repeated efforts in the preceding five years to purchase nuclear weapons and sensitive nuclear technology.[7] There is evidence that Libya has continued to seek the purchase of nuclear weapons on the black market since it became a party to the NPT.[8] The lack of substantial nuclear technology and the generally restraining influence of the Soviet Union on Libya's nuclear program, however, are likely to minimize the prospects of a Libyan nuclear weapons capability, at least in the short term.[9]

The situation is less favorable with respect to South Africa. Not only does it have the technical capability to develop and deliver nuclear weapons, but political and military disincentives to do so no longer clearly outweigh the incentives. Because of South Africa's international pariah status, the ability of outside parties to influence South African nuclear policy also is limited.

The military utility of South African nuclear weapons, either for deterrent or defense purposes, has been questioned by a number of analysts.[10] They note that South Africa possesses overwhelming conventional military power vis-à-vis other African states and that the threat of nuclear violence is not likely to deter domestic guerrillas. As Robert Jaster points out, however, the key issue is not the objective assessment of the balance of forces in southern Africa, but the perceptions of military threat by the South African leadership.[11] That leadership and the white electorate, more generally, appear to believe that they face "a massive communist-supported conventional assault . . . in the short or medium term."[12] The leadership may also regard possession of nuclear weapons, or a "bomb in the basement" (i.e., the capability quickly to deploy a nuclear weapon) as a means to boost the morale of the Afrikaner population and as a device to obtain international bargaining leverage.

The absence of effective U.S. and Soviet leverage over South Africa's nuclear program, such as exists in the U.S.–South Korean or Soviet-Libyan cases, leaves the superpowers with few policy alternatives.[13] Therefore, South Africa's announcement during the September 1987 IAEA General Conference that "it will soon be able to sign the NPT and has decided to open discussions with others to this end" is extremely significant.[14]

The timing of the announcement, immediately before the General Conference was to vote on the IAEA's Board of Governors' recommendation to suspend South Africa from the IAEA, was clearly calculated to influence the vote. The precise wording of the statement by President P. W. Botha also raised a number of questions regarding South Africa's intent. Nevertheless, the statement, and the subsequent conference vote to postpone action for one year on the suspension of South Africa (extended for an additional one year at the 1988 General Conference meeting), opens the door for joint U.S. and Soviet diplomatic action to gain South African adherence to the NPT.[15]

SOVIET–U.S. COOPERATION FOR NONPROLIFERATION IN AFRICA

The recent expression of South African interest in discussing adherence to the NPT provides an unusual opportunity for joint U.S.–Soviet diplomacy.

Every effort should be made to gain South African ratification of the NPT and to put in place full-scope safeguards on South African nuclear facilities. South Africa's major incentives for acceding to the NPT appear to be improvement of its international standing, particularly with other African states, and avoidance of a Western embargo of its uranium exports, already in effect for the United States and likely to extend to Western Europe and Japan if South Africa is suspended from the IAEA. South Africa also would like to gain some assurance that its position in the IAEA is protected and that it would be able to participate in future General Conference meetings.[16] It is with respect to the latter concern that U.S. and Soviet diplomatic activity should be directed. Both countries must make a concerted effort to persuade the Group of 77 nations, which pushed for South Africa's suspension from the IAEA, that their security would be enhanced by strengthening the nonproliferation regime and making the NPT and the IAEA universal organizations.[17] The United States and the Soviet Union must also persuade South Africa that NPT membership is in the RSA's best interests and that, although the two powers cannot guarantee protection at the IAEA, South Africa's positive decision on the NPT would assist U.S.–Soviet efforts to depoliticize that body.[18]

The United States and the Soviet Union could also work toward the declaration of a nuclear-free zone in Africa. Both superpowers have endorsed the principle of nuclear-free zones as a nonproliferation measure. The Antarctic Treaty of 1959 and the Treaty of Tlatelolco are products of this convergence of interest. Without underestimating the difficulties of negotiating a comparable agreement for the African continent, more attention should be directed at the possibility of creating an African or sub-Saharan African nuclear-free zone. Should South Africa accede to the NPT, the prospects for a continentwide zone would improve. The major reservation is likely to come from the United States, which may be concerned about transit rights of nuclear-armed ships through the Suez Canal.

Soviet adherence to the seven-nation Delivery System Agreement would enhance Soviet–U.S. efforts in nonproliferation. In April 1987 seven countries—the United States, the United Kingdom, France, Italy, Japan, the Federal Republic of Germany, and Canada—reached an agreement to limit the export of critical equipment and technology for nuclear-capable missiles.[19] This agreement should make it more difficult for emerging nuclear states to obtain nuclear-capable delivery systems. At the present time, however, the missile technology control regime does not include a number of established missile suppliers, including the Soviet Union, or emerging or potential suppliers such as Brazil, India, Israel, and South Africa.[20] Soviet adherence to the new agreement to control missile technology would be a useful nonproliferation measure and one that could reduce the speed of nuclear weapons to the African continent.

In addition, the two powers could expand the focus and raise the level of bilateral consultations. As previously noted, U.S.–Soviet consultations on nonproliferation already take place in a number of bilateral and multilateral forums. To date, these consultations have tended to focus on technical issues rather than political ones. They also have rarely been the subject of high-level superpower deliberation. A successful U.S.–Soviet nonproliferation effort requires more attention to the political dimension of the spread of nuclear weapons, a dimension that can be effectively dealt with only by the highest political leadership.

CONCLUSIONS

Measures for U.S.–Soviet cooperation in nonproliferation are not without political costs. Soviet sensitivity to Third World charges of superpower collusion and discrimination, in particular, may inhibit cooperation even when the nonproliferation objectives of the Soviet Union and the United States coincide. Nevertheless, U.S. and Soviet perspectives on nonproliferation appear to be close enough to make significant cooperation possible, especially on the African continent.

NOTES

1. See William Potter, "Nuclear Export: A Soviet–American Comparison," in *Foreign Policy: USA/USSR,* Sage International Yearbook of Foreign Policy Studies, eds. Charles Kegley and Pat McGowan, (1982), 291–313; and Potter, "Nuclear Proliferation: U.S.–Soviet Cooperation," *The Washington Quarterly* (Winter 1985): 141–154.

2. May 1974, the date of the Indian nuclear explosion, was a critical juncture in the evolution of U.S. policy. The comparable learning experience for the Soviet Union was much earlier, in 1958, when the Chinese announced that they intended to produce their own nuclear weapons.

3. Not reflected in the table are the numerous African countries with demonstrated or estimated natural uranium reserves. They include, in reverse order of the size of reserve, South Africa, Niger, Namibia, Algeria, Gabon, Central African Republic, Zaire, Somalia, Egypt, Madagascar, and Botswana. See Daniel Poneman, *Nuclear Power in the Developing World* (London: George Allen & Unwin, 1982), 23.

4. See Leonard Spector, *Going Nuclear* (Cambridge, Mass.: Ballinger, 1987), 236–237.

5. Ibid., 222.

6. Cf. Mohammad Heikal, *The Cairo Documents* (New York: Doubleday, 1973); S. El-Hattab, *The Evolution of the Egyptian Military Doctrine: Some Factors Influencing Strategy and Defense Policy Toward Israel* (Ph.D. dissertation, Carleton College, 1976); Tunde Adeniran, "Nuclear Proliferation and Black Africa: The Coming Crisis of Choice," *Third World Quarterly* (October 1981): 673–683; Julius Emeka Okolo, "Nuclearization of Nigeria," *Comparative Strategy* 5, no. 2 (1985):

135–157; Robert D'A. Henderson, "Nigeria: Future Nuclear Power?" *Orbis* (Summer 1981): 409–423; Ronald W. Walters, *South Africa and the Bomb* (Lexington, Mass.: Lexington Books, 1987).

7. For accounts of Libya's attempts to acquire nuclear weapons see Steve Weissman and Herbert Krosney, *The Islamic Bomb* (New York: Times Books, 1981), and Zivia S. Wurtele et al., *Nuclear Proliferation Prospects for the Middle East and South Asia,* a report prepared for the U.S. Department of Energy by Pan Heuristics, June 1981, 2-24 to 2-29.

8. See Spector, *Going Nuclear,* 150–154.

9. For a discussion of the Soviet–Libyan nuclear relationship see Potter, "The Soviet Union and Nuclear Proliferation," *The Slavic Review* (Fall 1985): 477–481.

10. See, for example, J. S. Spence, "South Africa: The Nuclear Option," *African Affairs* 80, no. 321 (1981): 445–446; and Richard Betts, "A Diplomatic Bomb? South Africa's Nuclear Capabilities," in *Nonproliferation and U.S. Foreign Policy,* ed. Joseph A. Yager (Washington, D.C.: Brookings Institution, 1980).

11. Robert S. Jaster, "South Africa," in *Limited Nuclear Proliferation,* eds. Jed Synder and Samuel Wells, Jr. (Cambridge, Mass.: Ballinger, 1985), 170.

12. Ibid.

13. The option of offering South African security guarantees as a means to dissuade it from going nuclear, for example, is precluded by the need for the superpowers to distance themselves from the government in Pretoria. See Jaster, "South Africa," p. 172, on this point.

14. "Statement Issued by South African State President," *IAEA Newsbrief* (5 October 1987): 2.

15. See "IAEA Postpones Contentious Issues to Next Year's Meeting," *Nucleonics Week* (29 September 1988): 9–10. The Soviet Union was not prepared to support suspension of South Africa from the IAEA at the 1988 General Conference.

16. Although South Africa would undoubtedly like to regain a seat on the IAEA Board of Governors, it probably recognizes that this is impossible. These considerations were noted in a personal communication from David Fischer, who recently conducted a series of interviews in Pretoria and Vienna with very senior South African officials. See also David Fischer, "South Africa As a Nuclear Supplier," in *International Trade and Nonproliferation: The Challenge of Emerging Suppliers,* ed. William C. Potter (Lexington, Mass.: Lexington Publishers, 1990).

17. The Soviet Union voted to recommend suspension of South Africa at the June 1987 IAEA Board of Governors meeting, but altered its position at the September 1987 General Conference following the South African announcement.

18. The Soviet Union may be concerned that the suspension of South Africa from the IAEA would increase pressure to also suspend Israel, a move that would likely lead to U.S. withdrawal from the agency.

19. See Leonard S. Spector, "Nuclear Delivery Systems in the Threshold States," in *International Trade and Nonproliferation,* ed.William Potter, and Lewis Dunn, "Nonproliferation: The Next Steps," *Arms Control Today* (November 1987): 4.

20. Although South Africa does not now possess a missile delivery capability, it probably has the technological know-how to develop one. See Robert D. Shuey et al., *Missile Proliferation: Survey of Emerging Missile Forces* (Washington, D.C.: Congressional Research Service, October 1988).

21

Nuclear Nonproliferation in Africa

YEVGENY A. TARABRIN

By late 1987 the NPT had been signed by 137 countries. Apart from two nuclear powers (China and France), the treaty had not been signed by countries that either possess nuclear weapons or may possess them in the near future (India, Israel, Pakistan, Brazil, Argentina, and South Africa) and a number of others, including African countries (Algeria, Mozambique, Angola, Niger, Nigeria, Tanzania, Zambia, and Zimbabwe). Though the countries that have not signed the treaty form a minority, they account for 45 percent of the world's population.

Although there are only five nuclear powers, ammunition depots, command posts, communication centers, and other elements of nuclear war infrastructure are found in sixty-two countries, all oceans, and all continents except Antarctica. In addition, according to numerous reports, fissile material secretly moves from country to country and can be used to produce nuclear weapons. A black market supply of enriched uranium and plutonium, which could easily be used to produce military loads, cropped up in Khartoum, Sudan.

In 1988 Mikhail Gorbachev and Ronald Reagan met in Moscow and signed a document putting into force the INF Treaty. The public welcomed this act as a step made by the two great powers toward complete elimination of nuclear weapons. Three international forums held during the same period paid major attention to the nonproliferation of nuclear weapons. These were the Thirty-eighth Pugwash Conference (Dagomys, USSR, August–September 1988), the Conference of Foreign Ministers of Non-Aligned Nations (Nicosia, Cyprus, September 1988), and the forty-third session of the UN General Assembly.

The Pugwash Conference voiced serious concern over the fact that the NPT had not been backed by a number of states capable of producing nuclear weapons. This problem is to be considered at the next regular conference (they will be held every five years) of treaty participants in 1990 at Geneva.

The Non-Aligned conference stressed in its Final Document (35 and 36) that implementation of the declaration on nuclear-free zones would be a crucial measure to prevent proliferation of nuclear weapons in Africa. It also resolutely condemned the intention of South Africa's racist regime to have such weapons, as well as the assistance that certain NATO powers and Israel gave the regime. Such acts undermine the promise of keeping Africa as a nuclear-free zone, and compromise efforts at disarmament, conflict resolution, and security in the region. The ministers have called on the UN Security Council to take effective and concrete measures to prevent the South African regime from having nuclear weapons of its own. The Final Document reiterates once again that the issue of nonproliferation should not serve as a pretext for restricting the right of states to acquire and develop nuclear technologies for peaceful purposes.

Finally, in his statement at the forty-third session of the UN General Assembly, Soviet Foreign Minister E. A. Shevardnadze noted that the UN should be more deeply involved in the process of nuclear disarmament, achievement of universal agreement on the termination and banning of nuclear weapons testing, and creation of nuclear-free zones in different parts of the world.

All this is further proof of the timeliness of discussion of the problem within the framework of the project Soviet–U.S. Cooperation for Africa.

The acquisition of nuclear weapons by certain African countries is not as difficult as it may seem. Experts claim an atom bomb can be produced in laboratory conditions and does not need to be tested in a series of explosions.

The critical issue for concern remains the position of South Africa. The question goes beyond discussions of whether it has nuclear weapons or not. The point is that South Africa has the raw materials, technology, and trained personnel sufficient to produce a number of nuclear weapons. One should not ignore Pretoria's 1987 maneuver with respect to IAEA. To prevent its expulsion from IAEA, South Africa declared its readiness to sign the NPT. This would have placed uranium enrichment in that country under international control—South Africa went back on its word.

There are other issues related to the nonproliferation of nuclear weapons in Africa: the role of Africa in the production of nuclear weapons, and in their storage and transportation.

First, Africa accounts for over a third of the uranium available in the capitalist world. It is available to Western countries at $80 to $130 per kilogram. Second, such considerable stocks of uranium can, if appropriate technologies are developed on the spot or bought, increase the temptation to produce nuclear weapons or to sell uranium to countries that have not signed the NPT. Third, in view of the strategic position of Africa, the appearance of nuclear weapons, of whatever origin, in any one African country would trigger a chain reaction. It should be borne in mind that the continent is teeming with military installations.

Therefore, the proclamation of Africa as a nuclear-free zone assumes both continental and global importance and can contribute to the success of the inevitable process of elimination of nuclear weapons on the planet.

It should be stressed once again that restating the principles laid down in the NPT and strengthening the international regime for halting the spread of nuclear weapons would be a weighty contribution to the cause of peace and security. Nonproliferation of nuclear weapons is a sphere of mutual interest to the USSR and the United States and a good example of Soviet–U.S. cooperation.

The nonproliferation of nuclear weapons is an imperative demand of our time. It should be worked out today, because tomorrow may be too late. Ruling out the possibility of nuclear war between the great powers, it is vitally important to rule it out also in the Third World, including Africa.

PART 8

Arms Transfers

Developments in the 1980s have opened up possibilities for the Soviet Union and United States to cooperate effectively on arms transfers to Africa. Not only have the two countries themselves come to share the view that their activities in Africa (and elsewhere in the Third World) have an important bearing on their mutual relations, but many African states have been conscious of the problems of promoting economic development in the face of heavy military expenditures. Indeed, the GNP per capita of a large number of states has actually declined since the mid-1970s. Arms imports make up a substantial share of the military outlays for a high percentage of those states.

African–Soviet–U.S. cooperation in this area should follow several basic principles. Cooperation should be approached on a step-by-step basis, with modest and realizable goals. Efforts to engage in collaboration should focus initially on active conflict situations in which the Soviet Union and United States have at least an indirect involvement. Joint ventures in the realm of arms transfers must be treated as a component of an overall attempt to stabilize conditions in the places selected as targets of concentration. African states and governments there will resent and oppose undertakings that tend to have adverse effects on their own security and interests with no compensating merits. It should be made clear, however, that such a search for stability does not imply an endorsement of the political status quo. Rather political change through peaceful means should be encouraged. The Soviet Union and United States should also endeavor to incorporate other arms suppliers into their joint efforts at cooperation in the sphere of arms transfers. The two powers might also take the following steps:

• Publish data on their respective arms deliveries to Africa and other Third World countries and encourage the recipient countries to publish figures on both their total arms imports and the sources of those imports.

• Agree to devote their primary attention regarding arms transfers to the situations in the Horn of Africa and in southern Africa. These are the conflicts on the continent where the two powers have the greatest involvement and thus where the strongest potential for increased confrontation exists.

• Commit themselves to a fixed schedule of high-level consultations to monitor conditions in both the Horn of Africa and southern Africa. These consultations would provide a regular forum in which to discuss a whole range of stability-related issues, including arms transfers.

• Convene jointly with African nations representatives of current and potential arms suppliers to the African participants in the conflicts in the Horn of Africa and southern Africa. The attendees at this conference might seek to work out some qualitative restrictions on arms deliveries to these participants. Candidates for mutual exclusion could be items of advanced technological sophistication such as "smart" weapons, highly destructive weapons (e.g., multibarrel artillery pieces), advanced fighter and bomber aircraft, and intermediate-range missiles. To render these sorts of limitations more palatable to the particular African actors involved, the conferees might consider a ban covering the continent as a whole.

• Explore with other participants in such a conference how to cap the number of arms going to the African disputants in the Horn of Africa and southern Africa. Such a cap need not entail uniform restrictions on the quantities of arms that the various parties may receive; rather, the overall distribution of limitations should be designed to ensure a reasonable military balance in each region and to promise general regional stability.

• Mutually search for a joint mechanism through which the two powers could channel modest numbers of arms to Mozambique and perhaps other small countries in the two regions to improve these countries' defense capabilities, particularly to deal with internal military challenges. This mechanism might take the form of a special arrangement with the United Nations or the Organization of African Unity in which other powers could also participate; but determination of its exact nature may be left to negotiations between the two powers and other interested parties.

22

Cooperation on Arms Transfers to Africa

DAVID E. ALBRIGHT

Recent developments in the outlooks of the United States and the USSR, and in the situations of African countries, have greatly increased the possibilities for Soviet–U.S. cooperation on arms transfers to Africa. The United States and the USSR now share a common perspective on linkage between the state of their mutual relations on the one hand, and their undertakings in the Third World on the other. The two powers have long recognized that confrontation between them in the Third World could escalate to the nuclear level and have sought to forestall that possibility. But for many years they disagreed about the extent to which they could or should pursue activities in the Third World independently of their bilateral relations. Indeed, controversy over this issue played a major role in undermining détente between them in the 1970s. In the last half of the 1980s, however, both have come to accept that their behavior in the Third World has a critical impact on their mutual relations. Hence, they have concluded that any improvement in relations between them will depend in substantial degree on the nature of their interaction in the Third World.[1]

As for the African states, many now suffer from the burden of heavy military expenditures at the same time that they face serious problems with their economies. In 1985, according to U.S. estimates, thirty of the forty-eight countries for which data are available devoted 2 percent or more of their GNP to military expenditures, and of this total, eleven channeled 5 percent or more of their GNP into military outlays. Yet, twenty of the thirty states recorded lower GNPs per capita (in constant 1984 dollars) that same year than they had in 1975. Worse still, the 1985 figures on GNP per capita for fifteen of the twenty were less than $500.[2]

Arms imports accounted for a not insignificant portion of the average annual military expenditures (in constant 1984 dollars) of the central governments of virtually all thirty states during the first half of the 1980s. In six cases, the share did run less than 10 percent. But in nine others, it fell between 20 and 30 percent, and in another six, it was 30 to 50 percent. For the remaining nine countries, it exceeded 50 percent.[3]

COMPLICATING CIRCUMSTANCES

Some considerations pertaining to the United States and the attitudes and viewpoints of some African states, however, still make Soviet–U.S. cooperation on arms transfers to Africa difficult. Let us begin with those factors associated with the United States and the USSR directly.

Both powers today concur that neither has "vital" stakes in Africa (i.e., stakes that would justify going to war with the other to defend), but each also believes that it has "legitimate" interests on the continent and a role to play in its affairs.[4] Since Africa's transformation from largely colonial status to political independence commenced in the mid-1950s, the United States and the USSR have each established diplomatic links with the vast bulk of the countries on the continent; moreover, each power has forged close ties with a number of these countries and enjoys significant influence in them. Thus, no matter how much one power may agree or disagree with what the other defines as its own "legitimate" interests, neither will probably show much enthusiasm for measures that could weaken the position it now enjoys. To the extent that any Soviet–U.S. attempt to collaborate on arms transfers to Africa might entail curbs or controls on arms deliveries, this likelihood raises potential problems. Unless the steps involved promise to have no adverse effects, or at least equitable ones, there appears to be little chance that the two governments would acquiesce in such undertakings.

The asymmetries between the arms transfers of the United States and the USSR to Africa introduce further complexities into the situation. Throughout the 1980s, the USSR consistently delivered more arms to the continent than did the United States. According to U.S. calculations, those arms that the USSR supplied in 1982–1986 ran to about $191 billion in value, while those from the United States amounted to roughly $4.6 billion. Furthermore, the two powers have tended not to provide arms to the same African states. During 1982–1986, for instance, the USSR furnished arms to nineteen African countries, and the United States delivered arms to fifteen. But in only three cases—Algeria, Egypt, and Nigeria—was there overlap. No less striking, Nigeria constituted the only one of the three countries to which the two powers supplied arms worth about the same amount. Algeria got vastly more arms deliveries from the USSR than from the United States, while the reverse was true for Egypt.[5]

Such asymmetries would make working out a rational cap on arms transfers to Africa hard in practice even if the United States and the USSR proved amenable to this step in principle. Of perhaps greater consequence, the asymmetries would compound the possible problem of the differential in impact of such a cap on the two powers.

Even if the United States and the USSR consented to impose some mutual restrictions, other powers might move in to try to pick up the resulting slack. Certainly, the United States and the USSR are by no means the only sources of arms for countries on the continent at present. In 1982–1986, according to U.S. estimates, France shipped nearly $3.8 billion in arms to African states. The totals for China, the United Kingdom, and West Germany were about $1.2 billion, $1.0 billion, and $330 million, respectively. Equally telling, as arms suppliers these four powers constituted greater competitors to both the United States and the USSR than the two are to each other. France provided arms to twelve of the same African countries that the United States did; China, five; the United Kingdom, seven; and West Germany, six. As far as overlap with the USSR was concerned, France furnished arms to nine of nineteen Soviet clients; China, five; the United Kingdom, six; and West Germany, four.

In recent years, France and China in particular have looked upon arms they have sent abroad as revenue-producing items,[6] and many of the African countries to which the United States and the USSR delivered arms in the 1980s clearly do not have the resources to pay for all of them—at least over the short term. Nevertheless, states like Algeria, Libya, and Nigeria might conceivably afford France and China's lucrative markets for increased arms sales.

The prospect of adopting measures that could well be fruitless is enough to give both the United States and the USSR pause. This possibility might also cause additional misgivings, because measures to limit arms transfers inevitably entail a sacrifice of potential earnings of foreign exchange. Especially for the USSR, arms sales to African countries like Algeria and Libya have served as important sources of such earnings in the 1980s.

Soviet–U.S. cooperation on arms transfers to Africa, of course, could theoretically take forms other than mutual restraint on arms deliveries to the continent. The two powers might deem joint *supply* of arms desirable to ensure a military balance between two countries or within a region to promote stability. As noted earlier, neither the United States nor the USSR exercises total control over the flow of arms to the continent. Yet, such an undertaking would require the resolution of some thorny questions. A Soviet–U.S. decision to engage in a joint supply operation would probably come only if the proposed beneficiary or beneficiaries lacked the means to purchase the arms. In this case, presumably the two powers would share in the costs. But there would still be the question of who should provide what arms. In all likelihood no prospective recipient would welcome a mix of Soviet and U.S. arms of the same type (e.g., airplanes, rocket launchers, rifles) considering the problems of logistics, maintenance, and training that such a mix would create. Furnishing dissimilar arms, however, would require that the United States and the USSR arrive at some mutually acceptable method of determining the value of specific weapons and equipment. Otherwise, guaranteeing a just distribution of the burden of the venture is problematic. Furthermore, a Soviet–U.S. accord would have to be reached on how to prevent either power from acquiring undue leverage as a consequence of the precise kinds of arms delivered.

Turning to complicating factors related to the African states, there is, first of all, the risk that Soviet–U.S. attempts to collaborate would antagonize African governments. A substantial number of governments on the continent believe that they face external threats of one kind or another; not even their most severe critics would dismiss such judgments as sheer paranoia. In addition, the great bulk of African governments perceive actual or potential dangers from domestic sources. Their deliberately narrow political bases or their failure politically to integrate significant portions of the populaces of their countries, or both, have given rise to local opposition forces that question their legitimacy. Under such circumstances, many African governments might well see joint Soviet–U.S. restrictions on arms transfers to the continent as an intentional or unwitting threat to their security; and their negative reactions might be justified.

If African governments wished to circumvent Soviet–U.S. limitations on arms transfers in order to bolster their own security, most would also probably find it fairly easy to do. Of the forty-seven African states that obtained arms from abroad in 1982–1986, sixteen got none from either the United States or the USSR. Perhaps more directly to the point, only four of the thirty-one countries receiving arms from the United States or the USSR, or both, were totally dependent on the one or the other for their supplies. Three of these countries obtained arms from the USSR, while one bought them from the United States. Furthermore, only thirteen of the remaining twenty-seven states got more than half of their deliveries from either the United States or the USSR, or both together. In ten of these instances, the USSR provided all of the arms concerned; in two, the United States did; and in one, both furnished arms, although the USSR served as the primary source. Equally noteworthy, nine of the thirteen countries at issue received arms from one or more of the other main world arms suppliers besides the United States and the USSR. This pattern of arms transfers, then, makes it likely that few African countries would encounter difficulties in coming up with alternative sources.

Paying for arms from these other states could impede arms deals—particularly for African countries that need large quantities of arms and have a poor record of economic performance. After all, powers like France and China have placed a premium on arms sales that yield short-term economic returns. Nevertheless, even these powers have displayed an interest in increasing their average annual shares of the Third World arms market, and they might be willing to forgo some immediate benefits in the hope of reaping long-term rewards.

Finally, if the United States and the USSR agreed to cooperate with each other to curtail arms transfers to Africa, the states there might well ask the two powers to up their economic commitments to the continent commensurately. However logical and meritorious such a request might be in the abstract, neither the United States nor the USSR would necessarily accept such a linkage. Each confronts major problems in its own economy, and each has been seeking to reduce the costs of involvements abroad. Consequently, neither would in all likelihood welcome the idea of replacing old claims with new ones.

STRATEGY FOR COOPERATION

The foregoing considerations suggest several guidelines for successful U.S–Soviet collaboration on arms transfers to Africa. First, such collaboration should be approached as a step-by-step process. Attempting anything on a grand scale from the outset might shatter what is still a fragile foundation. The United States and the USSR lack experience in working together for common ends almost in any context, and they remain wary of each other. They need, therefore, to develop mutual confidence as they proceed to collaborate. Initially, limited goals that have the clear promise of being achievable should be established. Once defined objectives are attained, new ones of a more ambitious nature could be set. Joint efforts to realize these newly articulated goals, in turn, would afford opportunities for further confidence building on the part of the two powers. Over time, such a process could lead to both a widening and deepening of Soviet–U.S. collaboration in this area.

Second, Soviet–U.S. cooperation on arms transfers to Africa should focus to begin with on the continent's conflict situations in which both powers have at least an indirect involvement. Such situations produce the strongest incentives for the United States and the USSR to work together in the realm of arms transfers. Furthermore, this potential tends to reduce the significance of the disparities in quantities of arms that the United States and the USSR have been providing to the adversaries in these conflicts. This is especially true of conflicts in which the two powers have high political or strategic stakes.

Perhaps the situations that best meet the criteria are those in the Horn and in southern Africa (the region as a whole, not just Angola-Namibia). In the Horn, joint Soviet–U.S. undertakings to curb the flow of arms to Ethiopia and Somalia might facilitate dialogue and encourage political settlement of domestic turmoil in both states. As for southern Africa, an initiative by the United States and the USSR to put a cap on arms deliveries to the region might lesson tensions and permit more extensive negotiations on all sides. At the same time, strengthening the internal defense capabilities of some of the smaller countries in the region might have a positive effect, not only on their own stability, but also on the stability of the region at large.

Third, Soviet–U.S. collaboration on arms transfers to Africa should be linked with common measures designed to enhance stability on the continent. African attitudes toward such undertakings are plainly crucial. Not only could African governments or states decide to reject joint offers of arms, but probably most would manage to get around restrictions decreed by the two powers. In addition, transfers that caused African hostility toward either the United States or the USSR, or both, could wind up precluding further cooperation between the two in the area. Further, a decision by the United States and the USSR to work together—particularly to cut the flow of arms—might convince African states that the two powers were merely pursuing their own selfish interests. Steps to persuade African countries that their security concerns are taken into account are essential. Credibility might depend upon a framework of a range of measures to promote stability.

One word of caution is necessary, however. African governments and states must not be left with the impression that Soviet–U.S. collaboration means endorsement of the political status quo there. The possibility that unpopular governments might fall should be specifically acknowledged, and anticipated methods of governmental transitions might even be articulated. But the stress should be on change through basically peaceful means.

Enlisting the support of other major powers would undoubtedly prove easiest in instances where actual fighting was taking place on the continent. In such situations, the benefits to be derived from lessening tensions and moving disputes to the negotiating table are not hard to discern. Even in these cases, however, reasons for the strife and the proper resolution of it might be viewed differently. Thus, substantive accord with the United States and the USSR might be a price for acquiescing in Soviet–U.S. initiatives.

As to mechanisms of coordination with other powers, the United States and the USSR should show flexibility. Informal consultation might be sufficient and/or desirable in most circumstances. Nevertheless, the United States and the USSR should not oppose contacts of a more structured nature. Indeed, formal interaction under the auspices of international organizations such as the United Nations might even be attractive. Certainly such auspices would help allay fears that a Soviet–U.S. condominium with respect to Africa was emerging.

CONCLUSION

A few final observations seem in order. To begin with, Soviet–U.S. cooperation on arms transfers to Africa does not offer a panacea for instability and insecurity on the continent. Africans themselves have generated the disputes and conditions that have sent them in search of arms abroad. Only they can reconcile their differences and turn their energies and resources in more productive directions. What the United States and the USSR can do, at most, is to give contending local forces the chance to settle their problems themselves.

No less important, it would be naive to assume that Soviet–U.S. collaboration on arms transfers to Africa or in any other sphere of concern on the continent will stop all competition between the United States and the USSR. Nonetheless, such cooperation can reduce the dangers of military confrontation and channel the competition into less risky forms of action. That is an outcome that has unquestionable merit.

NOTES

1. Compare, for example, the address of Michael H. Armacost, U.S. under secretary of state for Political Affairs, to the General Federation of Women's Clubs, Grand Rapids, Michigan, 22 June 1988, on "Regional Issues and U.S.–Soviet Relations," *Current Policy*, no. 1089 (Washington, D.C., U.S. Department of State, Bureau of Public Affairs), with the interview by Professor V. S. Zorin, Soviet television and radio political observer, with Y. M. Vorontsov, USSR first deputy minister of Foreign Affairs, and K. N. Brutents, then deputy chief and now first deputy chief of the International Department of the Central Committee of the Communist party of the Soviet Union, on the "Studio 9" program, Moscow Television Service in Russia, 28 February 1988.

2. These statistics are derived from information in U.S. Arms Control and Disarmament Agency, *World Military Expenditures and Arms Transfers, 1987* (Washington, D.C., March 1988). For other sources of relevant data, see the 1987–1988 and 1988–1989 editions of *The Military Balance*, published by the International Institute for Strategic Studies in London, and the 1988 edition of *World Armaments and Disarmament: SIPRI Yearbook*, put out by the Stockholm International Peace Research Institute. These documents, however, do not constitute as rich a source of information as the U.S. Arms Control and Disarmament Agency document. Even though the estimates of the burden of military expenditures that their data yield do differ somewhat from those of the U.S. Arms Control and Disarmament Agency document, aggregation of the estimates from each of the three sources in terms of the broad categories used here reveals little, if any, variance among the three resulting sets of breakdowns.

3. This analysis is based on information in U.S. Arms Control and Disarmament Agency, *World Military Expenditures and Arms Transfers, 1987*. Its coverage of African states is more extensive than that of the 1988 edition of *World Armaments and Disarmament: SIPRI Yearbook*, the only other available source for such data.

4. Compare the speeches by Chester A. Crocker, U.S. assistant secretary of state for African Affairs, before the Council on Foreign Relations in New York, 5 October 1981, on "U.S. Interests in Africa," *Current Policy*, no. 330 (Washington, D.C., U.S. Department of State, Bureau of Public Affairs), and by George Schultz, U.S. secretary of state, before the Boston World Affairs Council in Boston, Massachusetts, 15 February 1984, on "The U.S. and Africa in the 1980s," *Current Policy*, no. 549 (Washington, D.C., U.S. Department of State, Bureau of Public Affairs), with the Soviet discussion on the "Studio 9" program cited in note 1.

5. This subsequent discussion of arms flows relies upon information in U.S. Arms Control and Disarmament Agency, *World Military Expenditures and Arms*

Transfers, 1987. No other source with such extensive, detailed data on arms transfers to African states exists. It should be underscored, however, that some of the data are estimates. The USSR and a number of other suppliers do not publish figures on their arms deliveries to African countries in general or to specific African countries, and some African states display equal reserve about the sources and amounts of arms that they receive from abroad. Thus, the absolute values set forth here and elsewhere in this chapter must be regarded as subject to a fairly substantial margin of error. Yet, the broad comparative judgments of the analysis appear beyond challenge. Indeed, all other available evidence (see the 1988 edition of *World Armaments and Disarmament: SIPRI Yearbook*) sustains these conclusions.

6. See Morton S. Miller, "Conventional Arms Trade in the Developing World, 1976–86: Reflections on a Decade," in U.S. Arms Control and Disarmament Agency, *World Military Expenditures and Arms Transfers, 1987*, 20–22.

23

Arms Transfers and Reductions in Africa's Military Spending

A. M. LISEVICH

Regardless of the form that they take, sales and grants of military aid contribute to the arms race on a global scale and sap resources that the developing countries need to overcome poverty. In the 1980s, yearly volumes of assorted arms transfers have amounted to $30–58 billion (as estimated in the 1986 prices), with the bulk of those arms supplied to Third World countries. West Germany, Italy, Great Britain, France, the Soviet Union, and the United States are six nations that supply 90 percent of those arms, the latter two countries accounting for up to two-thirds of the total.[1] Reductions in deliveries of conventional weapons would, no doubt, promote progress in global disarmament, cuts in military expenditure, and faster-paced social and economic development in the most backward regions of the planet.

Numerous research projects, books, articles, commission reports, decisions taken by various international organizations and forums, and statements issued by political figures treat the linkage between the cessation of the arms race and development mostly in terms of the need for the most advanced nations to reduce their military allocations and to transfer a part of the funds saved to developing countries. The world-scale expenditure of trilions of dollars for military purposes over the past few decades has, however, diverted attention from the growing military spending of developing nations.

Over the last two decades the growth rates of the Third World's arms race have outpaced those of advanced countries: developing nations accounted for 23 percent of the world's military budget expenditure in the mid-1980s.[2] Given the changing ratios between advanced and developing nations' military spending, it now appears that the traditional approach to the interrelation between disarmament and development needs revising. Problems relating to reductions in military allocations and to resource transfers should, it seems, be tackled comprehensively, with due attention allotted to the funds spent by developing countries on their armed forces and to their opportunities for reallocating those funds to development. We shall examine this problem as it relates to Africa.

Over a period of twenty years, from 1957 to 1977, the military spending of African LDCs shot up 15.7 times in real prices, while their proportion of global military expenditure grew from 0.4 to 3.5 percent. Excluding Egypt, Africa's military expenditure would multiply almost twenty-two times over during that period, climbing from 0.2 to 2.34 percent (a twelvefold increase) of the world's total.[3] Such trends should serve to put us on our guard, despite the fact that the original level of spending was very low.

In only the decade from 1976 to 1985 Africa's newly independent countries spent about $130 billion to equip and maintain their armed forces (these and all following figures are computed in 1980 constant prices). Following two decades of rapid and continuous increases, the record-breaking year of 1977 saw their military spending climb to $14.6 billion. In subsequent years, however, military spending in these countries showed a somewhat downward trend, with important exceptions. It amounted to $11.3 billion in 1985, down by 22.6 percent from the 1977 level.

At first glance, it may appear that the percentage of nonproductive expenditure has declined in most of these countries. But this view is refuted by even a cursory examination. Most of the funds saved on Africa's arms race are limited to Nigeria, which reduced its army's strength from 230,000 to 90,000 troops over those years: this accounts for $2.7 out of $3.3 billion saved throughout Africa. Excluding Nigeria, the decrease appears less impressive—only about 4.6 percent.[4] Therefore, we ought to talk in terms of unchanging military spending in Africa rather than of downward trends (see Table 23.1). And this persistent drain on resources should be considered in light of the continentwide economic crisis, including drought, hunger, rapidly growing foreign debts, and declines in real GNP per capita in the early 1980s.

Table 23.1
Military Expenditures in Some African Countries
(Millions of Dollars, 1980 Prices)

	1980	1981	1982	1983	1984	1985
Algeria	890	792	830	912	885	856
Egypt	1,464	1,488	1,679	1,883	1,948	1,868
Zimbabwe	459	361	395	384	328	321
Kenya	319	229	285	268	199	197
Libya	3,276	3,439	3,518	—	—	—
Morocco	1,118	1,140	1,187	1,329	953	969
Mozambique	97	114	127	200	209	211
Nigeria	2,613	2,077	1,639	1,326	810	608
Tunisia	194	256	539	549	573	680
Ethiopia	359	359	349	353	365	—
All newly liberated African nations	13,116	12,423	12,726	12,978	11,595	11,319
South Africa	3,106	2,915	2,884	3,127	3,222	3,248

Source: World Armament and Disarmament. SIPRI Yearbook-86, no. 4, 1986, 231–236.

Two factors are chiefly responsible for the fairly high and sustained levels of military spending in these countries (averaging about $13 billion a year over the last decade): (1) maintaining large regular armies (roughly in one out of every three or four countries), and (2) meeting the growing costs of continuously upgraded military equipment.

Over the last two decades the military buildup has been rapid and considerable in many African countries. The strength of African armed forces has grown many times over, as has their acquisition of modern weapons. Prior to the mid-1960s modern armies were built almost exclusively in North Africa, but since that time the remainder of the continent's states have been busy arming themselves. For instance, in 1966 the armies of only two African countries possessed tank units, but in 1981 18 national armies had such units in service. Over the same span of time, the number of African states having combat aircraft went up from 6 to 21, field artillery units from 7 to 36, and various armored vehicles from 13 to 36.[5]

Subsequent increases in armed strength were such that by the mid-1980s various indicators of military power for some national armies in Africa were comparable to those of industrially advanced countries, as may be seen in the following statistics. Egypt has more ground troops than does France, and almost twice as many as Britain. Somalia's field army has 1.5 times as many servicemen as the armies of Denmark and Norway combined. The Moroccan army numbers over three times as many troops as Portugal's. And Tunisia has more ground troops than Canada.[6]

It is only natural that in this age of scientific and technological progress the combat power of armed forces depends primarily on their combat equipment. The defense departments of numerous African countries seek to equip their troops with weapons that measure up to the standards of the times. For instance, Egypt's tank inventory, which numbered over 2,000 as of the mid-1980s, exceeded numerically that of any Western European country, with the single exception of West Germany. The Moroccan army has as many tanks as do the Portuguese and Norwegian armies taken together, and Somalia has as many as Denmark. Numerous countries focus on expanding their air forces. For instance, the number of Egyptian airmen exceeds that of any Western European country, and Egypt's (and Libya's) stock of combat aircraft is on a par with that of West Germany. To give another example, Morocco has more aircraft than Denmark.[7]

Egypt and Libya lead the continent in combat air power, having the most modern aircraft. As of the mid-1980s, Egypt's air force included over 100 French-made Mirage-5 fighter-bombers and 40 U.S.–manufactured F-16 fighters. At that time another 80 F-16s were on order from the United States, as were 40 Mirage-2,000 fighters from France, with plans calling for the purchase of an additional 40.

Numerous countries on the African littoral have naval fleets capable of guarding their coastlines rather effectively. As a rule, these navies include missile-carrying vessels, speedboats for guarding coasts, small antisubmarine ships, and mine sweepers. Some North African countries have an offensive capability, as well. For example, in addition to its auxiliary ships, Egypt has over 160 attack craft, including 14 submarines, and 10 destroyers. The Libyan navy has 8 submarines, and 8 frigates and corvettes.

Experts maintain that the six militarily strongest states in Africa are Egypt, Libya, Algeria, Morocco, Ethiopia, and Nigeria. Most of the continent's armored units, combat aircraft, and naval forces are amassed in those countries. Nine other countries—Somalia, Angola, Kenya, Tunisia, Sudan, Tanzania, Mozambique, Zimbabwe, and Zaire—have the potential to conduct intensive combat operations on a subregional scale, but their military power is largely inferior to that of the six states noted previously. Yet another ten to twelve states in Africa have armed forces capable of conducting effective defense. The armies in the more than twenty remaining countries are used mostly to maintain law and order domestically.[8]

Thus, over the last two decades the military capability of Africa's newly liberated countries has undergone considerable differentiation. According to some observers, the difference in levels of military power has so far not resulted in the use of force against weaker neighbors, but one should not rule out a likely situation where this asymmetry may become a source of some instability.

Most African countries have no capacity to manufacture their own weapons, except for some countries in North Africa. Egypt, in particular, is engaged in assembling or manufacturing some licensed types of aircraft; produces some types of missiles, artillery systems, and munitions; and has plans for manufacturing U.S.–licensed tanks (Abrahams M-1s). All in all, Egypt's military industries employ over 80,000 people, but large as it is by African standards, its military-industrial complex is not able to meet the country's armed forces needs. These gaps are filled with imports of weaponry.

According to the computations of foreign experts, from 1966 to 1985 African imports of modern weapons totaled over $21 billion (in 1975 constant prices and excluding Egypt), amounting to $7.1 billion from 1981 to 1985 alone. Over those years six African states topped the list of the twenty principal arms importers of the Third World. Egypt holds second place on the list. The total worth of major weapons delivered to the continent's newly independent countries exceeded $11.5 billion, or 27.1 percent of the total expenditure incurred by all developing nations.[9] As a result, Africa has taken first place in terms of the Third World's per capita arms purchases. Imports of highly expensive weapons create shortages of African currency reserves. According to some computations, since the mid-1970s the cost of weapons imports in Africa has been in the range of 6 to 10 percent of total imports, accounting for up to one-third of machines and transport equipment delivered.[10]

The desire to maintain massive and well-equipped armed forces causes some African countries to incur expenditures comparable to those of individual industrially advanced nations. Thus, the absolute amount of either Morocco's or Algeria's military expenditure exceeds that of Portugal; Egypt spends more money than Denmark or Norway; Libya's military allocations outpace those of Greece and Turkey. But it should be borne in mind that African countries have much smaller economic resources than those of higher income. And in terms of their GDP, numerous African countries spend a far larger portion of their national resources for military purposes than industrially advanced countries. For instance, while the NATO member countries have only four states that spend more than 5 percent of their GDP on the military (the United States, spending 5.6 to 6.9 percent in the early half of the 1980s; Great Britain and Turkey, spending 4.8 to 5.4 percent each; and Greece, spending 5.7 to 7.0 percent), Africa has nine such countries, with Libya and Mozambique spending up to 12 to 14 percent of their GDP.[11]

Such considerable amounts of nonproductive expenditure serve only to aggravate the crisis affecting Africa's economies. Over the last ten to twelve years there has been an obvious correlation between the amounts spent on military needs and the growing total of African nations' foreign debts. These countries' military allocations are almost twice as much as the official aid granted on easy terms to Africa by the world community. If just one-half of those resources had been invested rather than spent on Africa's arms race over the last decade, production would have grown by $20 billion a year, as against the current level. This amount would be sufficient to have 30 million hectares of arid land irrigated, making it possible to feed up to 200 million people.[12] According to the calculations made by the ECA, foreign financial resources to the tune of $35.8 billion will be needed from 1986 to 1990 for Africa's economies to survive the present crisis.[13] The amount is just a little more than one-half of the sum African countries will be spending on their military requirements over the same period, unless effective measures are taken to reduce their budget allocations for that purpose.

Leaders of the majority of African countries are aware that nonproductive spending depletes their already scarce financial resources. The documents prepared by the OAU indicate that military allocations should be reduced.[14] Meanwhile, those resolutions are hardly implementable until African leaders take joint political action to reduce the strength of their armed forces to the minimum needed for defense and to stop increasing the importation of high-cost modern weapons.

The USSR, the United States, France, and Great Britain, the continent's major suppliers of weapons, could help considerably in this regard. Their joint action to restrict arms transfers to African countries could contribute to lowering the levels of military confrontation in the region. Invitations to attend negotiations on these problems, if extended to representatives from African countries, would clear the way for local agreements to be concluded on arms importation control and arms reduction. Such agreements should also seek to ban arms supplies from third parties. The Soviet Union is pressing for restrictions in the sales and deliveries of conventional weapons.

NOTES

1. *United Nations and Disarmament: A Short Historical Review* (New York, 1988), 87.

2. *Disarmament.* A periodic review prepared by the United Nations, vol. 9, no. 2 (New York, 1986), 259.

3. *Globalnye problemy sovremennosti i Afrika* (Moscow, 1983), 65–66.

4. *SIPRI-86* (New York, 1986), 231–236.

5. *African Armies: Evolution and Capabilities* (Boulder and London, 1986), 96.

6. *Zarubezhnoe voennoe obozrenie* (Moscow, 1985), 49 (no. 1); 47 (no. 2).

7. Ibid., 49, 64–68 (no. 1); 47, 66–67 (no. 2).

8. *SIPRI-85* (London, 1985), 304–305.

9. *SIPRI-86,* 342–344, 354–355.

10. *SIPRI-85,* 303.

11. Ibid., 281–283.

12. *Militarism. Tsifry i fakty* (Moscow, 1985), 238.

13. Africa's submission to the special session of the United Nations General Assembly on Africa's Economic and Social Crisis, vol. 1 (Addis Ababa, OAU/ECM/2xV/Rev. 1 1986), 37.

14. Ibid., 18.

24

Arms Transfers to Africa

SAMUEL M. MAKINDA

The term "arms transfer" is used here to refer to the flow of weapons and military technology from outside Africa to the continent. Most of the arms suppliers are industrialized countries, but in recent years they have been joined in the arms business by some Third World countries. Arms can be financed by military sales or grants, and they may be given in the form of services or equipment.

Over the past three decades, arms transfers to Africa have undergone various quantitative and qualitative changes. They increased dramatically in the 1970s, but according to some observers, arms transfers to Africa, and indeed to the entire Third World, have dropped in the 1980s, partly because of adverse economic conditions in Third World countries. Indeed, not only has the volume of arms sent to the Third World been changing, but so has their quality. The surge in Third World arms buying in the 1970s and early 1980s was accompanied by an increase in the sophistication of the weapons being acquired.

This chapter seeks to explain the main causes and consequences of arms transfers to Africa. It also suggests ways, through confidence building, of reducing the urge to acquire large quantities of armaments.

OVERVIEW

The transfer of military items and services is, in itself, neither good nor bad. The *uses* to which those arms are put determine whether a particular arms transfer is desirable. The effects of armaments on any region depend on various factors: (1) the sociopolitical character of the region, (2) the motives and influence of the suppliers, and (3) the intentions of the recipients.

In general terms, armaments often provide a means by which nations may achieve security or stability, or maintain their sovereignty. They can also be the means—as is often the case in some Third World areas—by which some regions are destabilized and some nations lose their territorial integrity. Whether arms are utilized as a means of attaining one goal or the other depends on the nature of the situation and the intentions of the parties involved. Armaments can be used by great powers to establish domination over weaker or smaller nations. But they can also be used by small nations or groups of people to defend or advance their freedom. In the nineteenth century, Europeans used superior weapons and organizational skills to conquer and subdue Africans. But a century later, African guerrilla forces in some parts of the continent used weapons, in addition to unconventional organizational skills and high morale, to drive the Europeans out of Africa.

In the past three decades, arms transfers to Africa appear to have played positive as well as negative roles. Foreign-supplied arms have been used in military takeovers and in all conflicts within Africa since the 1960s. The Nigerian civil war in the 1960s, liberation wars in southern Africa, conflicts in Uganda, wars in the Horn of Africa, and the conflict in Chad, have all been waged with arms obtained from outside the continent.

But it would not be accurate to argue that these conflicts emerged solely *because* of the availability of arms. The majority of these conflicts stemmed largely from underlying social, political, cultural, and economic factors. The availability of arms, however, not only determined the intensity of the conflicts, but also influenced the methods of resolving them. If the past has anything to teach us, it is that in the future arms will continue to play both negative and positive roles in Africa.

How can African states and their arms suppliers help reinforce the positive while reducing the negative attributes of arms transfers? This goal requires a recognition of the many sociopolitical and economic problems that African states face and of the need to address the symbiotic relationship between the traditional suppliers, who are largely outsiders, and the consumers of armaments, who are Africans.

William J. Foltz and Henry S. Bienen have perceptively observed Africa's dilemma in relation to arms transfers. They argue that increased arms transfers to the continent in recent years have been both a function of Africa's weaknesses and a reflection of some "newfound strengths":

> It is Africa's military weakness that has brought outsiders—as arms merchants, mercenaries, training teams, expeditionary forces and superpowers offering economic and military protection in exchange for military facilities. But some [previously] weak African states have now built up armies strong enough to threaten their neighbors, in effect strong enough to overthrow governments not their own.[1]

This statement suggests that to understand the level and intensity of arms transfers to Africa, one needs to examine at least three factors: the quest for arms by African states, the nature of inter- and intra-African relations, and the willingness by outsiders not only to meet the desire for armaments, but also to exploit the situation in Africa to their own advantage.

QUEST FOR ARMS

As it has already been argued, the quest for arms by a country's leaders cannot realistically be condemned outright, and increased arms transfers do not always automatically increase the risk of war. Historically, armaments have been a means by which international changes—both positive and negative—have been achieved. In Africa, armaments have been one of the means by which some colonized people have achieved their independence and realized their dignity. Nations have sought arms to secure their freedom or maintain their territorial integrity. The quest for arms to enhance national or regional stability or improve national security is, therefore, potentially positive—at least within the parameters of a still-Hobbesian world and despite the ideals of the OAU. The main difference between the role of arms in some parts of postindependence Africa *now* and their role in most developed countries is that in the already developed world, arms tend to enhance the political and territorial status quo. However, in some parts of Africa, arms have had the effect of changing the status quo, undermining still-fragile national independence and threatening the system of states. In developed countries, weapons have been used to assert independence; in Africa, weapons use has too often resulted not in independence but in a dependence—on foreign arms suppliers.

There is no doubt that arms transfers to Africa have occurred because African leaders or liberation movements have requested them. In the case of nations, leaders or statesmen have sought weapons for different reasons. Some leaders have sought them for traditional security reasons, that is, for reasons that can best be understood within the traditional international relations framework of competing interests and self-preservation. They would like to build up large military forces with a view to providing their own—personal, regime, and/or national—security.

The term "security" and its implications at the national or regional level are sometimes difficult to define. When African leaders talk of the need for national security, do they imply primarily the defense of the whole nation-state or the survival of the ruling faction? The second part of this question would not arise as easily in the case of genuinely democratically elected leaders, but in situations where the leaders do not have the mandate of the majority of the people they govern—as is so common in Africa—the term "security" is often used to denote the self-preservation of a particular ruling group. For some African leaders, their main adversaries are their fellow rival politicians. Indeed, in some African states, the search for national security focuses on the security of particular sets of politicians or special privileges for certain ethnic groups. Yet, it has become increasingly apparent that in some states, the preservation of a particular regime may exacerbate rather than alleviate real national security problems.

In a case where a state's borders are threatened by an external force, the need for weapons appears more legitimate. The trouble is that there is no clear way of determining how much military power is "enough." Even when the level of armaments acquired by a "threatened" state is considered adequate, there is, in practice, no correlation between quantities of weapons and military success. In other words, the accumulation of more arms, though they may deter an attack, does not necessarily ensure defeat of the adversary, and may increase internal security problems for an extraordinarily powerful army. The quest for arms in Africa has not been limited to legitimate security needs. Some statesmen who already have what would be considered reasonable levels of weapons for legitimate security needs have sought even more arms, basically for reasons of prestige. They may seek sophisticated weapons with a view to enhancing their international status; they may also want to display some of the best military equipment during the national day parade. The arms-buying sprees of many African nations in the 1970s were not entirely for reasons of internal order or self-defense. Some of the items they bought were for display: the desire to see a fly-past by a F-5 rather than a Strikemaster aircraft; or a desire to display T-62 rather than T-34 tanks. The net effect is that the money that could have been spent on development projects is diverted to prestigious military items, and this contributes to the economic stagnation of some countries.

INTER- AND INTRASTATE RELATIONS

Another significant factor that has led to arms transfers to Africa, and is likely to do so in the future, is the nature of interstate and intrastate conflicts. Some of the conflicts that continue to afflict Africa are a consequence of colonialism, which left fragile African state boundaries and which often divided nations between two or more states. Although colonialism has receded into history, conflicts in Africa range from internal disputes in which some ethnic groups may seek secession, dominance, or regional autonomy, to nationalist guerilla wars in southern Africa. Groups seeking secession often do so for various ethnic, cultural, economic, ideological, or historical reasons. The Nigerian civil war from 1967 to 1970, for instance, stemmed largely from ethnic differences.

The Ethiopian-Eritrean war is based on historical, ideological, and nationalistic factors. Eritrea, which was an Italian colony from the 1890s until World War II, was federated with Ethiopia under UN auspices in 1952. Ten years later, Ethiopian Emperor Haile Selassie dismantled the federal structure and reduced Eritrea to the status of a province within a unitary structure. Since the 1960s, Eritrean guerrillas have been waging war to try to regain their autonomy, if not full independence. Ethiopian leaders, however, have felt that the loss of Eritrea would undermine Ethiopia's integrity and encourage other ethnic groups in the country to seek secession. They have accordingly refused to grant Eritrea autonomy.

Another major conflict in the Horn since the 1960s has been the Somali-Ethiopian dispute, which has revolved around irredentist demands by the Somalis. Somalia's leaders have claimed that the Somalis were one nation until they were colonized in the nineteenth century by Ethiopia on the one hand, and by Britain, France, and Italy on the other. Ethiopia's leaders have, however, consistently refused to give up or even discuss the future of the Ogaden region, again for reasons of territorial integrity. Thus, in the Ogaden, as in Eritrea, Tigre, and some other parts of Ethiopia, there is a clash between demands for popular self-determination and the state's imperative to maintain territorial integrity.

In the 1960s and 1970s, Somalia accumulated weapons with a view to "liberating" the Ogaden from Ethiopia and expanding its borders into a Greater Somalia nation, and during those two decades it went to war with Ethiopia twice. Somalia also laid claim to northeastern Kenya, which is inhabited by ethnic Somalis, and that claim had the effect of persuading Kenya to seek an alliance with Ethiopia in 1977. This is a classic case where regional differences led to a "regional arms race" and resulted in a serious war that, in turn, had a negative impact on superpower relations.

Thus, Ethiopia had its borders threatened by both Somali and Eritrean nationalists. Given the nature of Ethiopia's problems, its leaders stop at nothing to increase their military force. Indeed, there have been strong arguments to the effect that Ethiopia has legitimate defense needs to protect its borders and maintain internal order. But some of the military hardware it has been acquiring in recent years has found its way—presumably intentionally—into the hands of rebel forces challenging governments in the neighboring states of Somalia and Sudan. In such a case, arms, which might have been provided strictly for purposes of internal order and self-defense, have had a strong bearing on the stability of other countries in the region. It appears, then, that the accumulation of weapons in the Horn by one state often creates insecurity for other states in the region. In the Horn, weapons have become both the result and the cause of conflict.

In southern Africa, especially Angola, Mozambique, Namibia, and South Africa, wars of liberation and civil wars have been going on since the 1960s. Most of these conflicts could conceivably be resolved peacefully, but because there has been no political will on the part of one or both sides to seek a political solution, at least until late 1988, the resort to arms has often become very attractive. In all of these conflicts, the combatants have sought outside military assistance.

In recent years, military spending in Africa appears to have decreased, for several reasons. The most critical of these has been the rapid decline in the prices of export commodities, which, in turn, led to internal budget deficits and growing foreign debt. African states have continued to pay higher prices for their imports at a time when their export revenues have been declining. The policies of international economic institutions such as the World Bank and the IMF have also played a significant role in reorienting the import patterns of most African countries. This factor is important because virtually all African states purchase the bulk of their weapons from abroad and pay for them in hard currency. Nigeria's defense budget, for instance, has declined from 975.7 million naira in 1985 to 809.80 million naira in 1987. The drop looks much more dramatic in U.S. dollars, having declined from $1.106 billion in 1985 to $202.13 million in 1987 (the Nigerian currency was devalued several times in the mid-1980s). Some of the major recipients of U.S. arms in Africa, including Egypt, Morocco, Sudan, and Zaire, also have fallen behind in their payments of U.S. government-guaranteed military loans or have had their loans rescheduled.

In some cases, armaments have tended to undermine stability by helping to cause economic stagnation or collapse. Because of the existence of various economic constraints, absolute reductions in military spending have not necessarily led to the relative redistribution of resources to other sectors of the economy. In other words, the economic burden of military expenditures, measured as a percentage of GNP, has not gone down.

The decline in arms transfers to Africa in the 1980s is also due to institutional factors. The military forces of some African nations have had to be retrained in order to operate, maintain, and repair the new sophisticated armaments. This process often takes several years, especially in countries that do not have well-developed industrial infrastructures and have not had experience in deploying high-technology military equipment.

ARMS SUPPLIERS

The interests of arms suppliers have also been a significant factor behind arms transfers to Africa. The motives behind arms transfers include the desire by countries that supply arms to exercise or enhance political influence in Africa and the need of arms manufacturers to make economic gains and to cover the costs of research and development.

The leading outside arms suppliers to Africa include the United States, the Soviet Union, Britain, and France. The latter two still retain important political, cultural, economic, and military interests in the continent. France is, in fact, one of the leading weapons suppliers to Africa. West Germany and Italy have also exported limited quantitites of weapons to Africa and other parts of the Third World. Other outside arms suppliers to Africa include Israel, China, Sweden, Brazil, South and North Korea, Poland, and Czechoslovakia.

But the most conspicuous arms suppliers to the continent are the superpowers. The Soviet Union and the United States have in the past supplied weapons to African states partly to satisfy demands for such arms in the continent, and partly to further their own interests. It could be argued that both superpowers have been involved in Africa for pragmatic political, economic, ideological, military, and strategic reasons. Superpower involvement in Africa is also determined by constant innovation in military and industrial technology and Africa's proximity to other areas of economic importance or to vital routes to those areas. In recent years, the United States and other Western powers have been redefining their security priorities in terms of access to energy resources of the Persian Gulf and strategic raw materials in southern Africa. By arming African nations, the super-powers—and other industrialized countries—seek primarily to protect their own interests and those of their African friends and secondarily to deny any advantage to the rivals.

Both superpowers have also sought to establish or have access to military facilities in Africa as an effective way of projecting their military power in the continent or of preempting that of the other. The United States has had access to military facilities in various countries, including Egypt, Kenya, Morocco, and Somalia. Most of these were negotiated in 1980 following the 1979 Soviet intervention in Afghanistan. These facilities were related to arms transfers, because the United States paid for their use indirectly, through military and economic assistance to host nations. Until 1985, Egypt, Kenya, Morocco, and Sudan received increasing amounts of military assistance from the United States for allowing U.S. military forces access to their facilities. And, according to various U.S. government offi-cials, these facilities had little to do with Africa itself. They were aimed at enhancing U.S. capability to compete with the Soviet Union in areas *adja-cent* to Africa. It was in this light that Chester Crocker, the assistant secre-tary of state for African Affairs, in testimony to a House subcommittee on foreign operations in April 1983, said:

> Our strategic interests in the Horn of Africa are strictly corollary to our broader interests in Southwest Asia and the Indian Ocean, and our military activity in the Horn, including our acquisition of access rights in Kenya and Somalia, is directed at protecting these larger interests.[2]

The Soviet Union also has maintained some military facilities in Africa over the years: in Egypt until 1972; in Somalia until 1977; and currently in Ethiopia. In all these cases, the Soviet Union has provided the host nations with large quantities of weapons. Although the actual amount of the Soviet Union's military assistance to its African friends is difficult to know, U.S.

government sources have estimated that the total Soviet military assistance to Ethiopia between 1977 and 1982 was over $2 billion.

Like the United States, the Soviet Union's military activities in Africa appear to have been driven by pragmatic military and political interests, as well as a broad strategic view of the Third World. But they have also been opportunistic to a considerable extent. Increased Soviet military activities in Africa coincided with the time when the Soviet Union became a global military power in the 1970s. This also was the time when the Soviets responded to "revolutionary" processes in Africa by exploiting targets of opportunity through low-risk and low-cost adventures or via proxies.

In the eyes of the superpowers, however, Africa ranks lowest in terms of strategic priorities. But this fact has not hindered them, until recently, from competing for influence in the continent. The involvement of the superpowers in Africa has meant that African conflicts could have repercussions far beyond the continent's shores. The combined Soviet-Cuban involvement in the Angolan civil war in 1975–1976 had the effect of changing the U.S. perception of détente; their involvement in the Somali-Ethiopian war in 1977–1978 had a negative impact on superpower relations, including arms control. It was partly for that reason that Zbigniew Brzezinski, President Carter's national security adviser (1977–1981), argued that "SALT lies buried in the sands of the Ogaden."

Other arms suppliers, who are likely to continue to play an increasingly important role in arms transfers, are African states themselves. It has been claimed by various Western governments and the media that Libya has built a chemical weapons factory, which, if true, portends serious security problems for Africa. There is no doubt that chemical weapons produced in Libya would be cheaply acquired by various combatants in African conflicts.

Some African countries, especially Egypt and South Africa, have become important small arms suppliers. Egypt's arms supplies fall into two categories: indigenously produced arms and old weapons, some of them supplied by the Soviet Union in the late 1960s and early 1970s. Egypt is one of those Third World countries that view the establishment of military industries as a useful mechanism for spurring the development of high-technology civilian industries. It also appears to perceive arms sales as a promising vehicle for improving its international trade position. But although the establishment of a domestic arms industry may generate con-siderable export earnings, it also requires a very substantial level of capital investment and can result in continued dependence on the major industrial powers for specialized technical products and services.

South Africa is another growing arms supplier in Africa. As a virtual pariah state, South Africa appears to have developed an indigenous military industry in order to circumvent or compensate for the international arms embargo that has been imposed on it since the 1970s. South Africa is the only country in Africa whose military industry appears to have clearly benefited the "national," predominantly white-run, economy. The small wars that have been going on in southern Africa for many years have provided a market for small arms, ammunition, and other combat items, which South Africa can easily satisfy, to groups such as UNITA in southern Angola.

A discussion of arms transfers to Africa must consider the indigenous arms suppliers who are likely to play increasingly important roles in future small wars. Many belligerents in recent wars in the Third World have discovered that high-technology weapons have not always performed as well in combat as in peacetime exercises. They have found also that many high-technology weapons require elaborate maintenance work, which most African countries cannot afford, especially in wartime. For these reasons, many African nations or potential guerrilla groups are likely to resort to cheaper, low-technology weaponry, which can be provided by African or other Third World arms suppliers.

WHAT IS TO BE DONE?

Arms transfers to Africa have, in the past three decades, been generally sustained by symbiotic relationships between the suppliers and the consumers of these commodities. Traditional concerns for security, interstate and intrastate conflicts, and the superpowers' desire for influence have interacted to sustain this trade in arms. The size and cost of the military in an African country—as elsewhere—ought reasonably to be related primarily to clear defensive needs, namely, to the likelihood of threats from neighbors or from domestic dissidents, provided the government is itself legitimate.

Now, what is to be done? As long as the possession of arms is deemed indispensable by African governments, which is the case and may remain so for a long time, no amount of effort from the superpowers and other outside suppliers alone will stop them completely from acquiring weapons from other sources. It appears that the most effective measures to reduce the incentive for acquisition of large quantities of arms in Africa have to aim at resolving the political, economic, social, cultural, and ideological problems that make the importation of armaments imperative.

Some of the practical steps that could be taken to reduce the need for weaponry—sophisticated or otherwise—in Africa would involve the establishment of a series of confidence-building measures. Such measures could include the publication of data on military expenditures, the withdrawal of troops from border zones, the notification of military exercises in border areas, and the establishment of direct and rapid communication systems between the states concerned. Provided most governments themselves become increasingly stable and legitimate, these measures are likely, in the long run, to increase trust among neighboring states and facilitate the peaceful settlement of disputes. These measures could also facilitate the redefinition of the strategic environment in terms that would make it less threatening and thus strengthen the case for low levels of armaments. In eastern Africa, the United States has encouraged cooperation between Kenya and Somalia since the early 1980s, and these two neighbors have in the last few years been establishing confidence-building measures between them.

The effectiveness of confidence-building measures in any African region will depend, of course, on the removal of some of the basic sociopolitical and economic roots of instability. Without the alleviation of these problems, confidence-building measures would soon run into difficulties. Moreover, these measures would be conceivable largely within the framework of the OAU and based on solid international security guarantees. This means that the cooperation of the superpowers and other arms suppliers is necessary to help African states resolve their internal or regional problems. In recent years, pragmatically, such superpower cooperation has become more possible.

Perceptions and misperceptions are perpetual problems in international politics. Nations usually take actions to advance their goals as defined and perceived by their leaders. But, while leaders may base their decisions on objective factors, they also make judgments on the basis of their values and perceptions, often subjectively perceived intentions and values. Since values take a long time to change, confidence-building measures, too, may take long to bear fruit. The time to start moving is now.

NOTES

1. William J. Foltz and Henry S. Bienen, eds., *Arms and the African: Military Influences on Africa's International Relations* (New Haven: Yale University Press, 1985), xi.

2. Statement by Honorable Chester A. Crocker, assistant secretary of state for African Affairs, before the Subcommittee on Foreign Operations of the House Committee on Appropriations, 26 April 1983, in *Foreign Assistance and Related Programs Apropriations for 1984,* hearings before a subcommittee of the Committee on Appropriations, House of Representatives (Washington, D.C.: U.S. Government Printing Office), 304.

PART 9

Development and Security
in Southern Africa

The presence of a dominant power in southern Africa, the Republic of South Africa, creates special problems and needs for the development and security of the region's states. In particular, South Africa attempts to contain the political, economic, and military independence of neighboring states, without regard to ideological preference. Estimates of the loss to these countries of South African destabilization are as high as $30 billion in national income (GDP) for the period 1980–1986. In recent years the Soviet Union and United States have been perceived in world opinion as the principal allies of antagonists in the area, yet their competitive conduct in southern Africa has netted them no substantial gains. Indeed, the countries of the region have a shared history of relations with both East and West in which a policy of nonalignment and political toleration has become an important building block of regional unity.

Soviet–U.S. cooperation for development and security in southern Africa can take place through joint commitment to both political and economic objectives, and by building on the desire of the region's countries for productive assistance without having to take sides in global rivalries. The political role that African–Soviet–U.S. cooperation is best suited to play is in connection with a dismantling of apartheid and the enhancing of security throughout the region. The Soviet Union and the United States can offer security assistance to specific countries and encourage the disengagement of antagonistic forces. Economically, African–Soviet–U.S. cooperation can provide resources and expertise. Specifically, Soviet–U.S. cooperation could take the following forms:

• The Soviet Union and the United States could make clear their commitment to peaceful resolution of crises in southern Africa and their intent no longer to be drawn into regional disputes on opposing sides. This could be accomplished through a joint statement and declaration on the principles of political settlement regionally and in specific areas. The effect of such a statement would be to dispel the perception, on which regional antagonists have thrived, of southern Africa as a compartmentalized battleground of conflicting global ideologies.

• With respect specifically to Namibia, the smoothness of the anticipated transfer of power may well depend in part on signals given by the Soviet Union and the United States concerning their likely response in the event of any attempt to circumvent the agreed procedures. There will also be a great need for economic assistance of all kinds during the period of transition, including the human needs of refugees and war victims, and the provision of financial and technical assistance, and support for a new government coping with the requirements of a transitional economy. In addition, steps should be taken to ensure against attempts by South Africa to return in force militarily to Namibian territory.

• Specific attention ought also to be accorded Mozambique, whose security and economic development has implications for the region as a whole. In particular, Soviet–U.S. cooperation should focus on enhancing the security and development of transport; developing agriculture, industry, and manufacturing; and alleviating Mozambique's debt burden. To these ends, the Soviet Union and United States should establish a commission to explore the potential for collaboration in the reconstruction of Mozambique.

• In the region as a whole, African–Soviet–U.S. cooperation should seek ways, possibly in conjunction with the SADCC, of improving infrastructural development, and reducing or canceling the debt burden of regional countries. Humanitarian assistance, in particular, should be forthcoming to groups affected by the instability of the region.

25

Southern Africa in the
Context of Soviet–U.S. Relations

VLADIMIR B. KOKOREV

The problems of southern Africa constitute a most intricate set of international tensions. One recent publication has claimed that there are no longer any direct or indirect conflicts between the Soviet Union and the United States in Africa, nor contradictions that could be an obstacle to their cooperation in rendering assistance to the continent.

While encouraging, such statements should not lull us. In certain conditions developments in southern Africa may bring to naught all our efforts to establish Soviet–U.S. cooperation on the continent. Though neither country desires such an outcome, declarations of goodwill are insufficient, on their own, to avoid it. New ideas and solutions are needed to rule out the slightest chance of a Soviet–U.S. clash in southern Africa. The declarations of the two countries to the effect that they have no special interests in that region are a weak guarantee against such a clash. The experience of preceding decades shows that we have often found ourselves on opposite sides of the barricade in spite of our will and interests. In an atmosphere of mistrust and suspicion, chance can play a much more important role than diplomacy and politics. Words alone will not cause another to believe you. Trust and confidence are a result of open and honest behavior, life experience, and human interaction.

One can hardly say there are no Soviet–U.S. contradictions in southern Africa when U.S. Stinger missiles shoot down Soviet-made aircraft. But one should also keep in mind that there have been quite a few cases in Africa when opposing sides in armed conflicts have both possessed a mix of Soviet- and U.S.–made arms. In any case, there is little cause for surprise if Soviet military advisers work in Mozambique side by side with NATO counterparts. The question is why joint efforts by the Warsaw Treaty Organization and NATO, the two most powerful military alliances of the East and West, respectively, cannot stabilize the military and political situation in Mozambique.

We all have lived through illusions and disappointments. In the mid-1970s, the United States thought the USSR was conquering Africa with the help of Cubans. Ten years later some of our U.S. colleagues thought Moscow was suffering a defeat in Africa. Such an interpretation of events might be possible if one tried to describe political developments in terms of military strategy. But politics differs from combat actions not only in dynamics but also in the range and diversity of its manifestations. The errors and miscalculations of the opposite side should be studied and analyzed, but should not be exaggerated. Exaggeration will not allow us to break away from the circle of illusions. The Soviet Union and the United States are real factors in the international relations of African countries, and this should be taken into account by all of us. True, recognition of this reality by journalists and some of our colleagues has often boiled down to labeling the parties involved in the conflict in southern Africa as puppets of the Kremlin or White House. Life has shown the fruitlessness and danger of such misreadings. Proof of this were the developments in Angola in 1975–1976 when misinterpretation of actions of the two sides actually dealt the first blow at détente. Unfortunately, the Angolan lesson was not analyzed quickly enough.

A more thorough examination of the state of affairs in the region has led both Soviet and U.S. researchers to the conclusion that it is not we who move the pieces on the chessboard of this conflict. At the same time, understanding, or at least near understanding, of the roles our two countries play in this situation has brought about another illusion, namely that the Soviet Union and the United States cannot have a positive effect on the course of developments. This opinion may seem very attractive to some. Indeed, one might think that as long as we do nothing and keep away from the conflict in southern Africa, there can be no contradictions between us in this respect.

But, first, marking time is also a position. Second, the refraining of our two countries from seeking solutions in southern Africa does not rule out our mutual suspicions. Since we cannot be absolutely sure that the opposite side does not take part in local developments, we are led to suspect it of attempting to gain unilateral advantages behind our back. Third, it is immoral to sit idly by when we can be contributing to the cessation of bloodshed. Political morality today is tantamount to a policy of survival.

The Soviet Union has more than once shown its readiness to cooperate with the West for the sake of settling the situation in southern Africa. Today, as we are reviewing our foreign policy decisions of the past, I am led to ask myself whether criticism of Soviet policy in southern Africa could not lay the groundwork for radical changes in our approach to the problems of the region.

There are certain general aspects of Soviet foreign policy that have had a negative effect on developments in the region. The Soviet Union's activities in southern Africa have often been misinterpreted because major foreign policy decisions have not been properly discussed—in the Supreme Soviet of the USSR or elsewhere. This has also made our genuine intentions in the region look somewhat vague and has provoked various absurd assumptions about the character and size of Soviet military aid to the frontline states, the African National Congress (ANC), and the South West Africa People's Organization (SWAPO). Hence the myths carried by newspapers that Soviet weapons delivered to Angola were sufficient to conquer South Africa. The authors of these myths seem to forget that weapons without trained personnel are heaps of metal. We have no data on the number of weapons supplied by the Soviet Union to the frontline states, ANC, or SWAPO, but proceeding from expert estimates based on an analysis of Soviet arms deliveries in similar situations in the past, say in the Middle East, we can say that they usually conform only to a justifiable need for weapons. Furthermore, the USSR does its best to keep an eye on the weapons it supplies so as to prevent their transfer to unauthorized forces or their sale on the black market. In any case, we have shown a maximum of responsibility in the question of arms deliveries, although failures sometimes do occur.

The same can be said about our military aid to national liberation forces. It is not very difficult to buy arms in any quantity on the world market. Eloquent proof of this is in the case of the Salvadoran rebels, who receive no military aid from the Soviet Union. As a man and scholar advocating the ideas of new political thinking, I am against violence in any form. But my personal opinion cannot affect the internationally recognized right of peoples under a colonial or racist yoke to armed struggle. Roman law long ago established the principle that violence may rightfully be rebuffed by force. Had this principle not been implemented, the United States would have never gained independence from Britain.

Hence, since the right of peoples to armed struggle has been recognized and the struggle waged in South Africa and Namibia has been caused by the cruelty and irreconcilability of the authorities, it would be better if the ANC and SWAPO were to seek weapons not on the black market, where one can buy such barbarous arms as portable ground-to-air missiles, but in countries that accept responsibility and are capable of controlling the lethal power of these weapons. Moreover, military aid should be rendered to the ANC and SWAPO not by any single country but via a special UN–controlled international foundation. This would minimize apprehensions about the intentions of the parties concerned and make it possible to control the escalation of conflicts.

It might be held that if such a plan were implemented, an organization could still acquire weapons on the black market as well as from this foundation. But if liberation movements were forced to choose between gaining official international support and losing it, they would be more careful about the rules of warfare. Anyway, my proposal could be a kind of intermediate solution that would diminish mutual suspicion under conditions where we cannot put an end to the conflict.

I agree that the smoke screen of secrecy around the Soviet Union's actions in southern Africa has led to a wrong assessment of our country's intentions in the region. At the same time, I do not wish to confirm the expectations of those who think that the USSR will radically change its policies in the light of new political thinking. The nature of the apartheid regime is such that there can be no pluralism of opinions concerning its preservation. I do not think the United States is interested in preserving racism as a principle of diversity.

The point is how one can put an end to it. It would be naive to think that the reason for different Soviet and U.S. approaches to this problem lies in the fact that the USSR is for the elimination of the apartheid regime by force and therefore supports the ANC and SWAPO, while the United States is for gradual evolution and therefore against any manifestations of extremism.

Obviously, apartheid is not just a result of the ill intentions of some political forces moved by the pathology of racism. It is a result of tragic clashes between cultures personified by racist distinctions. Without going too deep into the reasons for the rise and persistence of apartheid, we can say that the system of apartheid has created itself. This view is shared both by opponents of this system and by some of its advocates.

But will apartheid disappear on its own, gradually dissolving in various spheres of social, political, and economic life? The question is much more difficult than simply identifying social and political discrimination on the grounds of the color of skin.

A majority of visitors to South Africa say the level of life there is comparable to that in Western Europe or the United States. But South Africa ranks only between Argentina and Brazil in terms of GDP; per capita GDP is about $2,300 a year. Unfair income distribution creates an illusion of a high living standard in towns. On the average, a white South African has an income fifteen times that of a black. Nevertheless, the latter is still ahead of Africans from less developed countries.

An end to discrimination in the economic sphere, the leveling out of the incomes of racial groups, and, finally, the creation of a large black middle class—in other words, any measures based on income redistribution—would diminish the living standard of whites, above all the least well-off and the middle class. Naturally, even the specter of such redistribution is regarded by a majority of white South Africans as an aspect of socialism, which is not conducive to a higher morality or the elimination of racism.

The situation is worsened by the export-oriented character of South Africa's economy. Because South Africa exports limited numbers of raw materials, gold above all, they are dependent on the market situation. Unfavorable changes in the terms of trade for its exports and the resulting lack of confidence inside the country are an unreliable basis for consistent reforms aimed at putting an end to the system of apartheid.

The question of the future of a democratic, nonradical South Africa should be decided upon by South Africans themselves. But the world community, including the Soviet Union and the United States, can and should create favorable conditions for a political settlement of the conflict.

True, our opinions seriously differ as to what conditions may be regarded as favorable.

The U.S., British, and South African presses have recently stressed an evolution of the Soviet approach to the situation in southern Africa. True, it is sometimes difficult to understand what the essence of this evolution is, because these materials usually focus on the stand of the ANC and the South African Communist party. The Soviet Union supports the position of these organizations. But can this be identified with the position of the USSR on southern Africa?

The USSR has never set forth a comprehensive concept for resolution of southern African conflicts. Soviet leaders have, though, made a number of statements in meetings with representatives of African countries. These statements, at least those made since the early 1980s, boil down to the following:

- The Soviet Union is for eliminating the regime of apartheid and setting up a democratic, nonradical South Africa;
- The Soviet Union believes peace in the region can be attained only by political means; and
- The Soviet Union is ready to accept terms that will be acceptable to our friends and allies.

I do not think that the last statement, which refers to our relations with African countries and liberation movements, cancels out the other ones. As the results of the meetings of ANC and white South African community representatives at Dakar and Cologne have shown, there are fewer and fewer insurmountable obstacles between freedom fighters and those South Africans who are genuinely interested in radically reforming the existing system.

Changes in the Soviet approach to the region can hardly cancel out our obligations to other African countries. But these obligations can be supplemented, say, by a joint Soviet–U.S. declaration on the principles of political settlement in southern Africa.

It could, first of all, dispel suspicions about the intentions of our two countries, demonstrate the objectives of our policies vis-à-vis each other and toward African countries, frustrate the hopes of racists for support based on Soviet–U.S. antagonism, remove illusions about Soviet–South African rapprochement at the expense of the United States, and consolidate those forces in South Africa that demand change.

Both blacks and whites in South Africa should be allowed to see their future. It is immoral to draw a picture of inevitable apocalypse that allegedly will follow the abolition of apartheid. Though the situation in South Africa is unique, it is not the only country that encounters racial and ethnic problems. The task with which Soviet–U.S. cooperation must cope is to set a positive example based on our own histories.

26

Cooperation for Southern African Development and Regional Security

C. R. D. HALISI

The December 1987 Moscow meeting Soviet–U.S. Cooperation for Africa focused in part on the southern African region. Specific attention was paid to the importance of regional security and regional development projects. Unfortunately, a regional analysis must take into account the extensive destabilization potential by South Africa, the costs of which have been very high. Recent assessments by SADCC estimated the costs to be approximately $10 billion for 1980–1984, and perhaps as much as $30 billion in lost GDP for 1980–1986. The estimated regional GDP for 1985 was $25 billion.[1] Thus, as many donors now recognize, SADCC must include the cost of security in the cost of regional development, and also reckon on the seemingly twisted character of interstate relations. Interaction between South Africa and the majority-ruled states involves a complex reality of economic interdependence, coupled with often hostile political relations. Similarly, connections between the regional actors and the outside world reflect apparent ironies. Western and Eastern nations alike provide economic and military aid to African liberation movements and the neighboring independent governments threatened by South Africa's military incursions. However, most economic aid has come from the Western nations, while military support for liberation movements and their successors has come primarily from the Soviet Union. Both forms of aid have been necessary to contain South African aggression.

Collectively, the countries of the region share a history of relations with both East and West in which nonalignment and political toleration are important building blocks of regional unity. With respect to regional cooperation, it has been observed that "Southern African regional development must be designed and implemented by Southern Africans."[2]

Neither the Soviet Union nor the United States has achieved the desired outcome from their competitive foreign policies, while the region has suffered increased human misery. Over the years, black-ruled governments have maintained relations with both the Soviet Union and the United States; more recently, even South African officials have come to acknowledge publicly the role that the Soviet Union plays in the region. Neither the United States nor the USSR has "vital" regional interests that determine the entire range of bilateral relations. The primary consideration might therefore be what southern Africans desire for their respective nations and the region. That perspective might also allow the two powers to move beyond mutual distrust and to engage in new thinking regarding cooperative regional policies.

REGIONAL TRANSPORT

Although many factors inhibit economic development, transportation is a key area of concern for the states in the region. Indeed, Stephen Lewis has observed that transport, including rail links and ports, is the primary element in the overall contest for power in southern Africa.[3] In fact, the first commission established by SADCC was devoted to the coordination of transport and communications, and to date about $1.7 billion has been received from foreign donors. Emphasis is currently placed on rehabilitating the Tazara railway and Beira corridor. Preoccupation with security concerns has precluded development of the Maputo corridor, though expert opinion holds that this is the preferred export route for Zimbabwe and Botswana while plans for the development of Lobito's port and the Benguela railway are being readied.[4]

One reason for continued donor interest in transport is the fact that key lines have suffered from South African sabotage and destabilization. Historically these lines served to export the primary materials and bulk products that many donor countries still buy, providing significant sources of foreign exchange in return.[5]

There are additional reasons why the regional heads of state have sought to establish priorities for the regional transport systems. Intraregional trade and a strong infrastructure are essential to industrialization. At the same time, maximization of regional economic autonomy from South Africa poses two related issues.

First, South African ports are the least economical outlets for southern Zaire, Zambia, Malawi, Zimbabwe, Swaziland, and for select commodities and their destinations from Botswana. Presently, Zambia, Zimbabwe, and Botswana now rely heavily on the "southern" route. In 1985 alone, freight diversions into the South African transportation system cost SADCC countries an additional $100 million. While Botswana's membership in the Southern African Customs Union (SACU) may limit future options in this regard, Zambia and Zimbabwe would benefit extensively from the completion and full operation of the rail lines leading to the Beira and Maputo ports. Of the nine SADCC countries, only Lesotho would not benefit from a fully operational SADCC rail and port system.

The second issue is again of regional destabilization, because South Africa has long sought to employ military means to reach economic goals. Severing rail movement along the east and west coasts of southern Africa to eliminate routes from the center of the subcontinent to the sea has been an important objective of this policy. These closures force the region to use the extensive South African rail system, in turn providing South Africa with a privileged position as a primary supplier of goods and services to northward markets.

The Southern African Transport Services (SATS), a former parastatal that includes railways, harbors, an airline, and some haulage, together with the private company SAFREN, monopolizes the region's freight transport business. SATS operates 5,000 rail cars and fifty locomotives on the SADCC rail network, and SATS and SAFREN have worked together to cut rates and attract traffic away from SADCC ports. South African harbors have superior capacity at freight terminals and transport one-third of the international cargos shipped by neighboring countries. SATS freight charges account for $200–300 million of South Africa's annual net balance of payments surplus with SADCC nations.[6]

Similarly, the road network in the region is relatively undeveloped. Roads were not designed to complement the rail network, which prevents the formation of an overall infrastructure for industrial development. Integration of road and rail would lower costs and permit the development of a regional production network. Regionally and nationally, road construction is thus vital to an overall transport infrastructure strategy.[7] The centrality of a good road network is sometimes lost as planners and donors focus on the more expensive and high-profile rail corridors. Yet it is precisely in the area of road survey and construction that opportunity might exist for Soviet–U.S. cooperation in support of SADCC's priorities. Such a project, which could be relatively low in cost, would provide incentives for industrial location and clearly signal the commitment of both countries to regional economic development.

In southern Africa the politics of transport reflect the problem of pursuing economic development in the midst of political conflict. Indeed, transport questions dovetail closely with those of security. South Africa's "Railway Diplomacy" is an important part of its so-called Total National Strategy, coordinated by the State Security Council (SSC) for the purpose of employing all the nation's resources to counter pressures against white rule.

Alternately, emphasis on the region's rail system reinforces the historical function of the national economies to produce primary materials and bulk goods for export. Moreover, in its present condition, the rail network cannot handle all the goods that are produced for export.

Only the Tazara line to Dar es Salaam has not been a target of recent attempts to disrupt operations; thus, six of the seven regional ports of SADCC are operating at only 35 percent capacity.[8] In particular, the Beira corridor and the Nacala port projects are of great strategic importance to the Zimbabwean economy and the region as a whole. Over a decade ago, during the period when Mozambique and Zimbabwe were under colonial rule, 75 percent of Zimbabwe's goods passed through Beira and Maputo, which are only 698 and 1,178 kilometers from Harare, respectively, compared to Durban, the nearest South African port, which is 2,077 kilometers away. Armando Guebuza, the Mozambican minister of Transport and Communications, insists that ports in his country can provide for the needs of all but two of the landlocked SADCC countries as well as Zaire's Shaba province.[9] Zimbabwe's interests in the corridor are reflected in its assignment of six thousand troops to the task of protecting Beira's ports, rail links, and pipeline.

THE ZIMBABWEAN CHALLENGE TO SOUTH AFRICA

Black repudiation of President Botha's 1979 proposal for a Constellation of Southern African States (CONSAS), and the formation of SADCC, was encouraged by the establishment of majority rule in the region's second-largest national economy (Zimbabwe). Had CONSAS materialized, the South African government might have tempered the hostility of neighboring states, expanded its access to regional trade and markets, politically legitimated its economic hegemony, and placated the growing criticism of segments of the business community.

In contrast to South African objectives, the black-ruled states, through a carefully planned strategy of economic cooperation, have sought to redefine the region politically. A new emphasis on regional economic cooperation had the political advantage of including in a single organization a country like Malawi, which in the past had been ostracized for its political and economic ties to Pretoria, and the revolutionary FRELIMO government in Mozambique, with whom Mugabe and his Zimbabwe African National Union (ZANU) party enjoyed especially close political relations.

Zimbabwean independence was central to this effort. There is a direct correlation between the economic capacity of various countries in the region and their ability to contribute to resistance against South Africa. The South African manufacturing sector produces five times as much as the combined output of the other countries, contributing 40 percent of the region's population while accounting for 80 percent of its GDP.

That economic power has nourished its military and political clout is not lost on the leaders of the frontline states. Thus, Zimbabwe, with its large manufacturing center and impressive steel industry, was expected to help provide a counterweight by serving as the catalyst for a favorable economic realignment among the three largest regional manufacturing centers: Tanzania, Zambia, and Zimbabwe. All of these states are under black rule;

they are therefore in a position to formulate policies better designed than those of South Africa to relate industrial development to the goal of political liberation.

Zimbabwe especially was also in a position to assume a role of leadership in the region. At the time of its independence, it contributed 57 percent of the region's (excluding South Africa) combined Manufacturing Value Added (MVA), which, combined with manufacturing in three other countries (Malawi, Tanzania, and Zimbabwe), constituted 82 percent of the region's MVA in 1980.[10] By 1984 the Zimbabwean manufacturing sector was contributing 30 percent of the region's GDP. In addition, Zimbabwe participates in a larger regional group, the Preferential Trade Agreement of eastern and southern Africa (PTA), which aims to reduce trade barriers and tariffs among member countries. Zimbabwe is one of the two largest exporters in the PTA (the other is Kenya).

To a greater extent than any black-ruled country in the region, Zimbabwe, with its more diversified mining and manufacturing sectors, has had influence with the leaders of transnational business enterprise (TBE). Second to South Africa in this regard, Zimbabwe is host to a large number of nationally based TBEs and cooperates with them to achieve domestic and regional development objectives.[11] Zimbabwe's President Mugabe takes a pragmatic approach to the private sector and insists that, since Zimbabwe has inherited a capitalist economy, efficiency and profitability must be encouraged.[12] Regional projects important to Zimbabwe, such as Beira, have attracted Zimbabwean private investment. Zimbabwean investors have formed the Beira Corridor Group (BCG) and are joined in the Beira development effort by international firms registered in Oslo as shareholders of the International Beira Group and Mozambican business interests organized as the Empress Austral de Desenvolvimento.[13] Carol Thompson contends that Zimbabwe may soon be capable of helping to advance Angolan, Mozambican, and Tanzanian manufacturing.[14]

Although Zimbabwe's economy is the strongest of the black southern African states, it is not without problems. There has been a recent decline in the economic growth rate, a fall in agricultural production due to drought, and a retardation of import capacity that has tended to slow the expansion of industrial development.[15] Moreover, the public sector is burdened by a huge budget deficit, estimated at 12 percent of GDP for 1986/87 and 9 percent for 1985/86. The government's heavy borrowing has not been used to expand capital infrastructure, but rather to meet day-to-day operational expenses. In 1986/87, the rapid expansion of education absorbed 17 percent of total spending, with defense costs at 16 percent and debt servicing amounting to 25 percent.

The legacy of the historical relationship with South Africa continues to be an expensive and significant issue as Zimbabwe works to shift its economic orientation away from the south. In 1984/85, 94 percent of

Zimbabwean trade was routed through South African railways and ports. Moreover, 40 percent of its exports were sold in South Africa, and the same percentage of tourists arrived from there. The inflationary South African rand tends to undermine the trading position of all the SADCC countries, especially that of Zimbabwe.[16]

However, unlike Ian Smith's Rhodesia or contemporary South Africa, Zimbabwe no longer faces a costly crisis of political legitimation. Furthermore, Zimbabwe's internal situation gives it an immeasurable economic advantage in comparison with South Africa, a fact often ignored through too narrow a focus on purely economic variables.

In the RSA, the marriage of white nationalism and capitalism has required the reconciliation of two potentially conflicting management functions. The South African state has always pursued economic policies thought to be compatible with capitalist industrialization while not undermining white domination; this delicate balance has become ever more difficult to accomplish. Laying aside the academic controversies regarding their connection, Western governments and financial institutions increasingly insist that South Africa's white rulers choose between apartheid and capitalism. This demand was dramatized in mid-1985 when the international banking community, led by Chase Manhattan Bank, refused to roll over South Africa's short-term loans. This measure was in part designed to demonstrate disapproval of South Africa's political recalcitrance. Although South Africa replied by suspending debt repayments, the economy faces a persistent shortage of foreign exchange.

The government of President Botha, which promised reform, faced a declining economy, an intensifying international sanctions campaign, a prolonged state of emergency, and escalating defense expenditures needed to control the townships and sponsor regional insurgency. In contrast to South Africa, whose capacity for economic readjustment is severely constricted by political considerations, Zimbabwe stands to benefit from reconstruction and development in the region.

The downward direction of the South African economy derives from both international and domestic politics. Yet, adverse international attitudes toward apartheid have probably hurt the South African economy less than the government's pursuit of costly, defensive, and ineffective social policies. The rate of economic growth and yields on investments have both been damaged by the government's tendency to subordinate economic decisions to the political cause of white domination. The decision to subsidize the movement of capital to the Bantustans and a determination to increase the number of segregated educational bureaucracies are examples. The deficit-financed public sector and the cost of the security system are major drains on the economy.

And as the international business community has become more circumspect about South African investments, regional trade has contributed a larger share to South Africa's balance of trade surplus. Under the impact of sanctions, South Africa will probably depend more on its neighbors for trade opportunities and as markets for its goods and services and as sources of hard currency. In 1984 southern Africa accounted for 44 percent of South Africa's annual trade surplus, 10 percent of its exports, and 20 percent of its nongold exports.[17]

At the same time, South Africa finds itself in a schizophrenic posture of having to destabilize its major regional trading partners. In the last twenty years the South African military budget has climbed from 1 percent to 30 percent of its GNP. Christopher Coker believes that this increase does not correspond to outside threat, but rather represents "a form of over-insurance, a quest for security, an affirmation of political power."[18] Pretoria's efforts to modernize the archaic structures of racial rule have allowed the National party to retain power, while gradually undermining economic growth. A shortage of white, skilled manpower affects industry as well as military recruitment. As a result, job reservation requirements have been waived and more blacks are being recruited by the defense forces. Given the shortage in white manpower and the rise of conscript desertions, South Africa's preference for proxy armies in Angola and Mozambique may well be a matter of necessity as much as choice.

SECURITY IN THE REGION

South African destabilization has been a matter of a clearly calculated plan to increase regional dependence and thus hold neighboring economies hostage; the strategic infrastructure is the major target. Notwithstanding the contrasting perspectives on the possibility of economic autonomy for SADCC countries, South Africa considers certain forms of free trade a threat akin to political independence in neighboring states. The destabilization strategy has constrained the development options of regional economies. In the government budget of smaller countries, basic infrastructure, the extraction of primary resources, and government services compete with investment in manufacturing.[19] Military strategy designed to incapacitate normal economic activitity requires the affected countries to divert prohibitive amounts of their resources into expenditures related to security, repair, and additional transport.

While able militarily to intimidate the region, South Africa has to face the fact that military intervention does not necessarily translate into political influence and that there are serious limits to military capacity. In several respects the military dimensions of South Africa's regional policy have proven counterproductive. For example, the South African–backed MNR, also known as RENAMO, has on occasion been known to destroy infrastructure, such as pylons from the Cabora Bassa, curtailing the supply of hydroelectricity to South Africa itself.

Christopher Coker suggests that the policy of destabilization has demonstrably failed politically. Pretoria has not won a reliable security system, nor has it forced its neighbors into submission.[20] Growing resistance by the independent states of the region indicates that implementation of *"Pax Pretoriana"*—regional peace on Pretoria's terms—has collapsed. Contrary to South African objectives, diplomatic initiatives now recognize the security of the independent states as a corollary of development strategy. While there may have been some near-term successes, the long-term failures of destabilization as a political policy are evident in the negotiations now taking place among Angola, Cuba, and South Africa, with the encouragement of the Soviet Union and the United States.[21]

The susceptibility of the Pretoria regime to Western influence, particularly that of the United States, is fiercely debated. While it is often argued that Western economic and political policies create problems for the system of apartheid, the historical evidence also suggests a long-standing ambivalence in relations between the white state and the arbiters of international capitalism. The South African government has reiterated that it is not wedded to the West. Kobus Meiring, deputy minister of Foreign Affairs, is on the record as having said that the USSR and the United States have legitimate interests in Africa, but that both must consult South Africa. Meiring also questioned whether South Africa should "rely only on what the US tells us how the Russians think about southern Africa and South Africa."[22] Whatever the real motives, South African policy does appear in a state of flux, and the government is very interested in recent changes in Soviet–U.S. relations.

The MNR has emerged as a security threat not only to the government of Mozambique, but to several neighboring countries. Initially nurtured by Rhodesian and South African security forces as a means of denying sanctuary to the ANC, the MNR retains the support of the South African military. Consequently, the FRELIMO government is forced to divert money and manpower to a costly internal war. Conceived initially as a means of thwarting FRELIMO-ZANU cooperation, the protracted nature of the conflict has proven costly to all concerned. Coker estimates that after the Nkomati Accord the military cost of supporting MNR was higher than earlier, more overt, destabilization of Mozambique.[23]

Furthermore, there is a growing consensus that the destructive policy of the movement is without any real political goal. The "Gersony Report," distributed by the U.S. Department of State, found no evidence of any program. In fact, the MNR's political objective appears to be a purely negative one of "resistance," conducted through an extreme policy of terror and slavery. Gersony concludes that

> the violence is systematic and coordinated and not a series of spontaneous, isolated incidents by undisciplined combatants. . . . It appears that the only reciprocity provided by Renamo for the efforts of the civilians is the possibility of remaining alive. There are virtually no reports of attempts to win the loyalty

—or even the neutrality—of the villagers. . . . The refugees report virtually no effort by Renamo to explain to the civilians the purpose of the insurgency, its proposed program or its aspirations.[24]

The destructive effects of MNR activity reach considerably beyond Mozambican borders. The prime example is Malawi, which in March 1988 had been inundated with over 500,000 Mozambican refugees (with 30,000 more arriving monthly).[25] On occasion, Malawi has been used as a sanctuary for some MNR troops. This caused such tension in the area that neighboring heads of state threatened that if President Banda did not take steps to curtail Malawian support for the MNR, they would deny Malawi rail access through their countries.[26]

SOVIET–U.S. COOPERATION AND MOZAMBIQUE

The desire of the Mozambique government to have both Soviet and U.S. participation is a basic aspect of any proposal for Soviet–U.S. cooperation in that country. In addition, there are several reasons why Soviet–U.S. cooperation should begin in Mozambique.

First, there is a moral imperative to assist the country most affected by the ravages of international conflict in the region, although Angola is also important in this respect. Soviet–U.S. encouragement of internationally coordinated efforts to counter hardship and South African aggression in the region could have a major impact, with governments, nongovernmental agencies, and private investors taking part. In this connection, food aid for refugees and resettlement of dislocated segments of the population should take precedent. The World Food Program has apparently gone a step further and even provided food for soldiers protecting the Beira Corridor.

Second, Mozambique is one country of the region in which there is already a degree of parallel Eastern and Western economic involvement. An informed observer notes that President Joaquim Chissano, like the late Samora Machel, will continue to pursue an autonomous nonaligned policy, meaning that he will seek to extend his country's ties with the West while also seeking to sustain improved relations with the Soviet Union.[27] The Soviet Union does not oppose the Mozambican government's reinvolvement with Western financial and international development institutions. And, for whatever reasons, it was determined that admission of Mozambique to the Council for Mutual Economic Assistance (COMECON) would be un-realistic. For its part, the Mozambican government has had some success experimenting with decentralization and free markets.[28] However, much depends on the defeat of the MNR, which is shattering the national economy.

Third, Mozambique is central to the reconstruction and extension of the region's infrastructural network, a SADCC priority. Projects that link infrastructural repair and development with security concerns should be emphasized. The reconstruction of Mozambican ports and infrastructure will have more benefits for the region than any comparable effort in any other country. In particular, Zimbabwean industry and development, crucial to regional development, stands to benefit from such a focus. As Mugabe reportedly once remarked, "Mozambique is our window on the sea." Colin Legum astutely points out that destabilization of Mozambique has had adverse effects on economic and political conditions in Zimbabwe. According to Legum, "South Africa's policy of promoting instability in Mozambique is also a means of directly applying pressure on Zimbabwe."[29]

Fourth, the Nkomati Accord, whatever it has meant in de facto terms, commits South Africa to security and reconstruction in Mozambique. Despite the continuous South African involvement with the MNR, there are recurring reports that different branches of the South African government are split over whether to support it. According to these reports, the Foreign Ministry would like to distance South Africa from the MNR although the military leadership is opposed to such a policy. This internal dissension is most clearly captured in the reported view of intelligence chief C. J. van Tonder who "swears he will not let [RENAMO] go [and] regards Pik Botha as a traitor at worst, naive at best."[30]

Politically and economically, the MNR has inflicted real costs on the region. While the threat to Mozambican, Zimbabwean, and Malawian development and security is obvious, the fissures caused by MNR policy inside the South African government are less obvious. The contradictory nature of destabilization as a regional South African policy is implicit in the havoc the MNR wreaks. While the MNR has virtually no legitimacy and no positive political agenda, it has become a conduit for virtually all of the forces opposed to the FRELIMO government, including ex-Portuguese Mozambicans, rural bandits, pariah capitalists, mercenaries, and ex-FRELIMO dissidents. Once set in motion, these forces are not easily controllable, not even by the governments and agencies that sustain them.

Finally, given the growing consensus that the MNR is a mercenary movement with no other political objective than to hold Mozambique hostage, the possibility of joint East-West security cooperation should be considered. Such cooperation could include African, U.S., Soviet, Eastern bloc, and European countries in an effort against the MNR. A host of countries are already providing security assistance and these efforts could be formalized and coordinated. The Nordic countries, which provide the largest amount of development aid to Mozambique, have begun to include the toll of security costs. At SADCC's Arusha Consultative Conference in January 1988, Spanish Secretary of State for International Cooperation Luis Yanez-Barnuevo also called for donors to "reach a formula whereby the financing of development projects likewise includes the necessary security factor."[31] India has taken the important step of providing a small naval presence to thwart the resupply of the MNR by sea, and this is another important area to consider.[32]

The security situation in Mozambique and the region was not created by independent southern African states. In many respects, these states face problems beyond their capacity to solve alone. The United States and other Western nations, the Soviet Union and the Eastern bloc, the SADCC countries and the numerous donor nations that have invested in the region through regionally based projects can together become an important diplomatic force for cooperative political initiatives. As a first step, a Soviet–U.S. commission for joint coordination of reconstruction and security in Mozambique, working closely with the Mozambican government, could serve as a vehicle to assess specific projects and programs beneficial to that country.

NOTES

The author ackowledges the valuable research assistance of Ed Brown.

1. *SADCC Annual Progress Report* (July 1986–August 1987), 8.

2. Amon J. Nsekela, *Southern Africa: Toward Economic Liberation* (London: Rex Collings, 1981), 6.

3. Stephen R. Lewis, "Economic Realities in Southern Africa (or One Hundred Million Futures)," unpublished (April 1987), 13.

4. D. S. Tevera, "Regional Transportation in the SADCC Countries," *The Zimbabwe Science News* 22, nos. 5/6 (May/June 1988), 57–61.

5. See, for example, UNIDO, *Industrial Co-operation Through the Southern African Development Co-ordination Conference* (15 October 1985), 84.

6. Lewis, "Economic Realities," 13.

7. UNIDO, *Industrial Co-operation*, 84.

8. *The Herald*, Harare (21 July 1988), 10.

9. André Astrow, "Interview with Armando Guebuza," *Africa Report* (July–August 1987), 64.

10. UNIDO, *Industrial Co-operation*, 27.

11. On the relation between TBEs and state-led development in Southern Africa, see Richard L. Sklar, *Corporate Power in an African State* (Berkeley: University of California Press, 1975), and Ronald T. Libby, *The Politics of Economic Power in Southern Africa* (Princeton, N.J.: Princeton University Press, 1987).

12. "Mugabe Takes the Hard Road," *South* (May 1984), 21.

13. *AED* (4 October 1986), 14.

14. Carol B. Thompson, "Cooperation for Survival: Western Interests vs. SADCC," *Issue: A Journal of Opinion* 16, no. 1 (1987), 32.

15. A. M. Hawkins, "Zimbabwe," *The African Review* (1987), 260.

16. Ibid.

17. Lewis, "Economic Realities," 5–7, 32.

18. Christopher Coker, *South Africa's Security Dilemmas* (New York: Praeger, 1987), 94.

19. UNIDO, *Industrial Co-operation*, 80.

20. Coker, *South Africa's Security Dilemmas,* 94.

21. For a recent summary, see J. Gus Liebnow, "Southern Africa: 'Not Yet Quiet on the Western Front'," *UFSI Field Staff Reports,* Africa/Middle East, no. 3 (1988–1989).

22. "Soviets Get Friendly Signals," *The Daily News,* Johannesburg (12 September 1988), 4.

23. Christopher Coker, *The United States and South Africa, 1968–1985: Constructive Engagement and Its Critics* (Durham, N.C.: Duke University Press, 1986), 236.

24. Robert Gersony, "Assessment of Mozambican Refugees," U.S. Department of State, Bureau for Refugees, Mozambique (1988), 11.

25. Ibid.

26. Colin Legum, *The Battlefronts of Southern Africa* (New York: Africana, 1988), 412–413.

27. Allen Issacman, "In Machel's Footsteps," *Africa Report* (January–February 1987), 26.

28. "After Machel," *AED* (25 October 1986), 2.

29. Legum, *Battlefronts,* 213.

30. "Mozambique: Marketing RENAMO," *Africa Confidential* 29, no. 18 (9 September 1988), 1.

31. "Donors Boost Front-Line Assistance," *AED* (5 February 1988), 28.

32. Maggie Jonas, "Tide Turns Against MNR," *New African* (May 1987), 20.

The Southern African Development Coordination Conference and African Security

VICTOR I. GONCHAROV

The dilemmas of development, combined with increasing global interdependence, call for constructive and creative cooperation among states and nations on a global scale. The solution of acute problems, the settlement of crises, and the search for ways to reduce tension can and should be participated in by all states—big and small—regardless of their level of development, geographic location, or external political affiliations. Objective conditions exist for the development of meaningful and mutually advantageous Soviet–U.S. cooperation in southern Africa, where an explosive situation has been creating a serious threat to the security of African nations and to the world at large.

The Soviet approach to a comprehensive system of collective security emphasizes the solution of regional conflicts by peaceful means. This may be feasible only if continuous confidence-building measures are taken. An atmosphere of confidence for solving the problems of southern Africa would be enhanced by Soviet–U.S. cooperation in ensuring the region's economic security. Keeping in mind that neither country has "vital" interests there that affect the entire range of Soviet–U.S. relations, a positive record of such cooperation, if it materializes, could be utilized to defuse conflicts in other parts of the world.

We believe that recognizing the goals of the SADCC, particularly as reflected in the developmental priorities and methods stated in the 1980 Lusaka Declaration, could become a cornerstone of our cooperation. These goals are essentially as follows:

- First and foremost, reduction of the economic dependence of SADCC member states (not only on South Africa);
- Strengthening of links for building up a genuinely meaningful and equitable system of integration;
- Mobilization of resources to support national, interstate, and regional policies; and
- Joint efforts to ensure international cooperation within a strategic framework for economic liberation.

A clear understanding of SADCC objectives is essential to correct decisions in any joint Soviet–U.S. approach to the region. For instance, SADCC member states reject the IMF and World Bank's demand to privatize state-operated agricultural marketing boards on the basis that "free" markets had never existed in the region, or that they are the creation of South Africa.

To give a more specific example, Botswana plans an irrigation system to attain self-sufficiency in grain and to cut its imports of corn from South Africa. These plans, and the purpose behind them, must be respected. SADCC states have set—both jointly and independently—an objective of relieving themselves from dependence on the apartheid state even at the price of extra production cost. It seems that "free market" principles will not be applicable to the realization of certain development projects, especially where this entails dependence on South Africa. In general, the structural economic changes insisted upon by the IMF and World Bank have proved to be quite inapplicable to southern Africa. The unhappy experiences of Tanzania and Zambia with such policies provides telling evidence in support of this point, and may serve as reference points to guide other regional states in the direction of economic and political consolidation or "collective self-reliance" designed to overcome economic backwardness as an alternative to structural adjustment.

From the point of view of SADCC member states, the advantage of joint Soviet–U.S. dealings with SADCC as a collective unit lies in avoiding the danger of diminished political sovereignty, which may result from direct bilateral dealings. Planning for projects should be made with great sensitivity to this concern. In this context, small- or medium-sized projects in a variety of fields seem most acceptable. Of utmost importance, planning and implementation of such projects should follow SADCC's developmental priorities rather than those envisaged by the Soviet Union or the United States. For example, since in SADCC countries industrial priority has been assigned to production of simple agricultural machinery and fertilizers, it might be interesting to consider establishing a joint Soviet–U.S. medium-scale venture for their production. Similar joint ventures could be set up in agrobusiness in Zimbabwe or Botswana for the production of canned meat. Keeping in mind the difficulty of finding international market outlets for such products, the USSR could agree to become in future a large importer of canned meat produced in these countries.

Fortunately, contemplation of a possible joint Soviet–U.S. contribution to regional development is made easier by the fact that SADCC has already fixed its development priorities. Transportation is one of them. The urgency of need for development of SADCC's transportation infrastructure is made clear by figures that relay the region's dependence on transit through South Africa. While in 1981 South Africa handled 26 percent of the export-import traffic of SADCC countries, in 1984 the rate rose to 31 percent. This is a field in which there is a possible contribution to be made via joint

Soviet–U.S. action. Only in recent years has substantial progress been made in improving the regional transportation infrastructure. Extensive work is under way at the moment on transportation lines linking the countries of the region with the ports of Dar es Salaam, Beira, Nakala, and Maputo. If the plans for the restoration of the transportation network are accomplished, by 1990 SADCC member states (with the exception of Lesotho) will no longer need to use the ports and railways of South Africa. Yet, a great deal remains to be accomplished. Of 111 projects developed by SADCC's Commission on Transportation and Communications, financing has been acquired in full for twenty-eight and partially for thirty, while forty projects are yet being considered and finalized.

Conscious of the constraints imposed by these conditions, the SADCC countries have started working out plans for accelerated industrial development. They plan, first of all, to restore and modernize, with the help of foreign capital, existing industrial enterprises. Speaking in Harare in February 1988, SADCC Executive Secretary Simba Makoni said that SADCC was ripe for a decisive investment push in the production sphere, with a major role assigned to the private sector. The Tanzanian minister of Industry and Trade, J. Rwegasira, has said in this connection that Tanzanians have come to the realization that private investment will of necessity be involved in future plans for accelerated industrial development.

The Soviet Union and the United States could contribute to the SADCC countries' efforts to increase the pace of their industrialization in several ways. One of these could be to assist with developing the region's power supply system. Another would be to help with building or modernizing some factories. Finally, joint projects could aid with the training of personnel.

The urgency of support to SADCC is made vividly apparent by the victimization of its member countries in the form of South African economic sanctions. Among the many examples of this occurrence is the recent one of destabilization in Lesotho. The total damage to SADCC countries resulting from destabilization policies in 1980–1986 has been estimated by SADCC experts at $30 billion.

Serious deterioration of trade conditions is another important reason to give support to SADCC. For example, in 1975–1980 the purchasing power of one ton of copper, coffee, or cotton as against one barrel of oil was cut by 50 percent. Maintaining stable volumes of oil imports necessitated a twofold boost of production of exportable agricultural commodities in countries such as Botswana, Mozambique, and Tanzania. This decline in SADCC countries' terms of trade seriously aggravated the problem of foreign debt. Countries of the region spend 25 percent of their export revenue on debt service (Mozambique spends over 50 percent). Output of agricultural products in the region has been steadily decreasing at the same time as hunger has been on the increase. In 1978–1985 per capita agricultural production decreased at an annual rate of 104 percent. According to UNICEF, in March 1987 a baby under the age of five died every four minutes in Angola and Mozambique.

In assessing the situation in southern Africa, one must proceed from the fact that the countries of that region cannot successfully develop economically as long as they remain militarily weak and suffer huge losses through the policy of destabilization pursued by the racist regime. One cannot speak today of the region's economic development in isolation from the problems of its security and eradication of the apartheid system. These three elements are closely interrelated. Military aid to the countries of the region is needed if only to protect investments channeled there. It is natural that economic and military aid to the SADCC countries were discussed in tandem at the consultative conference in Arusha on 28–29 January 1988. There, representatives of Western nations spoke of their readiness to provide military aid to protect projects financed by them in the region. Each developed country must decide for itself what military aid it can give the SADCC countries. As for the countries of the region themselves, they prefer that aid come in the form of military personnel, training, and arms supplies.

Willingly or unwillingly joint African–Soviet–U.S. ventures will create the need for political cooperation. We may be compelled to search out political solutions, for instance, to problems related to ensuring the security of joint venture operations in Angola or Mozambique. The very decision of the Soviet Union and the United States to cooperate in support of SADCC countries will come as an important political act. South Africa views the economic independence of SADCC countries as a threat to its regional hegemony and interests. Soviet–U.S. cooperation will demonstrate Soviet and U.S. determination to eliminate the shameful apartheid system, sending a clear signal to Pretoria. According to some estimates, trade between South Africa and SADCC countries runs to the tune of $1.5 billion. A big reduction of that trade could leave 2 million South African workers unemployed. Therefore, Soviet–U.S. joint support for SADCC's economic independence from South Africa would be an act of peaceful and effective pressure.

Meaningful African–Soviet–U.S. cooperation will compel the two global powers to give up a confrontational approach to solving regional problems and to recognize the right of peoples and governments of southern African countries to determine independently their destiny, socioeconomic policies, and the roles of the state-owned sector and private enterprise in line with SADCC general principles. The present conflict in the region is a result of socioeconomic and political developments, a legitimate outcome of the decomposition of an obsolete system of national and racial relations. It should also be noted that, because of the variety and differences in SADCC member countries' political orientations, the organization does not advocate socialism as necessary for its members. It merely aims to mobilize available regional resources for their development.

Development of African–Soviet–U.S. cooperation will presumably compel the United States to define more precisely its stance vis-à-vis the SADCC countries. In this respect, present U.S. policy may be described as containing a certain dualism. On the one hand, in 1980–1985 the United States provided Zimbabwe with $80 million in aid; on the other hand, the United States began recently to give regular material and military aid, worth dozens of millions of dollars, to UNITA. This actually constitutes support of destabilization policies conducted by South Africa against the countries of the region. A SADCC official has wittily noted that the United States gives money for the construction of one railway (Beira-Mutare) and for the destruction of another (Benguela).

The policy of the United States in southern Africa brings it only criticism. It is noteworthy that the July 1987 meeting of the Council of Ministers of nine SADCC countries condemned the U.S. decision to provide financial aid to member countries only if they denounce support to "terrorists in South Africa." It is worth mentioning here that EC countries signed a financial aid agreement with SADCC countries involving several multilateral projects within SADCC's institutional framework, and obligating themselves to respect its principles and priorities.

Economic security in the region is closely related to the elimination of apartheid. According to Botswana's Vice-President Peter Mmusi, "abolition of apartheid will constitute a major contribution to regional economic development." We are completely in favor of such an approach to ensuring economic security in the region. Therefore, it would be quite legitimate to consider giving aid to SADCC member countries in the context of efforts to isolate and apply sanctions to the Pretoria regime. If South Africa's destabilization policy toward independent countries of the region is not stopped, all efforts of the international community to help SADCC countries will prove senseless and ineffective.

An inequitable division of labor and the system of economic relations in southern Africa, picturesquely presented as "a white riding a black horse," must be stopped. Elimination of the imbalance will strengthen the economic security of the region and promote a political settlement of all the region's problems.

28

Namibian Independence and Soviet–U.S. Cooperation

SAM C. NOLUTSHUNGU

On 1 April 1989, Namibia began immediate progress toward independence under United Nations Resolution 435, on the basis of an agreement among South Africa and Angola and Cuba, brokered by the United States with Soviet support. The agreement came in the wake of the Soviet Union's decision to withdraw its forces from Afghanistan, and had been preceded by widely publicized signs of growing Soviet moderation in the southern African context.

The Namibian success has encouraged hopes of future effective cooperation on other problems in the region, including the dismantling of apartheid in South Africa itself. It also opened the way for direct contact between the Soviet and South African governments, confirming the Soviet Union in a path of "moderation."

The agreement calling for the withdrawal of South African and Cuban troops from Angola, and for Namibia's decolonization, was comparable to the Lancaster House Agreement under which Zimbabwe gained its independence nine years earlier. Like the earlier agreement (which was itself the subject of bitter criticism among Zimbabweans), the Namibia agreement is also deficient in many respects.[1] It excludes from the process of its negotiation key national actors in Namibia and Angola, SWAPO and UNITA, a factor that may have contributed to the decision that SWAPO (unlike its Zimbabwean counterparts) should completely disarm while the South West African forces created and used by Pretoria in the war against SWAPO remained armed.[2] That concession probably played a major part in the tragic decision of the SWAPO leadership to send some of its men into the country in late March and early April, and to the bloody massacre of those troops by South African forces.[3] The agreement is unclear about the role of South Africa during the process of the transfer of power, though it is difficult to imagine how conditions might have been made any more favorable for Pretoria, especially considering that the United Nations peacekeeping force is much smaller than originally envisaged.[4] Critical questions about voting arrangements, the making and adoption of the constitution, and the installation of an independence government remained unresolved. Also, the problem of Walvis Bay, over which South Africa claims sovereignty, was left unresolved.

For all that, an agreement was reached; and movement, tense and uncertain, toward democracy and independence was begun. The April crisis was contained and both South Africa and SWAPO were persuaded to continue to work within the agreed terms. Once again, the cooperation of the Soviet Union and the United States was evident. Yet, the defects of the agreement, perceived as one of the first fruits of superpower cooperation on regional issues, are also evident, and they threaten to compound the Namibians' own immeasurable political and economic problems.

It is early to measure accurately the extent of superpower cooperation and the two powers' respective shares in the Namibian "success" (and their respective responsibilities for what might follow). How important their overt and active cooperation was to the outcome of the agreement is hard to determine. The Soviet Union cast itself as an "observer" and the United States preferred to see itself as an "honest broker," the two countries distancing themselves from the antagonists. However, the agreement was in fact the culmination of U.S.–Angolan talks that had been going on erratically for many years—even though toward the end, the United States preferred the self-image of "mediator" with its suggestion of disinterest.[5]

As "broker," Washington made no significant departure from the policies it had pursued for nearly a decade, a period during which its relations with South Africa and its policies toward SWAPO and Namibia, Angola, and the Cuban presence could hardly be described objectively as amounting to mediation or the quest for a mediator role. The Soviet Union and its allies abandoned their opposition to linkage, and Moscow associated itself with what was essentially a U.S. settlement plan virtually without demur.

SECURITY PROBLEMS

Great uncertainty and nervousness prevails in Namibia as might be expected, not only about South Africa's intentions but also about the resolution of internal conflicts among Namibian parties and the various interests they represent. This unease extends to the base questions of whether a workable constitutional order can be found and whether a system of political power sharing that might secure the loyalty of all sections of the population can be created. Merely attempting to adapt the state structures created by South Africa will potentially constitute a major source of conflict between a popular party that wins and the state machinery through which it has to rule. Such problems will trouble the period of transition but will extend well beyond it. Yet, there seems little doubt now that South Africa does intend some real transfer of power and has no intention to restart the war. There is a great deal of doubt as to whether it has reconciled itself to the very high prob- ability of a SWAPO government or a coalition excluding its traditional collaborators from power. It is not clear, either, how Pretoria might respond to unfavorable outcomes in the elections, to the process of constitution mak- ing, or to the actual composition of the first independence government. The hope of South African financial and even military support might well encourage rebellion among the losers, as has occurred elsewhere on the subcontinent.

Internal conflict among Namibians will influence South Africa's options considerably. In this connection, the new nation will face a double security problem: the need to cope with a diversity of rival political forces embittered in many cases by past conflicts within the liberation struggle (and by their strong ethnic and racial identifications), and the threat of South Africa's intervention in various forms. A SWAPO-based government is South Africa's least preferred option; a Namibian government that excluded SWAPO, however, would have questionable legitimacy and little hope of securing internal political stability. Yet, given that SWAPO's support is less secure outside Ovamboland, a government consisting only of SWAPO members would cause considerable resentment among the larger ethnic as well as ideological minorities.

In any number of ways, South Africa's own internal problems are likely to have an impact on attitudes in Namibia itself, as has been the case for all the other southern African states. In addition, to a greater or lesser extent, there are potential security dangers from the still unresolved conflict in Angola. Should these uncertainties persist, northern Namibia will not be easy to stabilize, with or without South African involvement.

What regional military policies may emerge in place of the "total strategy" and what impact they will have on Namibia is impossible to say with any assurance. There are various indications that South Africa has no intention of renouncing all its military options or assets in Namibian territory, notably bases in the Caprivi Strip and Ovamboland and, most troublesome for Namibian nationalists, Walvis Bay. The South West African forces, including the notorious "Koevoet" brigade, now sometimes presented as "indigenous" (in reality they are no more so than the infamous Selous Scouts were in Zimbabwe), are presently the only armed force in Namibia. Their dismantling and the creation of a national military force are certainly needed.

The creation of a national army will pose other problems, such as integrating guerrillas with former proapartheid soldiers and training and arming the troops. This is one area in which the Soviet Union and the United States, either directly or through third parties, could easily cooperate to lend decisive assistance. However, it is by no means clear what kind of defense facilities they are willing to provide, especially as touches South Africa, or indeed, what Namibia itself will be capable of supporting, beyond the minimum of a ceremonial force directed toward the enforcement of law and order internally and, perhaps, immediately offshore (with respect to illegal fishing, etc.). Such decisions are for Namibians to take, but the prospect of external assistance will be of decisive importance.

Other problems of security are more complex, and even more require political commitments from the global powers, especially regarding South Africa. South Africa's role must be monitored, and its proclivity to intervene deterred or countered. This can be achieved partly by the United States and the Soviet Union helping to mediate internal conflicts in Namibia that might facilitate or provoke South African political and military interference. In the absence of international willingness to consider coercive measures against Pretoria, it is difficult to see how much could be achieved. Vigilance and candor about Pretoria's policies as opposed to an abject eagerness to appease, will alone help.

It is, however, only realistic to expect that South African intervention will not be the only likely source of insecurity and instability in Namibia. Support for the resolution of other regional conflicts that may strain the internal peace of the new state is imperative. No external power, however, can realistically be expected to bear the entire burden of international relations for a sovereign Namibian state. Rather, it is in regard to South Africa that there would appear to be clear international obligations, consequential upon Resolution 435 (as mediated by the Namibia/Angola agreement) and flowing from countless international resolutions and declarations against apartheid.

It is abundantly clear that the era of intense and violent struggle may not end with the formal attainment of independence; an even more bitter phase of civil and international strife could follow, indeed result from, the manner and circumstances of its achievement.

ECONOMIC ASSISTANCE

In principle, a less contentious area of cooperation is economic assistance (of which Namibia will have massive need). Depending on what kind of government emerges in Namibia, South African budgetary support and economic assistance may be significantly reduced.[6] But even were this to continue, the commitments of the new government and the expectations of its people regarding the rehabilitation of refugees, aid to displaced persons and war victims, expansion of employment, improvement of working conditions, and better provision of housing, education, and health services all will overtax the capacity of the national economy without substantial external aid. A higher volume of foreign investment, accelerated training, and technical and professional manpower in both the economy and the administration will be needed. Here, the tasks, though great, would, in principle, be relatively uncontroversial.

Perhaps more intractable difficulties may arise from restructuring the Namibian economy so as to reduce dependence on South Africa and serve Namibians. Doing that involves reorienting the current settler-dominated internal economy and making it more responsive to the needs of the African majority. A certain redistribution of wealth and income will be a sine qua non of legitimacy for any government. External financial and technical and political support will be necessary if it is to be achieved.[7]

An independent Namibia will have an evident interest in strengthening cooperation with other states within the region, notably, Angola, Botswana, and Zambia, and it will almost certainly seek membership in SADCC. With a small population of some 1.5 million, and even with a favorable resource base, Namibia, like the SADCC states, can achieve balanced economic development only in the context of regional development. The end of apartheid in South Africa could create great opportunities for mutually beneficial economic cooperation and accelerated growth in the region, but even with a nonapartheid South Africa, it would still be desirable for the less developed states in the region to strengthen the links among them. In this respect, external cooperation in aid of Namibia would be limited in its usefulness unless it were guided by a commitment to aid more significantly than in the past the accelerated development of the region as a whole.

The formidable security issues and the equally daunting problems of economic development highlight the pitfalls of "serial decolonization," which has characterized the end of colonial and racist rule in southern Africa. The notion taken for granted for over a decade now is that the liberation of the subcontinent must take place by gradual steps, one country at a time, culminating in the eventual deracialization of South Africa. This thinking has the obvious difficulty that, as decolonization has proceeded, the independent entity has become, in economic and security terms, increasingly more tenuous and more vulnerable to negation by conscious South African policy as well as by the unplanned consequences of internal difficulties. Thus, the newly independent country has had to make substantial concessions to Pretoria in ways that empty national independence of much of its intended content. In the extreme case of Mozambique, even the most extensive concessions to Pretoria's demands have not spared it from a scorched earth war of destabilization backed, and to some extent masterminded, by the South African state.[8]

In this light, action to overthrow apartheid and to replace it with a more beneficent political order is not an extraneous matter but a fundamental necessity, especially in terms of consolidating Namibia's independence.

THE LIMITS OF SUPERPOWER COOPERATION

It is easy enough to recognize the areas where superpower cooperation, and superpower initiatives to mobilize assistance, are most urgently needed.

Yet, it would be vain idealism to ignore the problems of such cooperation.

Not the least of such problems is the danger of subordinating Namibian interests to the preoccupations of the superpowers in their bilateral relations and in their policies toward South Africa. As regards South Africa, the USSR's present policy has a decidedly conciliatory ring, while Western policy has consistently sought to avoid confrontation with the apartheid regime, looking to the white oligarchy itself to initiate and realize reform. Africans might have to resign themselves to that reality, but it hardly expresses a perspective that they share. The majority of Namibians may soon find themselves in this position.

As to superpower cooperation, it is difficult to determine what measures of cooperation or competition would be most advantageous to Namibia. It remains a matter of opinion whether the period of confrontation and suspicion that led the Soviet Union to embrace the cause of radical nationalist liberation contributed to the eventual coming of independence or retarded that process—or once independence was achieved made it more vulnerable and precarious. By the same token, détente and like-mindedness on regional issues might remove the very rivalry and potential for conflict that made the resolution of such conflicts an urgent need. Once the international "crisis" aspect of the Namibian situation has been plausibly defused by superpower convergence or cooperation, Namibians might be abandoned to a worse fate.

The credibility of cooperation for Namibia turns on the question of whether there is on the part of either the United States or the Soviet Union any practical reason (as distinct from mere humanitarianism) to implement the major projects of assistance that are necessary.

Further, it is an entirely open question how far the spirit of cooperation is reciprocal or how long it may endure. In the southern African context, there is little doubt that the concessions, related mainly to ideology and self-image, have come almost exclusively from the Soviet side: deemphasizing the armed struggle, seeking contacts with South Africa, urging special recognition of racial minorities in a future South African constitution, and supporting a diplomatic process regarding Angola and Namibia that was in all essentials nothing other than the discredited policy of constructive engagement. There remains a strong feeling of skepticism in the United States and the West generally about the new Soviet policies globally, and great doubt about the utility of renouncing the strategic challenge to Soviet power and taking on face value its streamlining and reorganization.

In addition, there is a feeling in some official quarters that the Soviet contribution in southern Africa, while welcome and useful in some ways (e.g., encouraging traditional Soviet allies to cooperate with Western solutions), is largely redundant. Moscow does not appear to have much leverage in the region and is perceived as having failed to consolidate any secure gains in the area in the quarter of a century of decolonization there.

Associated with this skepticism is the persisting uncertainty as to the future of the "new thinking" in the Soviet Union itself and of its impact on foreign policy. Doubt, and even skepticism, for different, often opposed reasons, also prevail among southern African actors.

The important question raised by the Namibian case, which has far wider implications and is particularly important for South Africa, is to know what role there now emerges for the Soviet Union should Western policies remain unchanged. It is, specifically, to know what the Soviet Union can add to Western policies other than support by its abstinence from any actions that might derail Western initiatives.

Whether justified or not, skepticism about cooperation underlines a problem of fundamental importance, namely, that there has not emerged out of the new thinking a clear policy for Africa that is truly distinctive and that challenges or adds significantly to Western options. A mere disposition to conciliate the West, to "go along" with Washington in peripheral conflicted regions does not amount to much in the way of a change of policy. Conscientious cooperation on the scale envisaged requires clear policy, specifically directed to African issues rather than merely derivative of global superpower concerns, with a purpose and a well-articulated rationale. The apparent absence of this purpose provokes unease among Africans and to some extent undermines the positions of movements traditionally associated with the Soviet Union. If the new thinking proves to be infectious and such movements catch it, it is unlikely to represent much more than an ad hoc "tendency shift," rooted not in the realities of their own experience of struggle but in the pragmatism of the moment. In that regard, new thinking may not be much of an improvement on the "old" thinking.

Moscow will always have global and regional interests and perceptions of its own that will be different if not necessarily irreconcilable with those of the United States. That specter of difference between the superpowers, capable as it has been of producing mutually critical responses to situations as well as creative tension, has traditionally been considered a source of hope —one of very few—for oppressed peoples in the present international order.

To conclude, Soviet–U.S. cooperation on Namibia would have clear, urgent, and feasible tasks to perform in the economic field. However, it is likely that problems of security will remain compelling and urgent and are likely to be compounded by any deterioration in the country's economic situation. These considerations impose more dramatically than any others a need for the clearer definition of the aims and roles of the two global powers, not only as regards the formal attainment of independence in Namibia, but also for some considerable time and purposes beyond it.

NOTES

1. See J. Davidow, *A Peace in Southern Africa: The Lancaster House Conference on Rhodesia, 1979* (Boulder, Colo.: Westview Press, 1984); and D. Johnson and

P. Johnson, *The Struggle for Zimbabwe* (London: Faber & Faber, 1981), chapter 14.

2. It was no new departure to negotiate Namibia's future without SWAPO; what was remarkable this time round was the lack of a role for the frontline states who previously spoke for SWAPO. On this feature of diplomacy see, for example, M. A. Spiegel, "The Namibian Negotiations and the Problem of Neutrality," in *International Mediation in Theory and Practice, SAIS Papers in International Affairs No. 6*, eds. S. Touval and I. William Zartman (Boulder, Colo.: Westview Press, 1985).

3. See "Namibia Post Mortem," *Africa Confidential* 30, no. 8 (14 April 1989).

4. See *Africa Confidential* 30, no. 10 (12 May 1989); Antoine Bouillon, "Prétoria Joue les Divisions," in *Le Monde Diplomatique* (August 1989); David Beresford, "Bloody Road to Democracy," *Guardian*, 31 July 1989.

5. See Simon Barber, "Creating Realities: Some Final Thoughts from Dr. Chester Crocker," in *Optima* 37, no. 2 (June 1989).

6. According to figures in F. Tjingaete, "The Namibian Economy: Set the Market Free," *Optima* 37, no. 2 (June 1989), 76. South African budgetary aid for the period 1981/82–1988/89 totaled 2514.9 South African rand. No indication is given as to who were the beneficiaries of such assistance.

7. See R. Green, M. Kiljunen, and K. Kiljunen, *Namibia, the Last Colony* (London: Longman, 1981), especially chapter 11; see also Department of Information and Publicity, SWAPO of Namibia, *To Be Born a Nation: The Liberation Struggle for Namibia* (London: Zed Press, 1981), chapters 3–5.

8. See S. C. Nolutshungu, "South Africa and the Transfers of Power in Africa," in *Decolonization and African Independence: The Transfers of Power, 1960–1980*, eds. Prosser Gifford and William Roger Lewis (New Haven: Yale University Press, 1988).

PART 10

Conclusions

The hope of this project—to channel the enormous resources of the Soviet Union and United States toward assisting the development and security of the African continent—comes at a propitious time. It is a time of questioning the ideological rigidities that have precluded such cooperation in the past. Indeed, new thinking within both the Soviet Union and the United States is redirecting the goals of policy from the ideological to the practical; in other words, policy is increasingly geared toward facilitating increased human welfare worldwide, without political conditions. Just as important, it is a time when the countries of Africa need the benefits of cooperation more than ever.

Africans themselves may, with just historical cause, question the validity and beneficence of Soviet–U.S. cooperation. While some individuals and groups in Africa have actually profited from Soviet–U.S. competition, the great mass of African populations involved in conflicts in which either power has become a party generally suffer. To avoid perceptions that Soviet–U.S. cooperation for Africa is but a pause before worse things or that it might represent a "new hegemony," planning for cooperation must address these legitimate African concerns. Above all, cooperation must involve Africans and must incorporate their concerns into planning.

As a first step, perhaps paradoxically, it must be made clear what the self-interests of the Soviet Union and the United States in cooperating for Africa are. While statements of dedication to human welfare may be encouraging, skepticism of such statements can be overcome only through clearly stating what is at stake for those involved. In this regard, it must be emphasized that the global powers have a material stake in cooperating on behalf of Africa. This is because their conflict in Africa, as elsewhere, has consumed enormous resources, with little gain. Because it is an area of relatively low strategic priority to either the Soviet Union or the United States, Africa is probably the best region in the world for successful cooperation, which may subsequently extend to other regions.

Second, cooperation must be noninterventionary in substance and spirit, and it must be undertaken with modest goals in areas where benefits will occur reasonably quickly for all parties. The specific areas chosen for attention at the Airlie House conference constitute opportunities for cooperation where it is needed most, and where the Soviet Union and the United States possess a conjoint "comparative advantage" in providing assistance, as a result of their wealth of technical, educational, and financial resources. Through undertaking realizable goals, the achievement of productive results will be a major step toward overcoming skepticism.

African–Soviet–U.S. cooperation has the potential to produce great benefits for Africa, the Soviet Union, the United States, and for the world. For Africans to gain confidence in such cooperation the concerns discussed above must be treated with sensitivity, and the potential benefits of cooperation must be demonstrated. Cooperation in Africa can be an important confidence-building measure in another respect as well: it could improve the multilateral relations among the countries by reducing tensions, correcting misperceptions, promoting mutual understanding, and creating trust. In this improvement, the whole world benefits.

29

Cooperation for Africa as a Confidence-Building Measure

BOLAJI AKINYEMI

In 1975 détente floundered over the civil war in Angola. Henry Kissinger accused the Soviet Union of involvement in Angola, which he regarded as a violation of Soviet–U.S. understanding on regional conflicts. The Soviet Union did not agree with the United States that détente entailed any understanding on regional conflicts.

This chapter highlights ways in which the Soviet Union and the United States can cooperate in Africa to prevent African conflicts from spilling over in ways that damage their own relationship. *Can* the United States and the Soviet Union cooperate in the management of African regional conflicts so as to avoid damage to their bilateral relations? One might even broaden the scope of this question: Can successful Soviet–U.S. cooperative management of African regional conflicts reinforce a cooperative culture between the United States and the Soviet Union?

Although the question is more speculative than historical, it is best handled against a historical background. Afro-Soviet and Afro–U.S. relationships have never been independent of the Soviet–U.S. relationship. It would be erroneous to interpret this to mean that the United States and the Soviet Union have initiated African conflicts. On the contrary, an assessment of all the post-1945 conflicts in Africa will show that none was instigated by either power. African states have genuine grievances and differences among themselves that have sometimes resulted in conflicts. Of course, superpower intervention can, and often does, exacerbate these conflicts, changing their magnitude, direction, and even context. However well-intentioned, Soviet–U.S. cooperation cannot prevent African conflicts. The critical issue is whether the two powers can refrain from being dragged into them.

When the majority of African states achieved independence in and around 1960, they were confronted with an international environment that they perceived as alarming and perhaps threatening to their newly won independence. From their collective point of view, the cold war between the United States and the Soviet Union was not only at its peak, but was in danger of boiling over into a catastrophic world war. As Colin Legum has put it, "It was Africa's fate that it was required to find its feet in the international community at one of the most dangerous and complicated periods in all history."[1]

The newly independent African states, like most in the Third World, hardly desired involvement in any ideological dispute between the United States and the Soviet Union. Yet, the insistence of the superpowers—particularly the United States—that African states choose sides, coupled with their expressed abhorrence of the doctrine of nonalignment, was to create a rational fear among Africans of a menace to their newly won sovereignty and independence.[2]

It could be argued, quite correctly, that both the United States and the Soviet Union supported the African drive for independence; but this is not to imply that it was done in a spirit of cooperation. On the contrary, it was done in a spirit of competition, against a background of conflict, and as part of the overall strategy by each superpower to win the allegiance of the African states in their ideological struggle.

Certain things were obvious to concerned observers at the very beginning of this conflict. First, both superpowers regarded African and other developing states as not just important but crucial—though not critical—actors in the international system. In other words, there was no expectation by either of the superpowers that African states, having ascended to independence, would then fade into obscurity. Vernon McKay identified several reasons for this in his 1963 work.[3] The Soviet Union was the first of the two to have been innovative in courting African states. Unencumbered by the necessity to avoid offending allies, the Soviet Union staked out a position much closer to that of African states than to that of the United States.[4] In fact, as demonstrated by the maneuvering over the 1960 UN General Assembly resolution on the Granting of Independence to Colonial Countries and Peoples, the Soviet position was ahead of the African one.[5] Another example is seen in the Soviet rejection, following initial approval, of Dag Hammarskjöld's policies with respect to UN operations in the Congo, even when he was receiving the support of African states.[6]

The United States, on the other hand, in the period up to 1965, conducted its African policies under several handicaps: it had to tread cautiously through the minefields of African support for decolonization without offending its European allies, who not only still possessed colonies in Africa but who at the time showed varying degrees of enthusiasm for decolonization. Up until 1960, U.S. foreign policy was initiated by the conservative Eisenhower administration, whose basic ideological orientation did not dispose it to be supportive of Africa's aspirations for independence. The Kennedy administration sought to make up for lost ground through such programs as the Peace Corps, which, while not exclusively directed toward Africa, was well received there. As Richard Mahoney has shown, however, even though pro-African votes by U.S. delegations at international conferences became more regular, the Kennedy administration's policies toward Africa were spasmodic and included several false starts.[7]

Second, the African states, confronted with the cold war, did not opt for neutralism even though they were aware of the precedent of Austria and the Scandinavian countries. They opted instead for the Indian, Yugoslavian, and Ghanaian model of nonalignment. In this respect, there was a meeting of minds between the superpowers and the African states over the expectation that they would not be bystanders in international politics.[8]

Third, the African states were able to define not only the mode of their participation in international political deliberations—nonalignment—but also the content of those deliberations. As early as the First Conference of Independent African states, held in Accra, there was a marked difference in the attitudes of the two superpowers toward the African agenda. While the Soviet Union was supportive, the United States seemed bent on trying to change its contents. McKay refers to this historic event as "the Soviets ask[ing] the right questions,"[9] while for Mazrui, it was a case "of [the] Soviet Government's greater sensitivity to the aspirations of nationalists than has been the case among policymakers in Washington."[10] Differences between the Soviet Union and the United States in regard to African realities translated into opportunities for African states to exercise a measure of independence.

Initially, radical African states flirted with the idea of appealing to an international sense of solidarity and action in overthrowing "neocolonialist" regimes. This amounted to an invitation to the Soviet Union to meddle in African domestic affairs; but the OAU soon rejected that idea when it decreed that even African states have no right to overthrow any independent African government for any reason, ideological or otherwise. However, on continental issues such as decolonization, the movement to end apartheid, and economic development, African states conceded an active role for the superpowers. While African states were committed to the continental issues irrespective of the responses from the superpowers, it was nonetheless hoped that they would provide assistance in achieving Africa's collective goals.

As pointed out earlier, the African states became independent at the peak of the cold war and were apprehensive of its effects on their survival. Hence, Mwalimu Julius Nyerere, then president of Tanzania, expressing a common point of view, lamented that "when elephants fight, the grass suffers." The riposte by Lee Kuan Yew, the prime minister of Singapore, that "when elephants play, the grass also suffers" was to be much appreciated among Africans for several reasons. First, the strategy and tactics of the cold war changed from the threat of nuclear annihilation to competitively peaceful coexistence. Second, both superpowers set out to woo African states, competing with offers of financial and technical aid. Third, the concrete items on the African agenda, both continental and global, elicited different responses from the two superpowers. In sum total, the era of competitive peaceful coexistence was one in which the African states could and did engage in manipulation for their own purposes. However, it was not all unidirectional: the Soviet Union and the United States manipulated African states and conflicts between them in pursuing their own ends.

There is no doubt that Soviet–U.S. competition has influenced—often to the benefit of Africans—a number of historically critical events in Africa, such as the wars of liberation in Angola, Mozambique, Guinea-Bissau, Algeria, and Zimbabwe. This competition has also led to positive investments in developmental projects; examples include Soviet financing of the Aswan Dam and U.S. financing of the Volta Dam. On the other hand, the coup d'état against Nkrumah, the prolongation of the civil war in Angola, and several aspects of the Congo crisis are cases in which manipulation by outside powers had negative results.

In summary, then, it is obvious that apart from the period when there was a real danger that the cold war would degenerate into an actual shooting war, with African states the predictable losers, African states have, on balance, been the beneficiaries of the competitive relationship between the United States and the Soviet Union.

African problems are by no means over. Items remaining on the agenda are the antiapartheid struggle, the debt burden, declining standards of living, drought, epidemics, the dumping in Africa of industrialized nations' wastes, the struggle for the New International Economic Order, and several others. How will Soviet–U.S. cooperation affect these issues?

A brief historical excursus will provide some insight into this question. There was, some will recall, an ephemeral flowering of a minidétente following the Cuban missile crisis in 1962. The effect of this event on Africa was described by Ali Mazrui:

> This détente helped to reduce what little status Africa had as a "crisis area." From then on the Soviet-American scramble to buy the ideological souls of Africans lost its momentum. For as long as non-alignment had been regarded as dangerously near to communism, Africa had a chance of being regarded as "critical." The year of 1962 was, in fact, that peak year of American aid to Africa for that period. But in the fiscal year 1963 the economic assistance program for Africa began to drop back. From 12.5 per cent of the AID figure, Africa's share dropped to 10.4 per cent in 1963 and then 8.8 per cent in 1964. There are a number of reasons to explain this drop, including the overall global reduction of American foreign aid. But even the global reduction might be somewhat connected with the change in the tempo of the cold war following the Soviet-American détente. With that change Africa shrunk even further in her status.[11]

At the time of this minidétente, McKay raised certain questions that are pertinent to the discussion of the possible effects of the current climate of Soviet–U.S. relations. He wrote:

Considerable speculation has recently been devoted to the possibility of a Soviet-American détente and its effect on Africa. For example, would a détente lead to a reduction of armaments and thereby free more funds for economic aid to Africa? Or would it only weaken the United States Administration in its annual battle with Congress for appropriation for aid. On balance, it seems unlikely that a Soviet-American détente would change the underlying goals of the U.S. and the USSR in Africa.[12]

Conventional wisdom has it that in 1975 Kissinger thought that part of the understanding underpinning the Nixon-Brezhnev détente was that the Soviet Union would stop its military support for liberation movements and governments involved in civil wars in Africa. Hence, the continuing Soviet support for, and airlift of arms to, Ethiopia and the Angolan Popular Liberation Movement (MPLA) government in Angola, were regarded by the United States as a violation of détente. And yet support for the Ethiopian and Angolan governments has been reaffirmed year in and year out by the OAU, not only out of expediency but on a firmly rooted interpretation of articles (2) and (3) of its charter. The Kissingerian interpretation of détente is not peculiar to Kissinger but derives from a globalist tendency in U.S. African policy that is always in competition with an Africanist one. As regards the effect on Africa, Mazrui concluded that "détente between the Soviet Union and the USA reduced even the competitive motive behind the favours bestowed by the superpowers on the smaller countries of the world."[13]

Two conclusions can be drawn from the United States' position in 1975. First, on the surface, it would appear that Kissinger was advocating a policy of benign neutrality toward African conflicts. But was this benign neutrality global? Was abstention from intervention applicable to all countries, including the former imperial powers? Or was it applicable only to the two superpowers? If it was global, then it would have had to be applicable to both alliance systems. Yet, France, Belgium, Saudi Arabia, and, to some extent, Britain have a track record of political and military acts in Africa over which the United States has had no control. But the United States would have held the Soviet Union responsible for Cuban troops in Angola and for East bloc military assistance to Ethiopia.

In essence, then, the position of the United States amounted to this: Africa was not a traditional arena of Soviet diplomacy, and to that extent Soviet military assistance in conflict areas, even when that assistance was to established governments, violated détente. This conclusion is thus expressed by Peter Shearman: "The Nixon Administration never intended to give Moscow the equal status it sought. It rather hoped to contain Soviet influence in the Third World through a strategy of linkage, combined with sophisticated diplomacy designed to exclude the Soviet Union from areas where it already had a stake. [However,] the lack of ground rules for superpower behaviour in the Third World resulted in both sides seeking unilateral advantage in areas of regional conflict."[14]

If the Soviet Union had accepted the United States' position, the net result would have been to leave Africa at the mercy of the former imperial powers, as well as to circumscribe the external maneuverability of African countries. For example, if the Nigerian civil war had been fought during a period of détente, it would have been permissible for the Nigerian government to have turned to Britain for the purchase of arms, but not to the Soviet Union for the same arms. The second conclusion, as already shown by Mazrui, is the relationship between the level of aid for Africa and the state of the Soviet–U.S. relationship. So, Lee Kuan Yew's prophetic words— "when elephants play, the grass also suffers"—have been shown to be correct.

In assessing and predicting U.S. policy toward Africa, attention has already been drawn to the competition between the globalist and Africanist tendencies in U.S. African policymaking. Irrespective of the occupant in the White House, both tendencies will continue to push themselves forward; and which will predominate on any particular issue will depend on the ideological predisposition of the incumbent president.

In assessing and predicting Soviet policy toward Africa, a variable to be examined is the impact on Africa-related issues of perestroika. In the earlier parts of this chapter, reference was made to the fact that the Soviet Union was more sympathetic than the United States to African political goals and aspirations. It should be pointed out that this was done because it was in the Soviet national interest to do so. The Soviet Union at this time wanted to be accepted as a superpower. A superpower must have global interests, global presence, and global capability. The emerging Third World, which included Africa, seeking a world role and status independent of former Western colonial domination, represented opportunities for the Soviet Union to make new friends and to expand its areas of acceptability and influence. To that extent, there was a relationship that was beneficial to Africa between Soviet support for African causes and the Soviet need to be perceived as a superpower.

To what extent is perestroika going to affect the perception of this symbiotic relationship? A recent indication given by Vadim Medvedev, the new Kremlin chief of ideology, isolates two relevant factors. First, "peaceful coexistence" is no longer a tactic of the moment but a "long-term process." Second, common human values take precedence over "class struggles" in international relations. The full import of the new ideology will have to await a more comprehensive elucidation by the Kremlin and Soviet theoreticians. However, given the fact that the ideological basis for Soviet support for African liberation movements and radical African governments was the perception that though these political elements were of the "national bourgeoisie" variety they were still part of the international "class struggle," should we expect a reduction in support for liberation movements and radical governments in Africa?

Because of its colonial past, Africa still belongs to the free enterprise (capitalist) system. Programs that are advocated to solve Africa's economic problems entail structural and directional changes in the continent's linkages with the West. Even though the African states have not perceived themselves as waging a class struggle in making these demands, Soviet support for African demands has been predicated on ideological grounds based on the doctrine of class struggle. What will be the impact of the search for "common human values" on Soviet support for Africa on such issues as dealing with the debt burden and achieving the New International Economic Order?

In the new party program, the shift of emphasis has already been signaled; emphasis has shifted toward "newly liberated countries" and away from "national liberation movements," developing countries of socialist orientation are called upon to depend more on their own resources and less on Soviet aid, and there is explicit admission that the Soviet Union will seek to improve its relationship with developing countries "following a capitalist path of development." In other words, the Soviet Union intends to behave as an industrialized state operating in the Third World rather than as an ideological state. Presumably, the economic and technological challenges that this will pose to Western interests will be more acceptable to Washington than technical, economic, and military assistance to Angola and Ethiopia. And yet, will it always be obvious to Washington when the Soviet Union is behaving on a pragmatic rather than an ideological basis?

Earlier on I pointed out how Soviet support for Africa was based on an assessment of Soviet national interests. How is perestroika going to cope with the imperatives still facing the Soviet Union as a superpower? Among Gorbachev's objectives is the one of confirming the Soviet Union as a superpower. A superpower will hardly pass up opportunities to extend its influence and interests when they present themselves. This is no less than an imperative of power. How is Gorbachev going to confront this imperative?

President Gorbachev has stepped out boldly with imaginative proposals on disarmament that have struck a responsive cord all over the world, including Africa. Would this presage more aid for Africa? It is unlikely. One of the fallacies of the disarmament and development school is the untested and unproved assertion that disarmament will release more resources for foreign aid. There is no doubt that Gorbachev's embrace of disarmament has a lot to do with his perceived need to release more resources for the consumer sector of the Soviet economy. It is the Soviet economy rather than African economies that will be the beneficiary of disarmament. This point could be buttressed on two further grounds. First, even during the heyday of the conflict and competition with the United States, the Soviet

Union concentrated more on military than technical and humanitarian aid. Both the Soviet Union and the United States have justified aid on the grounds that it is a useful weapon in fighting the cold war. Without the cold war, will the moral concept of the global village be compelling enough for Congress or the Kremlin to vote more resources for aid in meeting African developmental needs? Assessing the forty-third United Nations General Assembly, Nigel Hawkes observed that "not everybody is wholly delighted about the cozy atmosphere that has developed between the big powers. . . . Neither the U.S. nor the Soviet Union, in their main statements of policy to the General Assembly, mentioned Third World debt, a sign of the times that stirs understandable resentment among the poor."[15]

It is difficult to controvert Legum's verdict that "Africa can claim a defensive interest in exploiting the existence of international rivalries to obtain benefits which otherwise it would be too weak to obtain by itself."[16]

If the Soviet Union and the United States follow through in their determination to cooperate on behalf of Africa, the impact of this cooperation will depend on the kind of consensus on which it is based. There are three possible scenarios. First, were U.S. African policy to continue in a globalist vein, it would have to be matched by the Soviet Union's refraining from pursuing an active African policy. Second, a consensus based on both the United States and the Soviet Union pursuing Africanist policies will result in their both supporting the same forces in Africa. The third scenario would see the Soviet Union pursuing an Africanist policy and the United States refraining from pursuing an active policy, an option that is not worth considering because of its high improbability.

The critical factor is that issues on the African agenda are determined initially by the Africans themselves, although the outcomes are subject to varying degrees of external involvement. In essence, Soviet–U.S. cooperation could not have prevented the civil wars in Angola and Ethiopia. It could not have prevented the Ethiopian-Somali war. It could not have prevented the breaking out of the antiapartheid struggle. However, the direction, intensity, and outcome of these and other issues are affected by the attitudes of the superpowers. It is only if both superpowers adopt Africanist-oriented positions on African issues that Africans and their interests will be served. If either or both the superpowers adopt a globalist approach, there cannot be cooperation, and whatever ensues cannot be confidence building.

NOTES

1. Colin Legum, "The Growth of Africa's Foreign Policy: From Illusion to Reality," in Robert K. A. Gardiner, M. J. Anstee, and C. L. Patterson, eds., *Africa and the World* (Addis Ababa: Oxford University Press 1970).

2. See Vernon McKay, *African Diplomacy: Studies in the Determinants of Foreign Policy* (New York: Praeger, 1961) for a brief but thorough discussion of the

hostility shown by both superpowers to nonalignment. See also Waldemar A. Nielsen, *The Great Powers and Africa* (London: Pall Mall Press, 1969), 191; and Ali Mazrui, *Africa's International Relations* (London: Heinemann, 1977), 180.

3. McKay, *African Diplomacy*, 149.

4. See Nielsen, *Great Powers*, 191; and Mazrui, *Africa's International Relations*, 180.

5. The Soviet Union wanted the UN to adopt a position of immediate independence for all colonies, while the African states settled for a phased and gradual granting of independence.

6. See Conor Cruise O'Brien, *To Katanga and Back: A UN Case History* (New York: Princeton University Press, 1962), and Rajeshwar Dayal, *Mission for Hammarskjöld* (Princeton: Princeton University Press, 1974).

7. Richard D. Mahoney, *JFK: Ordeal in Africa* (New York: Oxford University Press, 1983).

8. See Colin Legum, *Pan-Africanism. A Short Political Guide* (London: Pall Mall Press, 1962), 38–64.

9. McKay, *African Diplomacy*, 17.

10. Mazrui, *Africa's International Relations*, 180.

11. Ibid., 160–161.

12. McKay, *African Diplomacy*, 12.

13. Mazrui, *Africa's International Relations*, p. 183.

14. Peter Shearman, "Gorbachev and the Third World: An Era of Reform?" *Third World Quarterly* 9, no. 4: 1115–1116.

15. *The Observer*, 2 October 1988.

16. Gardiner, *Africa and the World*, 52.

30

From Confrontation to Cooperation: The Possibilities

MICHAEL D. INTRILIGATOR

African–Soviet–U.S. cooperation would be of enormous value to African people, countries, and regions, and also valuable to both the Soviet Union and the United States. It could facilitate more effective development in Africa and improve bilateral political relations among Africa, the United States and the USSR. It could also lead to cooperation in other regions or in other areas of mutual interest. Together with other initiatives for cooperation, it could even lead to a fundamental change in the overall relationships between the global powers, from confrontation to cooperation, with benefits to the entire world.[1]

But is cooperation between the Soviet Union and the United States for the benefit of Africa a realistic goal? What reasonably can be expected of Soviet–U.S. cooperation in and for Africa? At first glance, neither the historical record of Soviet and U.S. intervention and interaction in the continent nor traditional Western political theory is a source of optimism. Yet, thoughtful analysis suggests that there is, indeed, a basis for hopeful expectations for such cooperation in both fact and theory. Furthermore, there have been changes in the perceptions of all parties concerned, as well as in their real ability to influence the outcomes of international competition. The benefits of political and economic stability in Africa are now more clearly perceived and appreciated within both the United States and the Soviet Union. Africans have, on their side, realized the costs of Soviet–U.S. confrontation in Africa and may therefore be willing to consider, as a result of both the harsh lessons of experience and the realization of a real degree of power on their part, the possibility of African–Soviet–U.S. cooperation.

For those primarily concerned with the welfare of the African people, the appeal of Soviet–U.S. cooperation lies in its potential for effective development and improvement in the overall conditions of life. Cooperation in Africa would be valuable to both the Soviet Union and the United States, in acting as a confidence-building measure, helping move Soviet–U.S. relations toward cooperation on a world scale.

A POLITICAL AND GAME-THEORETIC BASIS
FOR COOPERATION

The "realist" school of political theory, whose principal adherents are Western and especially U.S. scholars, holds that the interactions of nation-states are typically guided along the lines of calculated national self-interest.[2] The question derived from the writings of these "realists" is: What incentive could there be for the Soviet Union and the United States to cooperate on behalf of third parties with little tangible benefit to either for their efforts? In fact, the realist position typically envisions the competition for relative power between the world's strongest states as the determining factor in global political relations.

The alternative point of view argues that the motivations, attitudes, and perceptions of decisionmakers are critical determinants of a nation's behavior in the international arena.[3] Although analysts differ sharply on the effects of misperception, many hold with Ayoob that "international relations, perceptions, whether they do or do not coincide with reality, are infinitely more important than reality itself."[4] On this view, the realist interpretation of the international system may be less an explanation of the real world than a description of the dominant mind-set of policymakers.

Something like this has apparently dominated (to differing extents of intensity, depending on a variety of factors over time) many state relations in ways captured in the most elementary form of game models that construct the world in "zero-sum" terms. Thus, policymakers in both the Soviet Union and the United States have believed that gains to one side are necessarily losses to the other.[5] In fact, the record of Soviet–U.S. competition in Africa is indicative. The worst scenario is that although involvement in a local conflict may not entail clear gains and might actually result in heavy costs, external antagonists will involve themselves nonetheless simply in order to deny gains to their opponents.

This way of "playing the game" reflects the attitudes, perceptions, and expectations of opponents, rather than any absolute realities or natural law of international competition. This has been illustrated in Robert Axelrod's now-famous experiment in game theory.[6] Pitting players against one another in a computer tournament involving the game of Prisoner's Dilemma,[7] he showed that when the game is repeated, an overall strategy that yielded the best outcomes was that of "tit for tat," leading to cooperation.[8] More recent studies have shown that an overall strategy of simply always cooperating can in certain game situations yield even better results.[9]

In fact, it should be noted that in any calculation of the national self-interest, both the Soviet Union and the United States have more to gain from cooperation than confrontation. Because this theoretical viewpoint poses the harshest challenge to disbelief in the possibility of African–Soviet–U.S. cooperation, the point requires elaboration.

There are two basic reasons Soviet–U.S. cooperation may be in the interests of all parties concerned. The first relates to the costliness to all of confrontation. In those conflicts on the African continent in which the global powers have been involved directly or indirectly as antagonists—the Congo, Angola, the Horn of Africa, and elsewhere—there are usually no "winners" or "losers" but protracted, costly, and politically damaging quagmires for the two. Part of the reason, as Alexander George has pointed out, is that Africa has been peripheral to the main concerns of both Soviet and U.S. foreign policy.[10] Gains of one at the expense of the other could be achieved, it appears to have been thought, at low cost. As such, both have repeatedly allowed themselves to become enmeshed in conflicts, with all too little forethought given to consequences.[11] Soviet–U.S. rivalry in Africa is not a zero-sum game. It is negative-sum. The benefits of such conflicts have often accrued to but a few opportunistic politicians and soldiers; the losers in the end are their powerful allies, and, above all, the people living in the areas of conflict.

The second reason Soviet–U.S. cooperation is in the interests of both is less immediately apparent but nonetheless real. It lies in the observation that conflict is a barrier to development. A rapidly developing Africa serves the interests of not only Africa but also the major industrialized nations and the world at large. If left in its current underdeveloped state and facing chronic natural and human disasters—from drought and famine to protracted and widespread warfare—Africa can only be a net drain on world resources. On the other hand, if Africa were aided to grow in economic potential, its enormous physical and human resources could contribute to the general welfare of the world.[12]

A further observation from a game-theoretic perspective is that the "game" was never, and is increasingly less so, between just the Soviet Union and the United States. African governments, rather than being passive witnesses to the "games" between the global powers on their own terrain, have been players in their own right. At a minimum, Soviet–U.S. competition for their allegiance has given them room for maneuver in strategically playing the one off the other. The negative implication of this situation is that unscrupulous leaders, lacking sufficient internal legitimacy to sustain their rule through domestic means, have been known with disturbing frequency to play the "great power game," threatening, for instance, to shift allegiance from one to the other if its principal ally fails to be forthcoming with resources.[13] A further implication is that the negative results of a zero-sum game or a single-play Prisoner's Dilemma mentality can be exacerbated by the even more negative blow to U.S. and Soviet claims to be leaders in the world movement for improved political and economic rights of the oppressed.

The positive implication of the observation that African states have acquired a measure of power in their own right lies in the increasing realization of leading African policymakers that they are the masters of their own fate. Increasingly, Soviet and U.S. policymakers are becoming aware of this fact as well, with consequences for their behavior toward each other. No longer can they hope to "score" gains at each other's expense, because they are likely to find themselves drawn into a game not of their own devising. The realities of Africa and the virtual impossibility that Soviet–U.S. competition can provide benefits to any but a few individuals, means that there is a need for changes in perception, insofar as competitive mentalities still exist.

Looking at the situation as a three-player game changes the game-theoretic analysis considerably. In such a situation one must take account of the possibilities for coalition formation.[14] In such a game "superadditivity" is typically found, where coalitions gain at least as much, if not more, than their constituent elements of individual players or smaller coalitions. If there are considerable gains from coalition formation, then such coalitions will eventually emerge, entailing cooperation among their constituent elements. Here the "grand coalition" of the Soviet Union, the United States, and Africa stands to gain considerably more than any smaller coalition. Each can play an important contributing role to the grand coalition.

WHY AFRICA?

There are compelling reasons Africa may be the most viable starting point for Soviet–U.S. cooperation in the international arena. As noted in the intro-dution to this book, there have been some examples of such cooperation in the past, which provide precedents. While Africa has enormous mineral resources and important sea lanes, as far as the Soviet Union and the United States are concerned, it is a lower priority for foreign policy than other parts of the world. Africa borders on neither country; trade between Africa and these two states, although important and growing in some areas, remains relatively insignificant; and conflicts on the continent have not contained high stakes, tangible or ideological, for either.[15] Although it may be extreme, in a sense, to cite the excellent record of Soviet and U.S. cooperation in Antarctica as a model for cooperation in Africa, the point remains that cooperation is most possible to achieve where the risks involved are lower.

The example of Antarctica, where there is excellent cooperation, may be an instructive one. An important foundation for cooperation there was the Antarctica Treaty of 1959. This was also one of the first arms control treaties, in that it banned nuclear weapons from the region. There were many arms control treaties that followed the Antarctica Treaty. In the same way, cooperation between the United States and the Soviet Union, which could be initiated in Africa, could possibly lead to cooperation not only in other regions but also in other substantive areas, such as cooperation in treating global ecological and health challenges.

This much said, however, it remains true that getting the point across to policymakers may entail some significant changes in perceptions on their part. This is because of the way Third World areas have been viewed historically in the context of Soviet–U.S. global rivalry. Mutual annihilation on the part of the Soviet Union and the United States has become a real possibility through their mutual deterrence regime, which implies that direct confrontation must be avoided at all costs. Not precluded, however, is indirect conflict, and competition has proceeded apace between the Soviet Union and the United States. The direct costs of this conflict have been borne by others, however. As Gupta puts it:

> The very stability of the global power balance and the determination of the Great Powers to avoid a confrontation makes them prone to seek lower levels of conflict and less dangerous ways of conducting their rivalries, which, in effect, means a concerted attempt to confine their conflicts to problems far removed from the areas where their vital interests are involved. To fight out their battles in the Third World is one way of ensuring that their own worlds are not touched by their conflicts and that they retain a great measure of option to escalate and deescalate their conflicts according to the need of their relationships.[16]

Because the perceived costs of conflict by proxy in the Third World were low, it became the preferred field of action for Soviet and U.S. antagonism.[17] That this perception was incorrect from the start is, of course, the subject matter of the preceding section. An increasing number of statements that are positive toward Soviet–U.S. cooperation in reducing conflict in Africa attests to an emerging change in the perceptions of policymakers as well.[18]

Policymakers in both the Soviet Union and the United States entered into conflicts on the continent of Africa, in part because the interests there of both were relatively low in priority. The apparent fallacy in reasoning on both sides was that low interests equated to low risks in conflict. Yet, just as low objective interest could, and did, lead to high costs in conflict, it may result in great benefits through cooperation.

AFRICAN CONCERNS AND THE POTENTIAL FOR COOPERATION

Opinion in Africa or in the Third World generally may be justifiably skeptical with regard to Soviet–U.S. cooperation, given the negative results of their interaction in past decades.

As reflected in several chapters in this book, Africans in particular may be skeptical about or even hostile to the idea of Soviet–U.S. cooperation for Africa, seeing it possibly as another colonial type of experience. After all, the longest sustained example of real cooperation among other external powers with respect to Africa was in the form of colonialism. Africans may also fear the imposition of a Soviet–U.S. hegemonic regime in Africa, which could then become one of exploitation. They may wonder if Africa will be the prize rewarded to the Soviet Union and the United States for changing from confrontation to cooperation. Even more immediate concerns will be the role of continuing assistance programs.

A major challenge will be that of reassuring African people and nations that none of these fears and concerns are warranted. Soviet–U.S. cooperation for Africa primarily benefits Africa, and not the United States and the USSR, although they can also benefit in an indirect way. Africans are justified in questioning such cooperation, but they should be reassured by previous instances of Soviet–U.S. cooperation and respect for the sovereignty of African nations. Still, the first instances of cooperation should be clear examples of the potential value of cooperation from the standpoint of Africa. African skepticism and hostility will have to be overcome and replaced by trust in the value of cooperation. While the discussion thus far has referred to "Soviet–U.S. cooperation," it is clear that there will have to be genuine three way cooperation—African–Soviet–U.S. —in order for it to be successful.

Such cooperation must be noninterventionary in character and spirit, and it must be undertaken with modest goals in areas where benefits will occur quickly for all parties. It is cooperation of this sort that is the objective of this project. The specific areas chosen constitute opportunities for cooperation where it is needed most, and where the Soviet Union and United States possess a conjoint "comparative advantage" in providing assistance. As a case in point, in one of these areas—that concerned with environmental protection—both the United States and the Soviet Union possess a wealth of technical, educational, and financial resources as a result of their own experience with combating desertification and other environmental problems. As another example, in the area of minerals development, the two countries could play a constructive, noninterventionary role by combining their resources in a way designed to facilitate the transformation of mineral-exporting nations into manufacturers of mineral-using industrial products. In these and all the other areas discussed at the conference, the goal of cooperation must be both modest and results-oriented in order for initial cooperation to succeed and the subsequent goals to be met.

COOPERATION AS A
CONFIDENCE-BUILDING MEASURE

If successful, African–Soviet–U.S. cooperation can capture the imagination of both Soviet and U.S. citizens perhaps more than other confidence-building measures. It could lead to cooperation in other regions and also in other areas of concern. At various times people have cited trade, cultural exchanges, exchanges of visitors, student exchanges, arms control agreements, and cooperation in space as initiatives that could be interpreted as confidence-building measures. All are valuable, and each can play a role in improving bilateral relations. Cooperation in Africa can, however, also play an important role in improving bilateral relations. African, Soviet, and U.S. people working together can inspire others to work together for common purposes. Such a program can be important to the people of the world, as well as to the people of the Soviet Union and the United States, and appreciated through the media of radio, television, magazines, and newspapers, as was done in the case of the famines in Ethiopia and Sudan. In fact, the creation of mechanisms for confidence building, beyond the personal experience of most, could provide hope and satisfaction. The clear need for help in Africa and the reality that the United States and the USSR possess the skills and resources needed to undertake this effort are the ultimate legitimating elements of a new order.

African–Soviet–U.S. cooperation for Africa, if successful, will capture the imagination of the world and lead to cooperation in other regions and also in other areas of concern. It might well be followed by cooperation for other Third World countries. It could buttress the approach of defining as global problems those of health, communication, energy, food production, and the environment. Soviet–U.S. relations can be transformed from confrontation and conflict to cooperation, and thereby promote a fundamental change in the structure of global international relations.

NOTES

1. See Vitalii I. Goldanskii and Michael D. Intriligator, "U.S.–Soviet Relations: From Confrontation to Cooperation Through Verification Deterrence," and Michael D. Intriligator, "Soviet 'New Thinking' and the Prospect for a New East-West Relationship" (in Russian), *MEMO* (journal of the Institute of World Economy and International Relations, Academy of Sciences of the USSR), September 1988.

2. For a classic summary statement and critique of the realist view, see Robert Keohane, ed., *Neorealism and Its Critics* (New York: Columbia University Press, 1986).

3. See, for example, Robert Jervis, "Beliefs About Soviet Behavior," in *Containment, Soviet Behavior, and Grand Strategy,* ed. Robert E. Osgood (Berkeley: Institute of International Studies, 1981).

4. Mohammed Ayoob, ed., *Conflict and Intervention in the Third World* (London: Croom Helm, 1980), 241.

5. For an exploration of the changing nature of U.S. containment policy, see John Lewis Gaddis, *Strategies of Containment: A Critical Appraisal of Postwar American National Security Policy* (New York: Oxford University Press, 1982).

6. For a thorough and rigorous introduction to game theory in application to political issues, see Peter C. Ordeshook, *Game Theory and Political Theory: An Introduction* (Cambridge: Cambridge University Press, 1986).

7. Prisoner's Dilemma simulates the tension inherent in much of international politics. In this game, two prisoners are faced with a choice between informing on each other ("defecting"), or cooperating by maintaining silence. This latter course (cooperation) yields the highest benefits to both: the "payoff" is that both are released from jail since the authorities have no information with which to convict either. If one prisoner informs while the other remains silent, then the informer receives a reduced sentence while the other is convicted. The "dilemma" (by assumption in "single-play" games) lies in the fact that neither knows initially what the other will do. Thus, the "dominant strategy" is for both to inform on the other. Yet, in doing so both prisoners are worse off than had they cooperated. The lesson of the game is that even when the benefits of cooperation are known, uncertainty or ignorance about the potential acts of others makes noncooperation the perceived safer course. The value of Axelrod's experiment is to demonstrate that when interaction between antagonists is repeated ad infinitum, both parties tend to gravitate toward a modus vivendi of cooperation even in the absence of communication between them.

8. Robert Axelrod, *The Evolution of Cooperation* (New York: Basic Books, 1984).

9. See Jack Hirshleifer and Juan Carlos Martinez Coll, *What Strategies Can Support the Evolutionary Emergence of Cooperation?* (CISA Working Paper no. 58, Center for International and Strategic Affairs, UCLA, Los Angeles, 1987).

10. See Alexander George, *Managing U.S.–Soviet Rivalry: Problems of Crisis Prevention* (Boulder, Colo.: Westview Press, 1983).

11. For a thoughtful and thorough examination of Soviet–U.S. involvement in a number of African confrontations, see I. William Zartman, *Ripe for Resolution: Conflict and Intervention in Africa* (New York: Oxford University Press, 1985).

12. For an elaboration of this point, which focuses on the benefits to advanced countries of trade with an economically strong Africa, see John W. Sewell and Christine E. Contee, "U.S. Foreign Aid in the 1980s: Reordering Priorities," in *U.S. Foreign Policy and the Third World: Agenda 1985–86,* eds. John W. Sewell, Richard E. Feinberg, and Valeriana Kallab (New Brunswick, N.J.: Transaction Books, 1985).

13. See, for example, Thomas M. Callaghy, "External Actors and the Relative Autonomy of the Political Aristocracy in Zaire," *The Journal of Commonwealth and Comparative Politics* 21 (November 1983): 61–83.

14. See Michael D. Intriligator, *Mathematical Optimization and Economic Theory* (Englewood Cliffs, N.J.: Prentice Hall, 1971), especially the discussion of the characteristic function description of a game.

15. For a detailed discussion of these points with respect to U.S. policy toward Africa, see James S. Coleman and Richard L. Sklar, "Introduction," in *African Crisis Areas and U.S. Foreign Policy,* eds. Gerald J. Bender, James S. Coleman, and Richard L. Sklar (Berkeley: University of California Press, 1985), 1–31.

16. Quoted in Ayoob, *Conflict and Intervention,* 242.

17. Those familiar with simple two-person game theory will recognize the situation as one in which the dominant strategy of both players in a zero-sum situation is to defect. It may be visualized as a game of "chicken," wherein two drivers are headed toward each other in the middle of the road on the dare that one of them will swerve away first, the winner keeping his nerve and heading straight. When conflict by proxy is involved, the incentive to defect (i.e., not to swerve) is enhanced

by the situation in which the principal antagonists are not even present inside the cars, but control them from afar, thus not risking harm to themselves.

18. For a summary of statements reflecting changed Soviet thinking on cooperation for peace in Africa, see Peter Shearman, "Gorbachev and the Third World: An Era of Reform," *Third World Quarterly* 9 (October 1987): 1083–1117.

31

Let Us Cooperate

ANATOLY A. GROMYKO

Ancient Romans used to say: *Sol lucet omnibus* (The sun shines upon all). For centuries this maxim would remain a moral call for curbing universal selfishness and the insidious policy of force. Now, when we are about to step into the third millennium of the Christian era, humankind has what is probably its last chance to turn this maxim into a political principle of universal survival. The sun cannot shine on only an elected few. Either it shines upon all, or none.

It is difficult at the moment to recollect in what African country I happened to hear this fable: A rhinoceros stole life-giving fire from the people, then went to hide in a cave. Darkness fell upon earth. The chief dispatched his bravest warriors to take possession of the fire by force. But the rhinoceros was stronger. The fire was shining on the tip of his horn. The chief's warriors were terrified by this sight and fled. But with the chief's order not yet executed they feared to face him. So they caught a poor and hungry man, pushed him into the cave and told him that they would never let him out unless he got the fire. The poor man had no other choice but to approach the rhinoceros. The latter decided against killing the man at once. The rhinoceros was very strong, he felt that the man was in his power, and being rather bored he wanted to amuse himself.

"Make me laugh," said the rhinoceros to the man, "and maybe then I shall give you back the fire."

"What can I do to amuse you?" answered the poor man. "I've had nothing to eat for three days. On account of my debt the chief has taken away all my possessions, even my wife. His warriors have seized me and pushed me into this cave for you to eat me up."

And the man started complaining to the rhinoceros of his misfortunes. However, the more he complained the merrier became the rhinoceros. The man's infirmity made him laugh. He enjoyed seeing the man miserable and helpless. In the presence of such a wretched creature the rhinoceros felt even stronger, more powerful. In the end he could not stand it any longer and fell rolling on the floor, roaring with laughter. The fire rolled off the tip of his horn and onto the ground. The man snatched the fire and ran out of the cave.

The man never attempted to outwit the rhinoceros. He was sincere with him. All the misfortunes about which he complained to the rhinoceros were actual and not imaginary. Moreover, the man did not lose a bit of his human self. Hopeless as the situation was, he went on looking for a way out. But what about the rhinoceros? He conducted himself as a rhinoceros might be expected to. The thing that draws tears from a man makes a rhinoceros laugh. And the rhinoceros paid dearly for such amusement.

We live in times full of peril. It is quite possible that some people may consider the present state of affairs hopeless. As oversaturated with arms as it is, poisoned with industrial discharges, tormented by the incompetent hands of man, inflicted with diseases, and torn apart by conflicts, our planet can bear such conditions only so long. But we are human beings and we are inspired not only by the hope that everything might turn for the better but also by a determined effort to find a way out of the labyrinth of despair. Once having perceived the grave dimensions of imminent danger, humankind may for once realize that the world is a single indivisible whole. While preserving the multiformity of social life, humankind may gradually come to understand that feelings of national egoism should be situated in a perspective that is framed by a willingness to combine the legitimate interests of separate countries and peoples with the task of preserving "the common home of earthly civilization."

Of course, people have different notions of what this "home" may be like. For some it may be a "glittering city on the hill"; for others, a "European home"; for yet others, a "new structure of socialist civilization." This latter notion corresponds to what we in the Soviet Union are now erecting, gradually getting rid of a multitude or out own mistakes and prejudices. We pay tribute to different visions of the future of world civilization; we respect these differences, but we must realize that the Golden Age of humanity will either come to all countries and peoples or it will come to none at all.

The Soviet Union and the United States shoulder special responsibility for the future of the world. It does not mean, however, that we have a right to tell other nations how they should shape their future, what future to dream of, or what ways to choose to solve the problems they have. Freedom of choice is one of the main principles of the new political thinking. Only the recognition of its universal nature can ensure stability in international relations under present conditions of growing diversity in the world. For centuries billions of people stayed outside the mainstream of the historical process, now they are becoming aware of their role as creators of history. There is no doubt that they will have a decisive voice in determining their own way of development.

Those who put barriers in the way of this process resemble the rhinoceros from that African tale. However, while being favorably disposed toward new states seeking their developmental paths, the Soviet Union and the United States should not keep aloof and ignore the problems these states have to face. A degrading quality of life—when it comes to millions of people—is a factor of political instability and uncertainty no less important than the confrontation between East and West.

Just as positive changes in Soviet–U.S. relations are contributing to reducing the intensity of confrontation between East and West, we have come better to realize that nuclear destruction is not the only danger to be encountered in the present situation. While we were looking at each other over the electronic sights of nuclear weapons and were much worried about whether we were doing enough to perfect them, humanity found itself encircled by other dangers. We are besieged by mighty forces of hunger and ecological degradation.

I would call attention to a time before the historic Soviet–U.S. summit in Washington, when prospects for signing an agreement on the elimination of two types of nuclear weapons were not yet clear. M. S. Gorbachev received, in April 1987, a delegation from the U.S. House of Representatives and displayed great interest in an idea expressed by House Speaker Jim Wright. Mr. Wright spoke about the possibility of joint Soviet–U.S. projects, including ones for combating hunger and disease in Africa. Gorbachev responded:

> We are quite sincere when we speak of sharing the experience of solving different problems, including national problems. However, to make it beneficial one must get rid of speculation, give up attempts to interfere into internal affairs, break oneself of gendarmes' and teachers' ways. One ought to repudiate "the image of the enemy." In the present situation it is intolerable. All this belongs to the past; it has just gone away. One should be considerate toward every people and every country, and one's attitude should be critical when addressing his own problems or the problems of his country. We must be mutually responsible, whether we like each other or not.

The progress that is beginning to occur in freeing the planet from nuclear weapons is opening up broad possibilities for international cooperation in pursuit of development. I am quite sure African–Soviet–U.S. cooperation is possible. More than that, it is necessary. This necessity is dictated by the realities of the African continent.

Beset by two superdeserts—the Sahara and the Kalahari—African countries constitute a disaster zone on a world scale. They are attacked simultaneously by hunger, drought, disease, and political and social instability; these are intertwined problems that cannot be resolved by African countries on their own. Despite all that has been said in the past by researchers from our two countries and sometimes stated by their official spokespersons, Africa is not a suitable place for a confrontation between capitalism and socialism. Of course, some African countries have declared adherence to opposing ways of future development, but we should not misapprehend the situation. Whether the self-proclaimed developmental paths of African states take on a socialist orientation, a capitalist one, or some mixture of the two, there is not in any case adequate reason for the global powers to allow their own differing sociopolitical orientations to stand in the way of the creation of conditions favorable to development. It is mainly a problem of whether we, the African, Soviet, and American peoples, will be able to overcome a certain narrowness in our ideological and political views in taking guidance from humankind's general moral standards as far as the fate of Africa is concerned. To address this issue is not easy. But I think that the work we have started will help to do it.

The organization of joint Soviet–U.S. research and a working out of well-grounded proposals on our cooperation are bound to assist African countries in solving their acute economic, social, and—to a certain extent—political problems. Such research is sure to contribute to the world community's struggle for the triumph of new political thinking, for a turn from confrontation on an international scale to cooperation in the resolution of the complicated problems now facing the countries of Africa.

Judging by the favorable reaction of African public opinion to the positive shifts that took place in Soviet–U.S. relations in 1988, the Africans are vitally interested in improved relations between our two countries. This is also the only conclusion I could draw from my many personal contacts with African public and political figures. I remember the president of Tanzania, A. Mwinyi, expressing his great satisfaction at the signing, in December 1987 in Washington, of the Soviet–U.S. treaty to eliminate all medium- and shorter-range nuclear missiles, and saying that it was "sheer folly" to spend a thousand billion dollars on the creation of cosmic weapons at a time when all countries of the world were experiencing great difficulties. In his opinion, an end to the arms race would create important prerequisites for making the concept of "disarmament for development" really effective.

At the same time, it should not be overlooked that some political circles in African countries are doubtful about what will follow the cessation of Soviet–U.S. confrontation as, in their view, it might be the first step toward the establishment of a condominium of the two superpowers, resulting in a "new hegemony." For all the speculativeness of these views they cannot be simply waved off; indeed, they may quite unexpectedly turn out to be obstacles in the way of implementing African–Soviet–U.S. cooperation for Africa.

The world public has grown accustomed to Moscow and Washington being in opposition to each other—always and on all issues. Our contradictions, real and imaginary, have acquired a character of permanency that is not easy to dispel. They must, however, be dispelled, as our two countries are not the only ones involved.

Africans realize only too well that the trend toward improvement in African–Soviet–U.S. relations contributes to lowering the level of military and political involvement of the Soviet Union and the United States in and around Africa. The imposing of sanctions by the U.S. Congress against the Republic of South Africa contributes to more effectively barring Pretoria from up-to-date nuclear technology. This policy is in harmony with the much stricter position taken by the Soviet Union, which has imposed sanctions on a much larger scale. This creates favorable conditions for holding African–Soviet–U.S. talks on turning Africa into a nuclear-free zone and nonadmission of nuclear weapons production in any African country, primarily in South Africa.

Once established, the African nuclear-free zone would do much to strengthen the Treaty on the Non-Proliferation of Nuclear Weapons and to tighten security in Africa and throughout the world. There are also good prospects for further development of Soviet–U.S. cooperation aimed at overcoming the economic backwardness of African countries and expanding production and distribution of agricultural products. It is quite possible to come to an agreement about joint support for separate projects of economic development in African countries, the examples being SADCC activities, and cooperation for the exploration and development of mineral resources.

The main task is to do away with the persistent underdevelopment of some African countries. It is to this general purpose that cooperation should be oriented. In the majority of African countries the problem of food supply shortages is particularly acute. Therefore, the immediate steps toward relieving this problem should be included in the program of cooperation.

Raising the volume of agricultural production in Africa, and that of food products in particular, is a task that must be viewed in relation to concomitant efforts at overcoming a number of complex problems—both internal and external. This perspective provides us with a variety of potential directions and areas for Soviet–U.S. cooperative efforts on behalf of the agroindustrial sector in Africa. In the framework of African–Soviet–U.S. cooperation for Africa project, experts from the Soviet Union and the United States have identified a number of specific steps, both technical and political in nature, that our two countries might take toward alleviating Africa's agricultural problems. They range from proposals to combine Soviet and U.S. resources for the study of well digging and irrigation projects to joint diplomatic action in international forums, such as the United Nations, in support of multilateral programs of price stabilization. Above all, the proposals are founded on the need to study and adapt implementation of any recommended actions to the specific conditions and needs of different countries and regions.

This line of action may contribute to the creation of more favorable conditions for African–Soviet–U.S. cooperation in other areas. I have in mind joint research work and technical assistance aimed at diversification of economies, industrial development, and other tasks vital to Africa's sustainable development.

At both the initial and later stages of such a program African countries will need help in carrying out a series of applied research projects (economic, technical and economic, technological, geological, prospecting, etc., including preinvestment surveys on some chosen objects) that could be jointly implemented by Soviet and U.S. consultative and engineering organizations. A propitious area for joint efforts of this nature is in the enhanced development of minerals production, which could become an element in national and regional plans for self-sustaining industrialization—one to integrate all sectors of developing countries' economies. Another potential area for joint research is in the development of alternative energy sources. Both the Soviet Union and the United States have accumulated some experience in sun and wind energy use. Research is also being conducted in our two countries on the use of biogas. Apart from physicists, economists and sociologists are needed to optimize proposals aimed at the development of ecologically secure energy systems for Africa.

While addressing questions related to technical and productive issues, we must not have our attention diverted from the delicate balance between society and ecology in Africa. To build modern society without upsetting this delicate balance between nature and man in Africa is hardly possible. However, no effort should be spared to minimize its social and ecological costs.

Thus informed, the proper use and application of technological solutions is indicated. Space monitoring, for example, is an area where the Soviet Union and the United States could jointly apply their technological capabilities in a way that is helpful to efforts to establish socially and environmentally sensitive programs of development.

As a scientist I share the enthusiasm of my colleagues who are engaged in space studies and who now dream of a joint Soviet–U.S. research expedition. Past confrontation extended into outer space, nipping in the bud the two countries' creative efforts at working together. Now that the process of détente has a chance of success, their hopes of cooperation may come true. However, as a humanist I cannot but think of questions of the applicability of this kind of research to humankind. I shall probably never forget the words I heard at the very beginning of 1988. It was at the time, right after the conclusion of the Washington INF treaty and prior to the Moscow summit, when the issue of joint Soviet–U.S. space projects was actively deliberated in the press. I was then a guest lecturer at Dar es Salaam University, where I was often asked about the prospects of Soviet–U.S. cooperation. When I started speaking to my students about the possibility of joint space projects, one of them interposed a remark: "Well, give our best regards to the Martians." I could discern bitterness in his words. He was probably quite justified in thinking that Soviet and U.S. scientists were too preoccupied with their own space problems to pay heed to problems on earth.

All this does not mean that I call for renouncing space technology. That is not the point. But what problems should be solved through the use of this technology?

Space technology is easily adapted to tackle the problems of developing countries. It can be employed to reduce the time and costs of prospecting for minerals, including prospecting on the continental shelf; or, it can minimize damage caused by environmental disasters through timely disaster warning. Communication satellites may be used to improve communication systems and to introduce new methods of raising the population's educational standards, both vocational and cultural.

The technology needed to accomplish these important economic and social tasks is available. Satellites and piloted orbital stations may be used to increase the efficiency of farming cycle operations, or to monitor seasonal climatic changes that have an impact on farming operations. Economists have estimated that a satellite system of distant monitoring will raise productivity on a world scale, by $1.8 billion in agriculture alone. Weather forecasts of two weeks in advance, made possible through the use of meteorological satellites and other technical means would ensure, UN experts say, yearly global savings of up to $9 billion.

These data testify to the fact that technological means such as joint space exploration and the use of space for peaceful purposes do meet the interests of developing countries. Therefore, we consider it advisable to carefully examine the following suggestion: In the event that a Soviet–U.S. agreement is reached on a 50 percent reduction of their strategic missile forces, the missiles slated for destruction could be put to use in the interests of development.

It is my opinion that under the present conditions this problem cannot be considered a purely technological one. No doubt, its political aspects have to be investigated, especially those pertaining to the creation of an appropriate international environment. For Africa, this work could be entrusted to African, Soviet, and U.S. nongovernmental experts.

In conclusion I would like to convey one more African tale, which I heard in Nigeria.

A jester fell into disgrace with the ruler. For an unsuccessful joke he was sentenced to a big fine, which he could not afford to pay. Then a rich peasant volunteered to pay the fine and demanded reimbursement: the jester would work for him for a year without payment. The jester had to agree.

On the very first day at supper time the jester offered the peasant a bet: if the jester correctly guessed the rich peasant's three thoughts, the latter would set him free to go home. Otherwise, the jester would work for him for three years instead of one. To exclude the possibility of deceit the jester would have to guess the peasant's thoughts in the presence of the ruler.

The peasant quickly realized that he stood nothing to lose—who could know his thoughts?—and he decided to lay the bet. So on the following day they came to the ruler.

"The first thought of this good man," said the jester, pointing to the peasant, was: "How lucky we are that we are ruled by such a wise and just man." The second thought: "Let God grant our ruler many years of happy life." The third thought: "Let his kin rule us forever!"

While the ruler was fair and wise he could not but like what was said. He asked the peasant whether he really had such good thoughts about his ruler. And the peasant had nothing to say but: "Yes, it is true."

Something we might wish to hear is not always the truth. In the framework of African–Soviet–U.S. cooperation, we have not come together for the purpose of paying one another compliments, only to part reserving judgment. Let us, then, openly and frankly confront the problems that we face. We start by establishing better human relations between us, a good starting point. Even an optimistic view of things stays on the solid ground of realism.

Acronyms and Abbreviations

ACMAD   African Center of Meteorological Applications for Development
ADB   African Development Bank
ADF   African Development Fund
AFCAC   African Civil Aviation Commission
AGRHYMET   Regional Center for Training and Application of Agro-Meteorology and Operational Hydrology
AMCEN   African Ministerial Conference on the Environment
ANC   African National Congress
ARCT   African Regional Center for Technology

BCCI   Bank of Credit and Commerce International
BCG   Beira Corridor Group

CCCE   Caisse Centrale de Coopération Economique
CIDA   Canadian International Development Agency
CILSS   Inter-State Committee for Combatting Drought in the Sahel
COMECON   Council for Mutual Economic Assitance
COMIDES   Conférence Ministerielle sur la Désertification
CONSAS   Constellation of Southern African States
COPUOS   Committee on the Peaceful Uses of Outer Space

DEL   direct exchange line

EC   European Community
ECA   (United Nations) Economic Commission for Africa
ECOWAS   Economic Commission of West African States
EDF   European Development Fund
EIB   European Investment Bank
EPA   Environmental Protection Agency
ESAF   Enhanced Structural Adjustment Facility
EXIMBANK   U.S. Export-Import Bank

FAO   Food and Agriculture Organization
FRELIMO   Front for the Liberation of Mozambique

GDP   gross domestic product
GNP   gross national product

HIV   human immunodeficiency virus

IACC   Inter-Agency Coordination Committee
IAEA   International Atomic Energy Agency
IBRD   International Bank for Reconstruction and Development
IDA   International Development Association
IDD   International Direct Dialing
IGADD   Intergovernmental Authority on Drought and Development
ILCA   International Livestock Center for Africa
IMF   International Monetary Fund
INF   Intermediate-Range Nuclear Forces
INILSEL   International Network for the Improvement of Lathyrus Sativus and the Eradication of Lathyrism
INMARSAT   International Maritime Satellite Organization
INTELSAT   International Telecommunications Satellite Organization Network
ITA   International Trade Administration
ITU   International Telecommunications Union

JAMINTEL   Jamaica Telecommunications, Ltd
JICA   Japanese International Cooperation Agency

KP&TC   Kenyan Post and Telecommunications Corp.

LDC   less developed country

MNC   multinational corporation
MNR (RENAMO)   Mozambique National Resistance
MPLA   Angolan Popular Liberation Movement
MVA   Manufacturing Value Added

NITEL   Nigerian Telecommunications, Ltd
NPT   Treaty on the Non-Proliferation of Nuclear Weapons
NTIA   National Telecommunications and Information Administration

OAU   Organization of African Unity
ODA   Official Development Assistance

PANFATEL   Pan-African Telecommunications
PATU   Pan-African Telecommunications Union
PTA   Preferential Trade Agreement

RASCOM   Regional African Satellite Communications System for the Development of Africa
RCSSMRS   Regional Center for Services in Surveying, Mapping and Remote Sensing

RDSS   Radio Determination Satellite System
RECTAS   Regional Center for Training in Aerospace Surveys
RENAMO (see MNR)
RSA   Republic of South Africa
RSP   Rural Satellite Program

SACU   Southern African Customs Union
SADCC   Southern African Development Coordination Conference
SAF   Structural Adjustment Facility
SATS   Southern African Transport Services
SCPC   single channel per carrier
SPA   Special Program of Assistance
SSC   State Security Council
SWAPO   South West Africa People's Organization

TBE   transnational business enterprise
TIPS   Technological Information Pilot System

UAPT   Union Africaine des Postes et Télécommunications
UNCTAD   United Nations Conference on Trade and Development
UNDP   United Nations Development Programme
UNEP   United Nations Environment Programme
UNESCO   United Nations Educational, Scientific and Cultural Organization*
UNFSSTD   United Nations Financing System for Science and Technology for Development
UNICEF   United Nations International Children's Emergency Fund
UNIDO   United Nations Industrial Development Organization
UNITA   National Union for the Total Independence of Angola
UNTACDA   United Nations Transport and Communications Decade in Africa
URTNA   Union des Radiodiffusions et Télévisions Nationales d'Afrique
USAID   U.S. Agency for International Development
USIA   U.S. Information Agency
USTTI   U.S. Telecommunications Training Institute

VSAT   Very Small Aperture Terminals

WASH   Water and Sanitation for Health
WHO   World Health Organization
WMO   World Meteorological Organization

ZANU   Zimbabwe African National Union
ZMDC   Zimbabwe Mining Development Corporation

Index

AID. *See* United States Agency for International Development
AIDS, 152, 153-154, 163
ANC. *See* African National Congress
afforestation, 46
African Center of Meteorological Applications for Development (ACMAD), 47, 49
African Development Bank (ADB), 82, 100
African Development Fund (ADF), 82
African National Congress (ANC), 221, 222
African Regional Centre for Solar Energy, 174
agriculture: in Botswana, 28; and colonial practices, 19; crisis in, causes, 16-31 passim; and the debt crisis, 14, 16, 29; and disasters, 17-18; and the environment, 20, 28, 71; export, 15-16, 19, 21-22, 28; government policies concerning, 22-24, 30-31, 33-39 passim; rates of growth in, 27; in Senegal, 33-39; in Southern Africa, 239; in Zimbabwe, 229. *See also* cereals production; food deficits; sectoral linkages; price
aid, 82, 64, 151, 226; military, 212, 221, 240
air forces in Africa, 203
All-African Seminar on the Human Environment, 43

Angola, 13, 214, 240, 244; Soviet and U.S. involvement in, 220
Antarctica Treaty (1959), 266
apartheid, 222, 230
armies in Africa, 203
arms transfers, 204, 208, 209; cost of, 193, 202, 212; from European countries, 195-196, 212; from within Africa, 214; from the Soviet Union, 194, 214; from the United States, 194, 213; growth in, 202-203; to the Horn of Africa, 211
Axelrod, Robert, 264
Ayoob, Mohammed, 264

banks, private, 79, 230
Bates, Robert, 22
Beira corridor, 226, 227-228
Beira Corridor Group (BCG), 229
beneficiation process, 121
Benguela, 226
Bienen, Henry S., 208
Botswana, 115, 226, 238
Beit-Hallahmi, Benjamin, 171
Botha, P.W., 182, 228, 230
Bowers, J., 51
Brzezinski, Zbigniew, 214
Burkina Faso, 157

COMECON. *See* Council for Mutual Economic Assistance
calcium: industrial applications, 124
Caisse Centrale de la Coopération Economique

(CCCE), 140
Canadian International Development Agency, 140
Caprivi strip, 245
cartography: in fighting desertification, 74
cassava toxicity, 163
Center for Disease Control in Atlanta, 158
cereals production: in Botswana, 238; in Senegal, 34-35
Chase Manhattan Bank, 230
chemical industries, 107-108
chemical weapons, 214
child mortality: in Angola and Mozambique, 240
Chissano, Joaquim, 233
cholera, 152-153
clay minerals: industrial applications of, 124
Coker, Christopher, 231
colonial governments: developmental legacy of, 19, 130
commodity diversification, 34, 118
communications development, 130-142 passim. *See also* telecommunications
confidence-building: and arms control, 198, 215-216; and cooperation, 7; in Southern Africa, 237, 268-269
Cold War: and United States foreign policy, 255-256
Committee on the Peaceful Uses of Outer Space (COPUOS), 142

DATE DUE

OC11 '00			

DEMCO